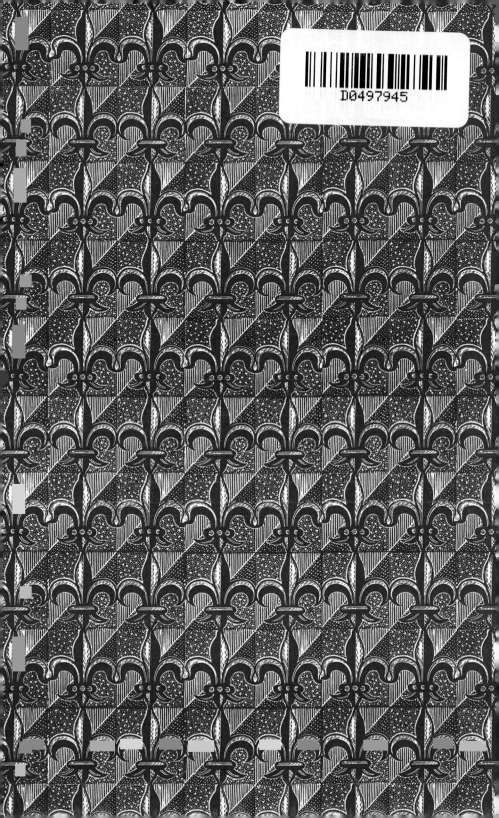

ARMS AND
THE WOMAN

ARMS AND THE WOMAN

KATE MUIR

SINCLAIR-STEVENSON

First published in Great Britain by
Sinclair-Stevenson Limited
7/8 Kendrick Mews
London SW7 3HG England

British Library Cataloguing in Publication Data
A CIP catalogue record for this book is available from the British Library.

ISBN: 1 85619 115 X

Filmset in Garamond by
Selwood Systems, Midsomer Norton, Avon

Printed and bound in Great Britain by
Butler & Tanner, Frome and London

For my Mother and Father

CONTENTS

ACKNOWLEDGEMENTS

Arms and the Woman would never have been written without the help of the following people: Flight-Lieutenant Heather Black of the WRNS who arranged for me to go to the Gulf and visit HMS *Brilliant*; Stuart Reed of MOD public relations in Dhahran; Flight-Lieutenant Caroline Forsyth of the WRAF; and Linda Grant de Pauw of the Minerva Center in Washington. Particular thanks go to Lieutenant Karen Mair in Canada and Captain Kate Martin of WRAC public relations in London for their encouragement, Alison Graham for her picture research and my editor, James Woodall. Without Charlotte Rastan who had the idea and Peter Robinson of Curtis Brown who made sense of it, I would have been lost. Finally, thanks and love to Ben Macintyre for his spelling and support.

LIST OF ILLUSTRATIONS

(between pages 114 and 115)

Dahomeyan Amazons of west Africa
  (© Peter Newark's Historical Pictures)
Soviet air-force fighter pilots in the Second World War
  (© Imperial War Museum)
Violette Szabo
  (© Imperial War Museum)
Senior Lieutenant of the Guards Rufina Gasheva
  (© Imperial War Museum)
Mechanics of the Women's Auxiliary Air Force
  (© *The Times*)
British Women's Auxiliary Air Force advertising poster
  (© Imperial War Museum)
Cartoon superhero Tank Girl
  (© *Deadline Comics / Penguin Books*)
Majors Dee Brasseur and Jane Foster
  (© Canadian Forces. Photograph by Joel Weder)
British Army Lieutenant Wendy Smart
  (© Stuart Reed, Ministry of Defence)
US Army Captain, JoAnn Conley
  (© DoD pool, Andy Clarke)
British women truck drivers in the 68 Squadron Royal Corps of
Transport
  (© Stuart Reed, Ministry of Defence)
Women's Royal Naval Service Rating Tanya Luffman
  (© Denzil McNeelance, *The Times*)
Private Heather Erxleben
  (© Canadian Forces. Photograph by Sergeant Ed Dixon)
US Army Specialist Hollie Vallance
  (© The Associated Press)
British Army launching new uniforms for women
  (© UPPA)
Soldier fainting at a Women's Royal Army Corps parade
  (© Cassidy and Leigh)

Man should be trained for war and woman for the recreation of the warrior: all else is folly.

Friedrich Nietzsche, 1883

1

OPENING SHOTS

She is wearing his trousers. They are khaki. Worse still, she is driving his tank. In the dust, crushed under its tracks, lies what remains of his machismo. The woman soldier has invaded the last place where the warrior could celebrate his masculinity in safety, and debagged him.

The appearance of the first female tank drivers, fighter pilots and warship gunners in this decade has rocked the military to its core. Never before in Western history have women been ready to go into combat as full and equal members of their armies. There have been isolated cases of heroism or terrorism by armed women in the past, but this is different. If the Falklands War took place again, British women as well as men would win medals and die on warships; if the Gulf War took place again, the British, Americans and Canadians would have women in the cockpits of Tornadoes and F-18 fighters. Over 34,000 women fought in the Gulf in 1991, and eleven came home in bodybags, despite the fact they were not officially supposed to be in combat. From now on, female soldiers cannot be shrugged off as an insignificant part of the forces, as mere auxiliaries to fighting men. Centuries of military tradition and assumptions about the roles of men and women are being turned upside down.

Through the first-hand accounts of female soldiers in the nineties, at war and peace, the following chapters build a picture of their lives in the strange world of the military, governed by rules and sacrifices incomprehensible to civilians. They also look at the arguments for and against putting women on the front line. Female soldiers answer the personal questions that their commanders would rather were not asked, and talk about their frustrations and fears about being allowed into some areas of combat, but not others; about a changing battlefield whose rear and front lines are blurred by high-technology missiles. Extraordinary and sometimes disturbing stories emerge: the two female helicopter pilots in the Gulf, one who lived and one who died; the British woman officer, alone in the Kuwaiti desert for three months with 300 Scottish squaddies; the infantrywoman and former lumberjack who carried her male colleagues' machine guns across the scrubland of California when they were too exhausted to continue; and the single mother, a cook in the navy, who left her two small sons behind with various babysitters for six months at a time.

The closeness of women to the danger zone varies by country and often seems far from logical. The British allow women to fire missiles and become gunners on warships; the Americans do not. Both countries allow women to drop bombs as fighter pilots, but still ban them from shooting in the infantry and firing missiles in the artillery. Yet the Canadians, Belgians, Dutch and Norwegians have opened all front-line jobs to suitably qualified soldiers, regardless of sex. Although full of discrepancies, the international picture is clear: women are becoming warriors of increasing significance to the military. It is extraordinary to think that ten years ago not one Western country had female soldiers in combat and now most do. The military change of heart has been sudden and precipitated by the Gulf conflict, when the policy of keeping women out of harm's way was found to be worthless; more American soldiers died in support services in the rear when a Scud missile hit their barracks than died on the front. The best form of defence is attack, and women soldiers are now in a position where they can be killed, yet only occasionally are they allowed to be killers.

But even this limited entry into combat, a foretaste of what is to come by the end of this century, has disturbed many military – and civilian – men. They find this role reversal threatening, or just downright perverse. Following the Gulf War, General Robert Barrow, a former commandant of the US Marine Corps, made an impassioned speech against women being allowed to encroach any further onto the battlefield:

> Exposure to danger is not combat. Being shot at, even being killed, is not combat. Combat is finding ... closing with ... and killing or capturing the enemy. It's killing.

2

And it's done in an environment that is often as difficult as you can possibly imagine. Extremes of climate. Brutality. Death. Dying. It's ... uncivilised! And women can't do it! Nor should they even be thought of as doing it. The requirements for strength and endurance render them unable to do it. And I may be old-fashioned, but I think the very nature of women disqualifies them from doing it. Women give life. Sustain life. Nurture life. They don't take it.

The general's views are common on both sides of the Atlantic – he cannot contemplate the idea of the bearers of life bringing death, nor does he think they are tough enough to do so. His last stand against the tide of American combative women – now 230,000 out of forces of two million – is also a way of covering his own back. He fears, understandably, that the Marines will be polluted by femininity.

The assault of female soldiers on the British psyche is infinitely worse. Military myth and reality play a disproportionate role in national pride. The army is held in deep respect by civilians, far more than in any other European country – Britain has no significant pacifist movement, possibly because it has not lost a war for over 100 years. Wars are remembered with pride and are the province of Tommy, not Tracey. The nation luxuriates in films and books about the Second World War and the Battle of Britain; Remembrance Day is a major event. The women of the war – so important it needs no date or place – were people who did ingenious things with dried eggs, or were land girls, munitions workers or army ladies bearing up splendidly on the home front.

Most older men define themselves largely by what they did in the war and even younger ones are touched by the military. Some politicians taking decisions on women's future came through the ancient route of Eton and the Guards to Parliament, or at least were part of the cadet corps at their public school. This baggage of male warring pride is combined with almost total ignorance of women's role in the modern British forces. With only 17,600 out of a total force of 288,900, female soldiers could easily slip by unnoticed, more so because they no longer wear their uniforms in public except on parade, such is the threat of the IRA. A deep consciousness of the male role, coupled with the invisibility of women, leads to an almost unshakeable prejudice against and incomprehension of women in combat.

The sort of army girl imagined by most of the public is extinct. Women no longer join the forces to find a husband or to dress up like an air hostess. They join for careers, education and travel, and expect to be promoted at similar rates to their male colleagues. The military is the only place left – apart from the priesthood – which is exempt in Britain from equal rights' legislation. Female soldiers will never be treated as equals or reach high command in large numbers until they have the choice to go into all areas of combat. Not all women want front-line jobs, but neither do all men. What women do want is to be respected as full soldiers and citizens, not half-hearted defenders.

Yet the road to combat, or just to soldiering, is not a pleasant one. It remains astounding that women – and men – put themselves through rigours which had they happened to a civilian might be condemned as a form of torture. Take an average day at boot camp – any boot camp in Britain or America – as new recruits learn the awful truth: they are in the army now. In summer they will be sweating, pallid and inevitably cleaning the linoleum of their barracks, inch by inch, with a very small scrubbing brush, as a sergeant of unparalleled viciousness bawls them out. In winter, they will be ordered on three-mile runs before dawn in sub-zero temperatures, wearing scarves over their mouths to stop their breath freezing. Next, they will be taken on exercise in the field, on short rations, and go sleepless until they start to hallucinate. On parade ground, if asked a question, their only permitted responses will be 'Yes, Sir', 'No, Sir' and 'No excuse, Sir'. And by the end of training, they will of course be proud, upright, confident and excited about their futures. Their parents will thank the military for doing in a few months what they failed to do in eighteen years.

Clearly women have the capacity to be moulded into soldiers. But do they have the capacity to be aggressive, to fire weapons of mass destruction, to fight hand-to-hand? How will their presence affect groups of fighting men used to being with their own kind? Will male bonding, which supposedly holds a platoon together, fall apart? Will

4

sexual relationships and desires affect combat readiness? Will men protect women at the expense of their own lives and military sense? Will mothers become soldiers and leave new-born babies behind to go into battle?

Later chapters attempt to answer these questions, analysing the physical and psychological aspects of going into battle. Certainly, women cite different reasons from men for joining the forces. Men talk about careers and travel too, but a few will say they joined because they wanted 'to see some action' or 'get my hands on a gun'. Not one of the 250 or so women interviewed for this book gave a Ramboesque reason for becoming a soldier. That may be no bad thing for the military, since calm and accuracy, rather than trigger-happy arousal, may result in fewer mistakes, such as the deaths by friendly fire in the Gulf. It will be fascinating to see whether a woman can fit the military psychology and uniform designed for a man without altering them. The alteration is physical as well as metaphorical – camouflage uniforms have now been issued in maternity sizes, adding another dimension to the female soldier. As mothers, they recount the painful decisions to leave their children and go to war.

This sudden injection of femininity, and its complicated and different demands, into a previously all-masculine organisation causes great upheaval. Integration – or rather the lack of it – is now a major issue. There is still a rich vein of misogyny running beneath the surface of the forces. Men who join up because they liked the camaraderie of the single-sex life are not exactly delighted at the prospect of sharing a missile silo or a tent with a woman. Others feel their importance is diminished by having a woman in the same job and they rarely trust her capabilities immediately. The female pioneer in a masculine field is frequently rewarded for her efforts with discrimination and sexual harassment. Far more than in the civilian world, a combination of fear and ignorance makes both sexes wary; soldiers live in extreme proximity, yet often know next to nothing about the workings of the opposite sex. For men, this book may begin to explain some of the supposed mysteries and myths about women in uniform.

Such male resentment sits oddly with the fact that army, navy and air-force women are some of the least avowedly feminist people around, although they are fighting battles for acceptance and equal rights that civilian women put behind them in the seventies. Joining the military and accepting its discipline in the first place requires a fairly conservative set of views and these women are often some of the more traditional – except when it comes to their jobs. They – and this book – are feminist with a small 'f' in the sense that they believe women can work from the inside to make the military change its policies and attitudes. But feminism also has its anti-militarist branch, which argues that standing armies only increase the likelihood of male politicians sending a country to war and that defence budgets would be better spent improving services for people. Woman, the peacemaker, should not throw in her lot with man, the warmonger.

It is true most women in the forces are not typical of their sex. Neither are they 'all lesbians', as is often suggested, although interviews later show that gay women do tend to have long and successful military careers. Those opposing female combatants should remember that clichéd arguments about the weakness of womankind are unlikely to apply to the kind of woman who decides on the military as a career, who has a different set of values and strengths from those outside.

The feminisation of the military and the militarisation of the feminine have implications not just for soldiers, but for the civilian world. For if soldiering is the ultimate seal on manhood, does it lose its significance if women do it too? If a woman can face the mental and physical challenge of battle, and sacrifice herself for her country as courageously as any man, can she still be routinely considered a member of the second sex?

Just as women gain from the military in the kinds of jobs they could not have as civilians, so the military gains from women. As modern warfare moves from the trench to the computer screen, the high intelligence levels of women compared to men applying to volunteer armies are increasingly important, as are female social and management skills. By moving from jobs as outer-office ornaments twenty years ago to centre stage now, women have made the atmosphere of the forces far more congenial. The image of an officers' or sergeants' mess filled with beer-swilling, punching men is dying out, because the addition of a few women tends to calm the worst excesses. Men start to form normal friendships and relationships, rather than swaying dangerously between near-monastic segregation and the brothel.

The catch is that normal relationships often lead to normal pregnancies and the military has found it has to do a little social work nowadays before going into battle. The British military, which only stopped discharging pregnant women in 1990, is about to discover that motherhood will be a major issue in the future. In theory, having soldier-mothers should not affect readiness to go to war, since each parent, male or female, fills out a family-care plan which designates a guardian in case of call-up. Practice – as the Gulf War showed – is more complicated.

In peacetime – and after all, very few soldiers actually see war during their careers – the US Army for one has started providing on-base crèches. Both the British and Americans find themselves in the interesting position that they now make provision for dual-career military couples, while instituting 'no-touching' rules which as far as possible prevent any more couples meeting. The problem is that the average soldier is in his or her late teens or twenties and extremely likely to form a number of relationships. Unless the military finds ways of controlling the growing sexual complexity of its soldiers lives' at work, discipline may go to the wall.

Presently, Western militaries are suffering from a sort of fever, as they either incorporate women into new roles too fast, or try to block their advance. The addition of women to previously all-male units causes an initial explosive reaction and the tremors from that reverberate throughout this book. Eventually, acceptance will take women out of the spotlight and into mundane ordinariness, particularly as the male-female ratio improves. Despite NATO cuts following the end of the Cold War, women are still expected to make up ten per cent of the British forces by the end of the century, increased from the present six per cent, and the Americans will go from eleven per cent to at least fifteen. Other countries are looking for even higher levels of female participation.

So the battle has begun and the army of the future will be female to a greater extent than ever before. At the same time, a number of military and civilian men are fighting a rearguard action to keep the second sex off the front. But if change continues at its present rate, the end of the decade will see Western militaries open all roles – including infantry, artillery and tanks – to suitably qualified women. It is, after all, in the nature of barriers that they fall.

2

THE INFIDEL WHO BROUGHT HIS WIFE

The British cannot be blamed for their ignorance. It was quite reasonable, until a small war occurred in a distant Middle East country in 1991, for the public to assume the work of their women soldiers largely consisted of flower-arranging in the officers' mess and typing for portly generals. Our girls would no more take up guns than their counterparts in the Salvation Army. They were not dangerous. They were decent.

That was how many of Britain's military leaders felt too. When the Gulf crisis blew up, only male troops were sent to the desert at first. A woman's place was in the homeland and there she would stay. The decision to keep female soldiers off the desert lines was partly because of Saudi Arabian tradition and partly because of old-fashioned Western male tradition. But as in all wars, the nurses going out tended to be female and more vulnerable than usual to attack, because Iraq's leader Saddam Hussein was threatening to use Scud missiles. Then the Royal Air Force took female air-traffic controllers and mechanics, and finally warships – which had just gone mixed a few months before – sailed for the disputed waters. There were already a few Sandhurst-trained women officers who had left with their largely all-male units, so it was, by then, pointless to try and stop the female flow of ordinary soldiers. Besides, if the female troops had not been with the units they had served for years in peacetime, the already-stretched allied forces would have been like a piece of bad knitting. A dropped stitch here, a hole there, and eventually the lot would have started to unravel.

Pressure from the Armed Forces Minister, Archie Hamilton, and from the Women's Royal Army Corps pushed the British forces into a unisex war. What was the point of making women into soldiers if they were never given the chance to do their job? The WRAC Director, Brigadier Gael Ramsey, said it was difficult to get women deployed, not just because of military policy, but because of Muslim customs. 'I was pushing it, saying a soldier is a soldier, be it in a skirt or trousers. Besides, all the women who went were volunteers.'

The British sent about 1,000 women, making about four per cent of their force, and the Americans sent over 33,000, making six per cent of theirs. Such a presence caused Saddam Hussein to become apoplectic with disgust. He told the Saudi Arabians they should be ashamed, for not only were they letting the Western infidel fight their battles, but the infidel had brought his wife. How could a great masculine-orientated nation bear to be defended by weak and feeble women? he ranted. The weak and feeble turned out to be pretty useful. It was women who loaded ammunition and set the computer coordinates on the Patriot anti-missile batteries which destroyed Saddam's Scuds. It was the women, alongside their male colleagues, who handcuffed Iraqi prisoners-of-war as they ran in surrender from their tanks and foxholes. It was the women – eleven of them – who came home as the men did in bodybags from Desert Shield and Desert Storm, despite the fact they were not officially 'in combat'.

Their performance in the Gulf War brought British and American women soldiers long-awaited respect. A few months' hard work in the desert did more for military women than years of public politicking and painstaking confidence-building. Traditional assumptions – that women would not cope with possible gas attacks, being prisoners-of-war, or that their countries would not be able to stomach their deaths – were all disproved. Plans on paper to keep female soldiers out of the combat zone were unworkable in a war of long-distance missiles rather than trenches. Out of necessity, women flew aircraft and helicopters over the front line and went far forward into the battlefields, outnumbered by men by thousands to one. In short, they broke most of the rules and the sky did not fall in.

In Kuwait close to the Iraq border the sand-covered salt flats stretched tediously into the dust haze. Occasional straggling herds of camels with no owners in sight skirted the edge of the tents and camouflage nets of The Royal Scots. The battleground was all around here, evidenced by razor-wired minefields, half-melted Russian tanks, shards of twisted metal and torn pieces of clothing which lay by the newly-etched sand roads. The camp was a large one, tall green tents each sleeping dozens of the 300 or so infantrymen. But in the centre of the camp, isolated in sand, there was one small tent. It was the women's tent. The woman was Lieutenant Wendy Smart, aged twenty-five. She was quite alone. She had not talked with someone of her own sex for three months.

Unlike the other British enlisted women, who were posted in small groups or all-female platoons, Lieutenant Smart had no support and no choice but to go it alone. In a war situation new to everyone, ordinary soldiers could afford to admit their ignorance and ask simple questions about field procedure. Being an officer, having to take the lead, was much harder, particularly when dealing with Scottish infantrymen, a species not known for its gentility. They showed their appreciation of the first female civilian to visit them in some months by standing in a row of five outside the only hole-in-the-ground ladies' toilet available, and cheering and whistling on entrance and exit.

It was not as if Lieutenant Smart had not proved herself. On G-Day, 24 February, the day the ground war began, she was in charge of the lead vehicle in a convoy of food and water trucks which followed a few miles behind the front-line fighting troops and tanks into Iraq. They travelled through the breach in the enemy's defences in their chemical-warfare suits and gasmasks in the dark and rain, avoiding cluster bombs and anti-personnel mines littering the track, hearing the roar of battle a few miles ahead, watching the flash of explosives ripping across the black sky, feeling the vibrations through the ground. Sometimes the trucks behind would get bogged down in the soft sand and they would have to wait for them to catch up. 'I had a grid point on the map where we were supposed to be and a compass, and if I got the distance and bearing wrong, we could have ended up on enemy lines. So it was on my head.' She stopped speaking and looked down at her boots in the sand.

Then Lieutenant Smart continued. She had been too anxious to sleep for more than one or two hours as her convoy travelled almost non-stop for four days and nights. 'I worried more about the boys than myself. I felt so responsible.' They followed the British armoured divisions which intended to surprise the Iraqi troops by coming upon them from behind. 'Usually we were thirty kilometres behind, but sometimes it was five, and at one position they were still fighting so we went round them. I don't think they realised we were that close.' Although women were banned from the front, Lieutenant Smart, like many others, found herself right in the combat zone. Hundreds of prisoners-of-war stood by as her convoy crossed the desert. 'We didn't have time to round them up, but we pointed them in the right direction. You should have seen the condition some of them were in. It was very, very sad. Some were smiling, some were subdued, some were wandering around vaguely in the middle of nowhere, some were burying the dead.'

In the same battlefields, a few miles from her unit, nine infantrymen from The Royal Regiment of Fusiliers died under friendly fire when two American A-10 Thunderbolt aircraft mistakenly attacked their two Warrior armoured vehicles. They had failed to see the allied markings on their roofs. The soldiers who died were mostly in their teens. Lieutenant Smart's convoy went past the site of the attack. 'They had put screens around while they were moving the nine bodybags... The boys here took it very hard. They were very young.'

Her tone was very different from that of the senior officers and NCOs briefing the House of Commons defence committee, who happened to have flown up to the desert just after the war for a guided tour of the same area. When their helicopter landed, they ran out in summer suits and were shown to a bench in a small operations tent with a large plastic board at the back set out with *Dad's Army*-style markings. The blue arrows were the British and the Americans. The big red circles were the Iraqis. The blue arrows swiftly wiped out the red circles.

Naturally, the aim of the talk was to ensure the select committee left thinking the defence budget was being well-utilised, but the officer giving the lecture could not resist being overtly gung-ho. He pointed his swagger stick as he described the assault by infra-red night sight, giving the impression his 'Jocks' were only too desperate to get out of the armoured vehicles and use their bayonets as bloodily as possible. But talking afterwards to the infantrymen themselves, there was a very different picture. They found their advance was

12

slowed by the numbers of prisoners-of-war, and the fact that they were throwing their own food rations and water out behind them to the starving Iraqis. Unknowing, the committee ate roast lamb with apricot sauce and fresh vegetables which appeared from nowhere on long tables shaded by camouflage nets, and continued their tour.

The gap between fiction and reality was to be found at every turn. Seeing war – or more like mass surrender – at its most depressing made it harder for Lieutenant Smart to put up with the trite idiocies of some newspaper reports which had arrived at her tent a few weeks later. On yet another boiling spring morning, she was thinking of writing to the Scottish *Sunday Post* about an article on exaggerated numbers of women soldiers escaping the war by getting pregnant. Having busted out of the stereotype herself, being the first woman on an armoured fighting-vehicle fleet managers' course and one of the few to see battle, she did not want to be reminded of unchanging perceptions at home. 'I think there is a place for women in a war. It may not be on the front line at the end of the day – although I would shoot if someone pointed a rifle at me – because in the infantry physical strength wins out, but I don't see why tanks should always be closed to us.'

In her small desert boots, with a red Arab scarf on top of her camouflage gear, short, dark, tousled hair, and wearing sunglasses, Lieutenant Smart just about reached the chest height of some of the men she commanded. In guts, she probably equalled them. Certainly, her staying power for three months so far as second-in-command of the headquarters company of The Royal Scots in the desert showed that. There were no difficulties with privacy. She showered by torchlight after the men had finished and did not ask for a special time to be set aside for her. If she wanted to sunbathe, she could always hide behind a nearby dune. She could cope with the practical side of being the one woman among hundreds of men. But the social side was much harder.

She was confident in her assessment of the situation, and not afraid to be honest. 'The Jocks have a brilliant sense of humour, but they don't like women in the army and they make it difficult at times. It is very lonely out here. I don't think they appreciate how nice it is to have other female company. The two warrant officers [commissioned from the ranks] are in their forties and don't particularly want to talk to me and I can only talk to the boys so much, in my position. I can't really talk to them as friends.'

A young spotty private arrived with bottled water at the tent and addressed her as 'Ma'am'. She distributed it to her first-ever guests in the tiny tent. 'It's nice for the boys to chat to a female. They can let go, be more honest. On the other hand, if I sit too long with one of them, that's it – I get accused of having an affair. It's unbelievable. Since I'm the only woman here that's all the gossip they have.' Supposedly professional relationships were not much easier. In watch keeping, she found soldiers ignored her and asked, 'Can I speak to someone?' – someone in this case being a man. They automatically did not trust a woman to pass on the message. 'When I used to make suggestions as a new subby [subaltern], it might be a perfectly good idea, but they would ignore it until a man made the same suggestion. It's an uphill battle and really frustrating at times.'

Frustration may be what makes competent and courageous Sand-hurst graduates like Lieutenant Smart eventually leave the army for a better-paid management job in civilian life. Although, in retrospect, she said she had enjoyed and got a lot out of her time with The Royal Scots, she was worried that future posts might not be so challenging. After the Gulf (and a much-needed holiday in the Caribbean), she was sent back to her regiment in Germany, as second-in-command of a fire-support company. In 1992 she was specially selected to be the first troop commander of women at the Army Apprentice College in Harrogate, Yorkshire.

The position of women in the British Army – unlike the American – was until recently archaic. Most men in the forces still had women mentally pigeonholed as secretaries and flower-arrangers. The British Women's Royal Army Corps had not got its fingernails really dirty since its formation in 1949. (The Second World War was a different matter.) The separate WRAC has now amalgamated with the main-stream army, but in 1991 it was in its death throes. Its revealingly unwarlike motto was 'Gentle in Manner, Resolute in Deed'.

Many of the female soldiers sent to the desert were used to being groomed and coiffed, wearing white gloves and tight dress uniforms in their regular jobs chauffeuring brigadiers in Vauxhall Cavaliers. Now, armed with sub-machine guns, fifty dust-grimed women were driving essential supplies for The Royal Corps of Transport in four-ton trucks, or petrol tankers, or JCB diggers somewhere in the roadless desert, without headlights in the blackout during Scud attacks.

At one point, there were two deaths a day on the main supply route from the coast to the desert battlefields. It was like playing chicken in a dust bowl. 'Suddenly the road would narrow to half the width and you'd find a whole convoy of extra-wide Saudi tank transporters coming towards you at fifty mph. You had no choice but to drive into the sand dunes,' said Private Sharon Thomas, one of the young truckers working out of the Al-Jubail coastal base. Being in an allied truck in this war was more dangerous than being in a tank. General Norman Schwarzkopf, along with the British, insisted on sixty days' supply of ammunition, food, fuel, spare parts and water for his front-line forces, so the potholed road parallel to the Saudi Arabia-Kuwait border was packed day and night. The sides of the road were dotted with twisted, burnt-out vehicle wrecks. The female truckers who were part of 68 Squadron RCT had no serious accidents. The men did.

Driving was hard enough, but locating army units on the move on a featureless landscape was even tougher. Sometimes the women would park the truck to sleep in the darkness and discover either by the sound of artillery practice or by the morning light that they were among tanks a few miles from the front line. 'They trained us before we went out with maps of the Brecon Beacons in Wales. That's fine – we know exactly where Merthyr Tydfil is now, but that's not much use here where it's just all yellow. So it's a compass, or you haven't got a clue,' said Private Katy Picken. Like her fellow truckers at the coastal Al-Jubail base, she was in her early twenties, tanned and comfortable in desert camouflage trousers and big boots. She strutted around, as though she had worn clothes like that all her life. She could not move in the same way in her best army driving skirt. It was a few weeks after the end of the ground war and the women's increased confidence following their metamorphoses from chauffeurs into truckers was visible, as was their pleasure in looking tough and grubby.

The drivers sat around on spare tyres in an empty freight container and talked. They had sometimes been only ten or twenty miles from the border, and that was more nerve-wracking after two American soldiers, one female, were shot at and taken prisoner by the Iraqis on the nearby oil-pipeline road. The trucks drove through the night, without headlights to avoid air attack during Scud-missile alerts, and out of contact with their base. 'You'd get this sickening feeling and your stomach would lurch when suddenly you'd go past a camp or another truck and everyone would have on their gasmasks and NBC [chemical warfare] suits, and you didn't,' said Private Thomas. Although chemical weapons were never used, the fear of them was very real and there was good reason to suspect if Saddam Hussein had used mustard gas on the Kurds, he would not hesitate to use it on a bunch of WRAC truckers.

At first there was no radio telephone, so the pairs of drivers in the women-only truck unit were entirely on their own on each mission. Battlefield units kept moving so they had no idea how long each trip would be, sometimes two days, sometimes three. They slept fitfully, often wearing gasmasks, wrapped round the steering wheel. Each time they returned to base, they got eight hours of uninterrupted sleep – depending on Scud attacks – and were back on the road again.

At first they drove with their sleeves rolled down, hair in their hats and sunglasses on, so at least they looked like men (Saudi religious law bans women from driving). Although the Saudis made an exception for allied women in uniform, no one was keen to test it out in a confrontation with Saudi police. It was rumoured that even in an accident the police would not speak to women. Other companies put men and women drivers together for safety. Some women soldiers found that Saudi coach drivers employed by the British Army would only take orders from them when threatened with sub-machine guns.

There were other more physical barriers to overcome, like changing tyres after blow-outs in the heat and doing basic maintenance, which was difficult, but not impossible, when one or two of them, at about five foot two inches, were hardly taller than the huge tyres on the fourteen-tonners and just reached the foot pedals. 'I don't want to go back to polishing the car and taking the boss's wife to the supermarket,' said Private Hazel Wakling. Private Thomas and the rest of the audience in the container agreed. 'I can drive a fourteen-tonner. I know what I'm capable of now. We've proved ourselves. We struggle to shut the big container trucks, so we work in pairs, but so do the men.'

Private Picken said that when they arrived the male drivers thought they were 'dollybirds' and were constantly dismissive of them. Later, they got more respect. Having tasted a real war, she would like to serve in Northern Ireland. Although women soldiers are not normally posted within six miles of the front or beyond the second echelon – the supply lines behind the front troops – Private Picken said she would be willing to go wherever her job took her and if that meant tanks at the front, that was fine. 'I don't suppose there will be any change. *They* decide for us. It's a male environment and certain divisions still don't want to have girls in them.' At present, women can make deliveries to the front, but they are not supposed to remain in the area.

As the women gained in responsibility and confidence in the Gulf, many realised that their jobs back home would not be challenging or fulfilling any more. Corporal Elaine Dargie, a driver with the nearby 77 Squadron RCT, said at this stage in her career, she had done everything, and the only thing that would keep her in the army was if they expanded the number of jobs open to women, right up to the front.

With Scuds landing everywhere but the front lines, the rule which kept both American and British female soldiers out of the combat zone was of little use. Often they would find themselves just behind the front, bringing supplies or replacement men. They often heard artillery fire or felt the vibrations from explosions. A missile landed in the sea just off the Al-Jubail camp and the drivers saw the debris. Another landed in one of the towns towards the Kuwait border. The last killed twenty-eight soldiers and injured ninety-eight when it hit American barracks in the city of Al-Khobar, near Dhahran. Three of the dead were women – Army Specialist Beverley Clark, Specialist Christine Mayes and Private Adrienne Mitchell. On 26 February, two days before the ceasefire, the Scud hit their corrugated steel warehouse which was being used as a canteen, dormitories and a gym. There were many injuries and deaths on the roads too – from mines and from crashes. Four men from the British RCT died in wartime accidents, as did three American women. Fear was evenly distributed across the desert, right back to the supply lines.

'You'd hear a blast nearby, and you didn't know what was on the warhead, so you'd spend the next two hours in your suit listening to the radio,' said Corporal Lorraine Dickie. After a while they became used to it and ended up sleeping in their gas masks and even writing letters in them. Corporal Dargie said the men had low expectations of their courage. 'They thought we would sit around crying and cuddling each other, saying "I want my Mummy". In the end the lads were coming to us with their problems and treating us like big sisters. There were just some things they couldn't discuss with other men. But although they would mostly try to treat us as equal, they would never stop reminding us, somehow, that we were women.'

The women truckers' gains in confidence during the war did not go unnoticed – they changed the army just as much as the army changed them and the RCT is presently opening far more trades to women. Major Bob Luke of 77 Squadron, which had drivers of both sexes, said his fears that the women would be passengers were unfounded. With some lyricism, he continued. 'The sky is black with the wings of chickens coming home to roost on the corpses of sacred cows which have been slaughtered.' What he meant by that was that many male officers had made the amazing discovery that women could drive as well as, if not better than men, something civilian insurance companies and women who served in the Second World War have known for a long time. It was a very simple thing, but in terms of the slow-moving attitudes towards women in the British forces, it was a huge advance.

Major Luke sat at a bench in the sun surrounded by his female driving team in a commandeered Saudi complex of concrete boxes which resembled a prison camp. At least it had showers. The rest of the women were in tents in the desert for up to eight months. Out there soldiers of either sex hated the dust storms, the stinking chemical latrines, the constant stress of Scud attacks and the boiling hot, charcoal-lined, chemical warfare suits that turned their skin black. All the women's fears of 'the hygiene problem' – the forces' favourite euphemism for periods – went and 'the separate toilets and showers problem' also dissipated in the desert, when creating a ladies meant no more than digging an extra hole in the sand and covering it with a lid. And when a shower was in fact a bucket with some holes drilled in it, which they stood under, it was easy enough to create an additional one.

But terror of the dirty word 'hygiene' knew no bounds. Most of the British women sent to the Gulf were encouraged by army medical advisers to go on the pill for six months without a break, so they had no periods at all. Normally, doctors suggest a week's break every month. The full-time prescription was suggested because women might have problems with menstruation in their chemical suits, though why this should be any different from once-daily male bodily functions was never explained. A few women did go on the pill for six months. Others thought that was unhealthy, if not downright dangerous. Also, only one variety of pill, Ovren 45, seemed to be readily available and it gave some women side effects.

It was not just the contraceptive pill which was a worry, but its combination with the other anti-chemical-warfare drugs given to soldiers. Staff Sergeant Jan Rees, aged thirty-three, was working in the RCT operations cell closer to the battlefields and talked as she sunbathed on a deckchair beside a captured Iraqi tank. 'It wasn't a direct order to take the pill so I didn't take it – not when we were being advised to have anti-anthrax injections and taking NAPS [anti-nerve agent] tablets all at the same time. They said the anthrax was voluntary and that put doubts in your mind.' The high doses, designed for male bodies, or perhaps the chemical reaction of such a cocktail of drugs, made the women ill and also forced them to go constantly to the toilet. Most of the Americans did not take the tablets, since they were not all approved by the Federal Drugs Administration. Nor were the Americans advised to use the contraceptive pill non-stop. Brigadier Gael Ramsey of the WRAC said pill decision was 'a legitimate proposal from the medical section. It was not an order. The pill existed to save them the punishment in the desert with no washing facilities, if they wished to swallow it.'

The pattern repeated itself with Tampax and sanitary towels. Obviously women brought their own, but they were not going to carry six months' worth. After all, no squaddie comes armed with six months' worth of toilet paper. There were no sanitary supplies at all at some of the camps. The Americans were also caught out, at first with too little too late, and then too much too late, after soldiers sent begging letters home. The parcels started to arrive for 'A Woman Soldier in the Gulf' and they contained cosmetics which were useless in the dust and endless sanitary supplies of various brands. 'I can do you Tampax, Lil-lets, Kotex, Simplicity and Boots. We've got about three years' supply here,' said a woman trucker digging into a four-foot-high box in the corner of a dormitory tent. An army unused to sending female soldiers to war had not had enough time to plan for their needs, and had done no medical research on the health risks to women of anti-chemical-warfare drugs.

Lack of forethought and coordination also dogged the business of whether women should drive at all. Those with 77 Squadron RCT, close to Al-Jubail, got on with their jobs when they arrived in January 1991. Then came the edict that they could not drive; so a compromise with the Saudis was reached – women could drive military vehicles in uniform, but not for recreation. Those at 68 Squadron RCT thought it was acceptable for two women to drive as a team. A few miles away 77 Squadron was quite convinced each woman had to be accompanied by a man. The women-only squad drove twenty-four- to forty-eight-hour shifts. The women on the mixed squads were not even allowed to do a twenty-four-hour loop, supplying 30,000 palletised missiles at a time to just behind the front. The system made very little sense and seemed arbitrary.

That was partly because although many of the officers were praising women volubly, there were a number of diehards who resented their intrusion and utilisation of women varied with the extent of their acceptance. 'Some commanding officers were reluctant to push their women too far forward. Some seized upon the opportunity to do just that and use them as professional soldiers. The women were on the whole fully employed, although a small minority were bored,' said Brigadier Ramsey. Those who trusted in female capabilities found them on the whole to be good workers and those who did not put a larger burden on their men. A few women were not pulling their weight, particularly in the initial stages of tent-erecting and trench-digging. That was partly because the then separate women's course had not taught these skills as thoroughly as that of the men, who had spent much more time on field and weapons training. Some women were not above encouraging a man to do the hard work for them. With the male-to-female ratio at twenty-to-one, offers of assistance were easy to come by.

There was more resistance to female soldiers from the enlisted men and non-commissioned officers, particularly those in their mid-twenties and thirties, who were not used to being around women in uniform, except those in traditional administrative or secretarial roles. Now six women drivers were not just in 77 Squadron, they were in the tent next door to Lance Corporal Kevin Carpenter, Sergeant Kevin Parkins and Corporal Steve Richardson, all in their twenties. After a hot and greasy 'compo' (tinned ration) lunch of quiche, ubiquitous baked beans and macaroni served on plastic airline-style trays in a sweaty cook tent, they had nothing better to do post-war than share their opinions. War is described as ninety per cent boredom and ten per cent fear, and when surrounded by sand and deprived of beer, the aftermath is guaranteed 100 per cent boredom. After a while in these conditions, little things begin to rankle.

'Half of them don't know how to use a pick or a shovel and they should be properly trained if they're expected to do it. The problem with the girls is they start off keen, but the moment they meet the challenge and prove they can do it, they lose interest and do less work,' said Sergeant Parkins, reclining on his American-borrowed camp bed. The tent wall above him was decorated with a poster of a topless model, greetings cards from home and a blue furry teddy bear. He claimed women were only too capable of persuading men to mend their trucks, help with their camouflage concealment and dig their trenches. Corporal Richardson was not pleased either, 'They're being paid the same as a bloke so they should do the same work.'

The men seemed aggrieved because women were doing the jobs which had been their sole province for a long time and also because double standards seemed to be operating. The girls had it easy was the opinion and not just in the workplace, but in bed. Lance Corporal Carpenter said, 'If we got up to what I hear women out here have got up to with other women, we'd be out.' He claimed there was a different standard for lesbians and for homosexuals, and the army turned a blind eye to the women.

This state of affairs had clearly irritated the red-blooded males in this particular tent. Aside from light pornography, battlefield souvenirs affirmed that these were indeed army men to the core. They eagerly displayed a huge knife, demonstrated possible uses of a sort of Iraqi tomahawk, and showed a shell casing and an Iraqi commanding officer's diary or logbook in Arabic. The women next door – or indeed anywhere else in the Gulf – seemed to have no interest in collecting Iraqi helmets or other gruesome relics. The men did not find that surprising. 'You've got to remember they *are* women at the end of the day,' said Lance Corporal Carpenter. 'Yes, there is that,' said Sergeant Parkins slowly. 'A lot of times my point of view is that they're almost as good a morale booster as they are a pain.'

Much the same views prevailed among the women when asked about their male workmates. It sounded like they had had a fairly rough ride to begin with. A sense of humour, they said constantly, was vital for survival. Private Sarah Smith, at nineteen one of the youngest women, provided an example of the survival technique. 'When we were down in Al-Jubail camp, we found the men were drilling spy holes through the wooden partition between their showers and ours, so we started filling them up with soap. Then after a few days we realised – if they can see us, we can see them. So we looked back at them. And that put a stop to it. Straightaway.'

Dealing with hostile fellow soldiers was something many of the women were used to. But this war had an added dimension – it was happening in a Muslim country and the female soldiers had to adapt to that. They had to wear combat jackets for modesty, working in fierce heat, while the men stripped down to T-shirts. Shorts were banned, except within closed camps, and a lot of women who were used to keeping fit by jogging had to desist. The Americans published a booklet, *Saudi Arabia: A Soldier's Guide*, which advised women they would be forced to ride in the back of buses and would be excluded from some shops. 'If you're a man,' it advised rather unnecessarily, 'DON'T try to date an Arab woman ... DON'T ask an Arab direct questions about his wife, or expect him to introduce any veiled woman who accompanies him.'

The sight of female soldiers driving sparked a minor revolution amongst fifty Saudi Arabian women in Riyadh, who dumped their male chauffeurs for a day and took to the wheel themselves in convoy through the city. The result: a few were suspended from their jobs and driving was made illegal for women not just under religious rules, but under state law too. In a country where women are expected to walk two steps behind their husbands, shrouded from top to toe in black *abiahs*, and are prohibited from travelling without permission from a male relative, the sight of female truckers and pilots was disturbing for both sexes. In Dhahran, one American woman officer was at a ten-pin bowling alley with the rest of her male unit, when a Saudi man started shouting at her, informing her she was a whore and telling her to go home. She drew her pistol and suggested he did exactly that himself. In another incident in a souk, a woman soldier was hit with a stick by one of the religious police for having the sleeves of her uniform rolled up showing bare arms. She floored him with a punch.

Such behaviour did little for Arab-American relations and some Western women found the customs hard to cope with at first, particularly when working alongside Saudi soldiers. 'We were deployed here to save these people and they don't want us because we're women,' Sergeant Sherry Callahan told the *New York Times*. As an assistant crew chief tending F-15 fighters in Dhahran, she found Saudi soldiers still looked shocked when she worked on the engine of her fighter next to a man, or worse still, gave orders. 'When I tell guys to do something you see them staring and saying to themselves, "Hey, it's not right for a woman to be ordering a man around".' But after a month of working in the same hangar with Saudi Air Force crews, there had been a thaw in their feelings. Eventually they even asked her to help on their aircraft if they were behind.

Saudi culture was also having a profound effect on the British doctors and nurses of 5 Armoured Field Ambulance, who had been on the wagon for three months. They drank crates of local non-alcoholic Moussy beer and ate too much chocolate as a substitute in the officers' mess tent, which was equipped with a board on a string for subordinates to knock on and show proper respect. Occasional illegal but strong drink would arrive from ingenious relatives disguised in Timotei shampoo bottles. It tasted a little soapy, but was set on with much relief by the bored medics who felt in many ways that this war had not been the real thing, although the boredom before and afterwards certainly was. The lack of alcohol – drugs too – meant that disciplinary offences in both the American and British forces were at an all-time low: the Americans had 1.45 serious disciplinary cases per 10,000 soldiers in an average month in the Gulf, compared to around fifty in peacetime.

The medics and nurses were not as stretched as they expected to be by the war. Most of the casualties were Iraqis, and after emergency 'tailboard treatment' on the back of armoured ambulances and trucks, they were helicoptered out to hospital across the border in Saudi Arabia. There were a few British casualties – mostly injuries from the unexploded ammunition and land mines which littered the desert, which went on long after the ground war was over. The women of the Queen Alexandra's Royal Army Nursing Corps, who received the Iraqi casualties at 32 Field Hospital in Hafra Al-Batin in Saudi, found the men gaunt, dirty and suffering from malnutrition.

Captain Anne Malcolm, a Scottish nursing sister in her thirties, said the majority of the 200 casualties were in for minor treatment. They were terrified, believing propaganda that they would be skinned, chopped up and fed to English people's dogs, if not to the dreaded Gurkhas, and might be experimented on medically without anaesthetic. 'We had one fifteen-year-old boy who was so scared. He was a wee lad, with his face stuck out under the blanket, and you just wanted to give him a cuddle – if he hadn't been so infested with fleas and lice,' she said. The nurses even had to taste the food before the Iraqis to prove it was not poisoned. After they gained confidence, the men, some of whom were barefoot, would show photographs of their families back home and speak a little English. Although sympathetic, Captain Malcolm and her team had no time for malingerers. 'They came in faking injuries and would lie there screaming the place down when there was nothing wrong with them. A major-general came in, like a little fat Buddha, complaining of back pain. We sussed him and threw him out. He was too frightened to leave his men.'

The nurses were very close to the fighting – too close for some. Medical technician Sergeant Liz Forrai said, 'There were fourteen of us and four stretchers stuffed in the back of a tracked ambulance, and suddenly we heard tank fire and personal weapon fire everywhere. So we turned the thing round and got out of there.' In their eagerness to reach casualties, they had ended up at the front.

The armoured ambulances were to have been driven by the all-male Gurkhas, but a mixed army medical unit was sent instead. 'At first the lads took a step back,' said Sergeant Forrai. 'They thought, "Oh my God – women". So we had to prove that we could do it, really get in there and pull our weight. Some did and some didn't, but now we're on board we get on very well.' Nursing Sergeant Delia McCarthy thought that in a unit of this size the men had to take on an extra one per cent of the work. 'That's fine, but I don't think physically we should be in a combat unit. I'm too slight and I don't think they could cope with women.' She felt women had the will, but not the strength. However, her boss, Lieutenant-Colonel Bruce Reece-Russell, seemed pleased with their performance. He declared he would be the first person to have women in a field ambulance at soldier level, since they had fitted in very well. 'And they don't half tone things down. They're good news.'

Both sexes seemed to cope equally well with the gore of battle, but unlike soldiers, doctors and nurses – often in the reserves – were used to pain and mess in their day-to-day jobs back in Germany and Britain. No one talked about nightmares following the war. It was more during the stressful period when Scuds were flying and soldiers slept in gas masks that the sound of men and women talking in their sleep filled the tents. One nursing major said that during raids she found men were showing more of the typical signs of stress – adrenalin rushes and dilated pupils – than most women. But for some soldiers, coming close to death and seeing the bodies of others made them reconsider their priorities in life.

Captain Penny France, a doctor in her late twenties, often found herself a little further forward than she would have liked. On the field dressing-station, in the rain and bitter cold that marked the start of the ground war, she patched soldiers up and resuscitated them before evacuation. They had multiple shrapnel wounds and some needed amputations. The experience of four months in the desert had changed her feelings about military service. She looked tired and drawn, not tanned like the rest of her colleagues who were treating the desert as a post-war sunbed. When she joined as a cadet at university and became a full-time doctor two years before, she never thought she would go to war. 'Ask any of us. Men and women. We never really considered it. Others are proud of having had a chance to do their job as soldiers, but I do this job every day and I don't need to go to war to prove I'm a good doctor.'

Captain France said she was planning to marry her boyfriend, an officer in the artillery, who spent the war with his regiment in Colchester. As the only female doctor still left in field ambulance – the other got an early flight home – she had a tent on her own with a dried-out red rose from her fiancé pinned to the canvas, copies of *Wedding* magazine and *Tatler* under the usual borrowed American camp bed (the British ones were deemed too uncomfortable), and a boxful of 'blueys' – the air-mail letters which had been their only means of contact. She had been intending to stay in the army and hoped they would get posted together as a married couple. Now, she was wiser and considering getting out. 'This sort of thing focuses your mind on what's important in life. I don't particularly want to be separated from my husband. When you go away you realise what's valuable in life, how important your family is to you and you think what you might have lost.' (In fact, once home and following her marriage, she remained, at least on paper, signed up until 1995.)

Others were resigned to the military invading sex and family life. 'Giving your ovaries to the army,' said one nurse, was part of the deal, and you stayed in and accepted it, or else you got out. Sergeant Forrai said, 'It's tough. If you stay in too long you become institutionalised and you can't manage outside. You have army-dictated relationships – you keep a man for a two- or three-year posting and then get another one. It doesn't work otherwise at long distance. With the best will in the world, you can't keep it going.'

A few do. Captain Alison Foster-Knight at the armour division rear headquarters nearby had been married to another officer for five years and they had yet to be posted together. He remained in Britain with the Royal Military Police, while she organised ammunition and food supplies for the front. Captain Foster-Knight said her husband was a little frustrated that she was the one living for four months under a tarpaulin attached to the side of an armoured vehicle in the desert, rather than him. Even a war did not help them to get posted together. For two and a half years previously, they had struck relatively lucky, being posted 'only 120 miles apart' in Germany, so they met at weekends. It was easier when they were both lieutenants, but now as captains, there were fewer postings for him and even less for her as a woman. She signed up for four more years and went to be an instructor at Sandhurst. She realised her sort of work precluded having children for the duration and was resigned. 'They spelt it all out when we got married, what the problems were going to be. As for the war, I think I'm more worried about him being anxious about me than anxious for myself.'

Captain Foster-Knight played down the danger inherent in being through the breach in the enemy's defences so soon behind the tanks. Her male colleagues were more inclined to go into detail. Major Steve Sanderson, the chief artillery logistics staff officer, whom she worked alongside under the sun-dappled camouflage nets of the headquarters tent, said, 'We arrived about an hour or less behind the brigades, sort of leap-frogging back and forth with the battle, and we saw hundreds of prisoners-of-war among the smoking wreckage. They were coming out of holes and waving white flags. Some even built themselves a barbed-wire compound and sat down in it so they'd be safe. They were dropping from hypothermia, dehydrated, with wounds only tended after a fashion.' But Captain Foster-Knight just muttered 'war stories again' and said it had happened so quickly all they saw were empty Iraqi posts.

Her colleagues in headquarters claimed it was good to have a woman around because she brought them back to reality and improved their language. They saw no reason why a woman should not be up at the front, but worried about families with both parents at war. Captain Foster-Knight absent-mindedly touched the 9mm Browning automatic pistol on her hip and said she thought the deployment rules which existed to protect women had become a little pointless. 'In practice, girls shouldn't be banned so long as they can do the job.' But doing the job again in peacetime – playing wargames in the barns and fields of England and Germany – would be hard when she had seen the real thing. Outside the tent, she paid absolutely no attention as male soldiers paused to urinate into the crotch-height 'desert roses', narrow pipes going deep underneath the sand, or to sleeping bags, unwashed for three months, aired on poles in the wind. 'I've spent seven years now in a male-dominated environment. I don't notice it any more. The person who notices the difference in me most is my husband when I get home.'

Delicacy and sensibility were not noticeably present around the battlefields, less so where the Americans were camped. Three young American military policewomen who patrolled the bomb-cratered road between the Iraqi border and Kuwait City were in mixed tents for three months. 'There is no privacy at all out here,' said Sergeant Jeremy Kopina. 'The first week I go home, I am *living* in the bathroom.' Her colleague, Private First Class Donna Bartlett, hung out the window of her HumVee – a cross between a Land-Rover and a beach buggy with an M60 machine gun mounted on top – and advised that she had not had a shower for two and a half weeks. Living in a mixed tent, they began by dressing inside their sleeping bags and later would just tell the men to turn their backs, hoping constant exposure would result in boredom rather than anything else. Clearly much less fuss was made about the presence of women among the American troops than the British. The Americans were used to mixed units and found women in the field ordinary, if not downright uninteresting. It also meant there was less pressure on the women, who were not treated as aliens with strange 'hygiene' problems. The policewomen's boss, First Sergeant James E. Smith, said, 'The military's got a job to do and if you leave it alone things work out. There's a lot of overprotecting of females in the outside world. It's better just to let them get on with it.'

The presence of women was decidedly more exciting for the prisoners-of-war they rounded up inside Iraq. Sergeant Kopina said, 'They were just begging for us to put the cuffs on. They couldn't believe we were women. They looked like they thought they were in heaven.' She worked eighteen- to twenty-hour days processing prisoners, but seeing the results of combat had not put her off. 'I think some women are capable of combat, but you need emotional stability, and there are a lot of men who can't handle it. It's not the dream of every woman to have a marriage and children and all that. Some women have different dreams.'

One or two of the Americans in the traditional marriage-dreaming category were lucky enough to be able to combine army and family life – they were posted with their husbands. In the Reserves' Civil Affairs unit down in what remained of Kuwait City, there were a number of married couples assigned together and, incidentally, two brothers, and a brother and sister. The units were there to advise the Kuwaitis how to clean up the mess, and to try and get essential supplies like electricity, food and water moving again. Captain Laurie Fisher and her husband Major Carl Fisher were involved in sending teams out to assess damage and check the fairness of Kuwaiti food distribution, since in some areas Palestinians and Asians seemed to be being sent to the back of the queue, while Kuwaitis went to the front. The unit also kept an eye on the roadblocks set up by vigilantes with stolen guns which peppered the city.

The unit's headquarters was in a warehouse complex just outside Kuwait, but subject to the same strange changes in light as thick, black oil clouds from burning wells blew over. At 9 am it might have been midnight and when the generator failed the soldiers worked by torchlight. The warehouse was bedroom, office and living room to about 113 reserves, of whom fifteen were women; the Fishers were assigned to separate beds on the opposite male and female sides of the room. 'I'm not complaining,' said Captain Fisher. 'At least we're together, and although they have rules about "conduct unbecoming to a soldier", we do spend a lot of private time together. But after lights out, we're supposed to be in our own place.' The army points out, quite rightly, that when everyone else is separated from their partner for months, those lucky enough to be posted together should not make it any harder for the others with amorous displays in public. In the regular army in peacetime, men and women are never sent to be under the same chain of command in a unit, either in America or Britain.

In Kuwait, it all sounded rather like the chastity expected of girls and boys at boarding school, when in fact this couple had been married for thirteen years and had a seven-year-old daughter, Megan, staying at home with her grandmother in Arkansas. The longest time the girl had been separated from her mother was two weeks, until these three months. 'She's probably doing better than I am, because she doesn't really have a concept of time. She sends me coloured pictures and I've sent her a couple of tapes, and since they set up AT&T phones here if you queue for a few hours you can call once a week.' Captain Fisher's lips smiled, but her voice did not. Major Fisher added, 'Taking Megan out of school and leaving her was the hardest thing about coming here. When there were two Scud alerts our greatest worry was what would happen to our daughter. Thank God they're so inaccurate.' As one soldier put it, 'If there's a bullet out there with my name on it, that's OK – it's my time. It's the ones that say "To whom it may concern" that worry me.'

Another reserve, Private First Class Melissa Benson, worked in the public-affairs unit on the same base. Despite the Scuds sometimes making the rear line interchangeable with the front, she still did not think women should go into the combat arms – the infantry, artillery and armour – because she thought men might get themselves killed trying to protect physically weaker women. The problem of women prisoners-of-war was also playing on her mind – after all, Army Specialist Melissa Coleman (née Nealy) had been captured on an oil-tapline road near the Saudi-Kuwait border when her truck came under fire.

She was shot in her lower arm during the skirmish, beaten in the truck by Iraqi soldiers and kept prisoner for over a month. It was discovered after Specialist Coleman was released that she had been treated better than her male co-driver, who was beaten regularly in his cell for the first two weeks. She was never beaten again by her captors and was given medical treatment for her wounds. The Iraqis had claimed they would treat women according to their own customs and certainly, once in prison, this was the case. It could easily have gone the other way. No one knows if a soldier commits a rape on a female POW out in the desert, whatever the instructions from his leadership, and certainly the male RAF pilots were tortured for information. This time, being a POW was better for women – in the next war it could be the opposite.

Another woman, flight surgeon Major Rhonda Cornum, broke both arms when her helicopter was shot down over Iraqi territory as the crew searched for a downed F-16 pilot. She was given medical treatment by the Iraqis and was returned along with about forty-five allied POWs after the ceasefire. A week or so after the ground war had ended, however, nothing was known of the prisoners, and Private Benson feared that Muslim countries and those which preferred women 'barefoot and pregnant are far more dangerous for women prisoners-of-war. They look upon women soldiers as sluts and whores, and they might treat them accordingly.'

She pointed out that there was a price for the capture of certain types of soldiers in every war. Before the Gulf, the most prized POW was a pilot, because of the millions of dollars it costs to train him. Now, with that extra emotional pull for the public back home, it was women – wives, mothers, girls, daughters. 'They run a higher risk of being tortured than men, because the enemy believes they shouldn't be there in the first place,' said Private Benson. The treatment of Kuwaiti women had left her in no doubt of the brutality of the invading Iraqis, who had raped, sexually abused and cut some women's breasts off, before leaving them dead in the street. The female POWs were lucky to come out unscathed, at least physically. Specialist Coleman certainly appeared at the Washington victory parade afterwards, in full desert uniform, and remained in the army to go on serving at Fort Bliss in Texas.

Private Benson, tall with blonde hair in a French pleat, was one year older at twenty-one than Specialist Coleman, and had driven media despatches in the same area and could easily imagine how terrifying the experience was for the POW. She had been in the war zone for seven months – normally she was a student in North Carolina. 'Back in February, I saw myself for the first time in a proper mirror and I seemed to have aged five years. In one way, I've noticed how much more vocal and confident I've become, but being in the field also brings you closer to the real things that matter in life, simple things like eating, finding somewhere to wash, surviving, and that really puts things back home into perspective. You realise more than anything that what's important are friends and family.'

The soldiers, like Private Benson, who travelled through the battlefields to Kuwait, saw the thoroughness of the devastation and heard at first hand of repression and torture, were much more aware of the reality of war than those in isolated camps in the desert. The desert had a safe normality about it, while around Kuwait everything was surreal. Even the warehouse complex housing the civil affairs unit was peculiar. There seemed on some days to be two dawns, one in the east and one in the west of the black sky. The fake one in the west was the bright orange light from oil flames.

In one warehouse, stocking educational books, the reserves found thousands of plain school exercise books, each with a photograph of Saddam Hussein on the cover and a patriotic message beneath for each Kuwaiti schoolchild. Outside, by contrast, there was a US Army 'Wolfburger' stall, a sort of portable McDonald's so the troops felt at home. There were creepier mixings of American and Kuwaiti culture, as in the story of the army officers' annual West Point dinner, held wherever its alumni are, to celebrate the founding of their academy. In March 1991, it was held in the most appropriate building available – the abandoned palace of one of the Al-Sabahs, the Kuwaiti royal family. The men and women officers ate dinner in one of the dining rooms, left untouched by the Iraqis, whose Republican Guard had used it as a headquarters. Downstairs in the basement, the American officers found a huge sandpit mapped out to show borders and troop encampments, with little markers. Upstairs in the attic – and possibly unknown to most of the officers – were the iron bedframes, electric-current machines, wires, drills, scraps of cloth for tying down victims and other paraphernalia used by the Iraqis to torture those suspected of resistance.

Like much of this war, nothing seemed quite real, and the Al-Sabahs' palace felt more like a film set than a place of torture. Because the British, Americans and Saudis came upon the ravages after the occupation, it was hard to imagine the real events which had created the results. For the women soldiers, who were not involved in the front-line combat, everything was seen through the anaesthetic of a time lag. After the war the British even organised rather ghoulish coach trips for soldiers to 'Bomb Alley' – the Basra Road leading out of Kuwait which had been strafed and cluster-bombed into two miles, six lanes wide, of twisted, blackened metal. The corpses had been removed from the tanks and civilian cars, but the smell still remained in some places, as did occasional shoes, sunglasses, chandeliers and bales of cloth belonging to, or stolen by, the escaping thousands. The soldiers looked on, took photographs and picked up shell casings, uncomfortable tourists with gruesome souvenirs. They felt at a loss, knowing they ought to see the devastation, but unsure what their reaction should be.

Driving out to Kuwait airport, a corpse in uniform hung by his neck from a window of one home flying a Kuwaiti flag, probably an Iraqi collaborator. Yet one of the British women soldiers who saw it said, 'My first thought was, oh, there's a dummy hanging there. Then I realised it was real.' And later when she saw a severed hand at the side of one torched Iraqi tank, she thought it was a black glove lying on the sand. 'I suppose in your head you go for the least frightening explanation as a way of coping. I mean, even corpses get referred to as "bodybags". No one really tells you how messy it is.'

The ghosts were everywhere. First Lieutenant Tracy McLaughlin, an American helicopter pilot at Kuwait airport, was billeted in a former airline office used by the Iraqis before and during battle. A patch about eight-foot square in the centre of the brown carpet had been cut out and replaced by artificial grass, presumably the only material available. 'I don't know why, but a lot of people died around here. You can see the bullet marks on the walls outside. Maybe bodies were left to bleed on the carpet and that was why they took it out,' she said. There was destruction all around after three weeks of allied bombing. A British Airways jet lay neatly spliced in two across the runway. The control tower was a shell. Everything that had not been smashed or strafed had been burned or booby-trapped as the Iraqis made their retreat. Escaped cows and horses roamed by the hangars. Lieutenant McLaughlin sat lankily in her green flying suit on a bench in the sun surveying it all from behind her pilots' shades. 'You get used to it after a while. It's not that bad. In a place like this you've got to find your own little piece of happiness.'

Aged twenty-five, she was one of the youngest and the only female pilot out of ninety, in an army aviation battalion of 225. But at least in the war zone, men were much more inclined to treat her as an equal doing the same job, because their lives depended on her if she made a mistake and vice versa.

She worked twenty-two-hour days at the start of the war, running flight operations and flying missions. 'I slept between eleven and one during the day; I was sleeping in the shower; taking cat naps when I was being driven somewhere. The hardest part of being a woman in this job is the motherly feelings you have towards the men you are sending out, although we haven't lost any.' She flew four or five hours at a time in her Blackhawk helicopter. In the previous few days they had been taking 'everyone and their mother' to the peace negotiations in Safwan on the border, including American Secretary of State James Baker, and Red Cross teams. They also had to avoid being shot down by Iraqi air defences near the border.

It was a very peculiar few months for someone who was normally a business administrator at the University of South Dakota. Lieutenant McLaughlin was called up as a reserve, but her husband, who is a full-time pilot, stayed in the States. He was flying search and rescue missions for the air force in Rapid City, South Dakota, while she was in the Gulf. 'He's not very happy about it.' They had been married for seventeen months and spent seven together. She was not in the army full-time partly because at that time flying opportunities were limited for women. 'I can't fly attack helicopters or anything with weapons, though I'd definitely like to. Anyway, I've been doing a lot of troop hauls, supplying ammo, and that's usually in hostile areas and you're not really expected to defend yourself with a little light M60 [the automatic machine gun on the Blackhawk]. They're not all that effective.' Following the performance of women in the US Air Force and Army airborne divisions in the war, the US Senate voted in August 1991 to change the law and allow women to fly fighter planes and combat helicopters. Lieutenant McLaughlin would no longer be frustrated.

There were twenty-two women pilots with 101st Airborne which sent more than 300 attack helicopters into Iraq during the war, carrying over 2,000 men, fifty HumVees, howitzers, food and ammunition. Major Marie Rossi was the lead pilot of a group of Chinook helicopters. Throughout the ground war she flew dozens of missions, sometimes carrying ammunition in the cargo holds, or with 2,500 gallons of jet fuel in tanks slung under her helicopter. She flew three missions in the first twenty-four hours of the war and told CNN in a television interview, 'What I am doing is no greater or less than the man who is flying next door to me or in the back of me.'

Major Rossi, a dark-haired thirty-two-year-old from Oradell, New Jersey, also talked about her fears of dying in the war. 'Sometimes you have to dissociate how you feel personally about the prospect of going into war and possibly seeing the death that's going to be out there. But personally, as an aviator and a soldier, this is the moment that I've trained for, so I feel ready to meet a challenge.' The day after the ceasefire, her Chinook hit an unlit tower at night in northern Saudi Arabia, and she and her two crewmen were killed instantly. Her body was brought back to the United States and buried with full military honours. Her last public words remained on the CNN tape. 'I think if you talk to the women who are professionals in the military, we see ourselves as soldiers. We don't really see it as man versus woman.'

3

SAILING IN THE GOLDFISH BOWL

The captain compared it to running a closed prison without any visitors. The inmates worked for eight hours, then slept for eight, in bunks they called coffins. There was no free time on board. Sometimes they sailed for nearly two months without a break, in cramped conditions that the average human-rights activist would call inhumane. HMS *Brilliant* was crossing the mine-filled waters of the post-war Gulf and its crew, mysteriously, were not complaining.

Fortunately for the sailors sentenced to this warship for six months, it had the one ingredient a prison does not – women. Usually the sailors' only contact was the girl in every port, but on HMS *Brilliant* there were a handful on every deck. Twenty of the 254 sailors were female, the first women to serve on a British frigate and the first to go to war.

The sixteen ratings – ordinary sailors – of the Women's Royal Naval Service shared one tiny mess with sweaty bunks a few feet apart and piled three high to the low ceiling, hence the nickname 'coffin' for the middle one. It was always hot and windowless below sea level, with a vague, darkroom-type red light, so at any time half the crew could sleep. 'There was a bit of animosity in the mess at first. You could feel the tension down there,' said Wren Radar Operator Helen Smithers. 'We kept picking one another up for petty little things. We got a bit ratty.' They were like the rats in the basic psychology experiment which become more aggressive as their enclosure gets smaller. Tension faded after a few weeks, when the war came closer. They spent time taping across the television and mirrors to stop them cracking, and securing the beds and lockers in case they were hit by mines. After a while, they were just too tired to argue.

HMS *Brilliant* was a more violent baptism for women sailors than the navy intended. The British followed the Canadian and

Scandinavian navies by making all ships mixed in 1990; the Americans are still keeping women off battleships and only allow them permanently on non-combat hospital and supply ships. When the British first offered women the chance to volunteer to go to sea, Saddam Hussein was still buying 'Supergun' parts from England and many people thought Kuwait was some kind of exotic fruit. The mixed ships were sent to play wargames, but the games became reality and HMS *Brilliant* was not going to be exempted from service, whatever the sex of its cargo. As the ship's Commander Chris Hadden put it, 'A mine doesn't distinguish between a man and a woman. If they're on the ship, they're in the war zone.'

Because a warship like *Brilliant* was built to fit guns first and people as an afterthought, the men and women lived in close proximity. There was almost nowhere on the ship to be alone. The navy banned the crew from forming relationships, battened down the hatches, sent the ship to war and hoped it would not explode – in both senses. But unlike two other ships in the allied fleet it was not hit by the floating mines that peppered the Gulf waters.

Throughout the war, women did the same jobs as men, keeping the Exocet and Sea Wolf weapons systems on twenty-four-hour alert, and operating radar and radio to track the Iraqis. If it had come to action stations, however, the Wrens would have been fighting alongside the men, loading explosives into the ship's magazines and using firearms. Women have now started training to fly Sea King and Lynx anti-submarine warfare helicopters with Sea Skua missiles, but in the Gulf the attacks on fifteen Iraqi ships were carried out by men. A large chunk of the Iraqi navy was not up to much. In the end the enemy was using rubber dinghies with rocket launchers, 'motorised lilos', as one pilot said with contempt. There was no direct confrontation, so *Brilliant*, riding shotgun guarding allied tankers and transporters, stayed on the edge of the action – which was fortunate, because there was plenty of action going on in the ship itself.

It was a military and anthropological first for Britain when the Type-22 frigate left Plymouth for the Gulf on 14 January 1991. The journey continued as the men and women officers took mid-morning toast and tea in the wardroom. Although the war was over the mines were not. The ship was still on yellow alert since the Iraqis had left one or two unanchored 'floaters' which occasionally popped up in previously swept channels. But this state of affairs had not affected the typically British stewardess service, silver toast racks and supplies of Rose's lime marmalade. There were realistic-looking fresh vegetables on board and newly baked bread, while fifty miles across the sea in the desert north of Kuwait, the troops lived for months on tinned pink meat, quite unrelated to any animal, and buckets of baked beans.

But the desert had one advantage: relative privacy, a luxury unavailable on board. On land, soldiers could at least walk away behind a sand dune for solitude. On ship, there was constant togetherness. Sailors who were used to part-time bachelorhood suddenly found their world collapsing. They were challenged by women who were present, but not available.

Publicly, the men's frustration, disturbance or even objection to the female invasion remained muted. But their true opinions – about subjects such as the pertness of a certain Wren's breasts, which female officers were sexy and which ratings were objects for admiration (or masturbation) – were noted in their departmental Dit books. Dit may be short for ditty (no one was sure); the books were originally intended to note misdemeanours and anecdotes relating to the boy-ratings who were training. But the grubby hardbacks were now filled with dirty jokes and cartoons. Locker-room humour was rife on the page, but muted in person. 'To tell you the truth I'm happy for them to come on. But then I'm still single,' said Seaman George Robb, who at seventeen was one of the youngest on the ship. He was in the darkened operations room, identifying blips of light on a radar screen, beneath the padlock over the bank of buttons which operated the Exocet missiles with live warheads. He whispered, 'A lot of the older lads who've been here ten or twelve years aren't too pleased, and they've made that clear.'

Some of their wives were not too pleased either when the prospect of women going to sea was first mooted by the British navy. About forty marched in the ports of Plymouth and Portsmouth in an attempt to keep the Wrens from sailing and, they claimed, stealing their husbands. The wives carried banners which said 'No Wrens at Sea' and 'Temptation is a Sin, Put this Idea in the Bin', gathered petitions and wrote to the Duchess of York, whose husband, Prince Andrew, was one of the threatened men. The wives were led by one

Jayne Green, married to a sailor and with two children. She told the press, 'We trust our husbands ninety-nine per cent of the time but there is always that one per cent doubt in your mind. If you confine people in small places and intimate situations like a ship at sea for long periods, you are going to get people attracted to each other.' Certainly, the plight of the wives engendered much debate, but in the end, there was little sailor-snatching. Mrs Green's words seemed ironic later, when she left her husband for an American sailor.

Despite a strict 'no-touching' rule on board all ships, there was one case on HMS *Brilliant* which resulted in a court martial and another in pregnancy. In the first, Lieutenant Mark Davies, a married man aged twenty-nine, and Sub-Lieutenant Jacqueline Ramsay, aged twenty-five, were found kneeling naked at either end of Lieutenant Davies' bunk. The court martial was told that they had not had nor did they intend to have intercourse. Senior officers had found the couple in 'non-action' when Sub-Lieutenant Ramsay was missing from her cabin after drinking coffee with Lieutenant Davies and they opened his door. On discovery, she said, 'Fair enough, you have seen enough. Now please shut the door while I put some clothes on.' They were each severely reprimanded and fined £750, despite the fact Sub-Lieutenant Ramsay was only on a trainee's salary and Lieutenant Davies was a fully-paid helicopter observer.

The relationship blossomed after a previous incident when they were reported together in a cabin and were banned by the captain, Tobin Elliott, from visiting each other's quarters; from leaving the ship for two months; and from using the bar for three months. Their punishment came at the end of the Gulf War and the two were unable to take shore leave after *Brilliant* docked in a number of ports. They stayed on board with little or no company but their own. Perhaps inadvertently, the captain, who was new to integrated disciplinary matters, had provided them with exactly the opportunity for friendship they wanted. The defence said the case was 'hardly earth-shattering' and a simple incident which caused embarrassment out of all proportion to the facts. It was just that it had come at a very inconvenient time for a gingerly integrating navy, and the press and wives pounced on it with gleeful 'I-told-you-sos'.

The second incident among the *Brilliant* crew was only discovered after the ship had finished its tour. Rating Wendy Clay, aged nineteen, and Able Seaman Darren Winter, aged twenty-one, had a secret affair, which might have continued unnoticed, had Rating Clay not got pregnant when she stayed in a hotel with Able Seaman Winter on shore leave in Dubai. Frightened that she would be flown home, or discharged, she kept quiet about it until her stint at sea was over, and then her doctor at home told her she was nearly seven months' pregnant. She had started to put on weight, but the ship's doctor decided it was stress due to the war, which had given a number of women overeating problems. In an interview with the *Daily Mirror*, she said, 'I know people must assume I was some sort of dizzy young girl, not taking proper precautions, but I was on the pill and never missed taking it. I think the tablets the navy gave us to counter the possible effects of chemical attack might have had something to do with it.' Now married to Able Seaman Winter, she has not been disciplined, since the events occurred on shore leave, but she has decided to leave the navy.

There was another case on the aircraft carrier HMS *Invincible*, just after mixing, when Sub-Lieutenant Callum Cowx, aged twenty-four, was caught asleep with a teenage Wren steward, Alison Grey, in his bunk. They were both still fully clothed and had come back to his cabin for coffee after dancing at a nightclub in Southsea. He was fined £350 at a court martial and severely reprimanded, and Steward Grey was fined £50 at an internal disciplinary hearing by the commanding officer of HMS *Invincible*. During the Gulf War, a nurse and a male medical officer were sent home from the hospital ship RFA *Argus* when they were caught embracing. Thereafter, the ship developed a somewhat racy reputation.

Despite a spattering of natural activity, the addition of women has not caused the entire fabric of the British navy to fall apart. Besides, on a ship 131 metres long and fourteen metres wide, with 254 people, it is fortunately rather hard to find a place to be alone. Anyway, what happens when the crew are on shore leave is their own business, so long as they do not get caught. Commandant Anne Spencer, Director of the Women's Royal Naval Service, said, 'I think it's inevitable that this happens occasionally. We really would be very naive if we didn't expect people to form relationships, but not on board ship where it could be prejudicial to good order.' Captain Elliott agreed, 'If people do break the rules, we mustn't get all upset and defensive about it. My philosophy is that we are all grown up and this is a very grown-up decision to have women at sea. All we have done is to make this ship normal.'

Generally, in terms of friendship, the women aboard HMS *Brilliant* had been a positive addition. Often a man and a woman would be stuck eight hours on, and eight off, on the same shift, in the same operations room below deck, for months. A male and a female radio operator (a former bus driver from Liverpool) had formed a platonic friendship so symbiotic they finished each other's sentences and had joint opinions on most subjects. 'What this really has proved is that men and women *can* be friends and nothing else. If I'm the only woman on my watch, then there's no choice,' said another Wren Radio Operator, Yvette Ellis, who used to do a day job in the navy information office in Whitehall. 'Some of my best friends here are men, and of course there's gossip-mongering and speculation, but you find yourself going home to meet their wives and that didn't happen on shore.'

Integration was difficult to begin with. The women ratings were billeted in one large mess and the four female officers in a couple of separate cabins. Because they all joined at once they were cut off from the experience normally passed down by word of mouth from sailor to sailor. Like any other institution ships have their own language. There are tannoy announcements, called 'pipes', and often the women had no idea whether they were being ordered to breakfast or to the bridge, so codified was the terminology. They also got lost in the lookalike, grey-painted corridors and had no idea of the names for particular areas. Constant enquiries became an embarrassment.

All the new sailors now have an older mentor called a 'Sea Dad', whom they can go to for advice. Knowledge can thus be swapped by the men and the women, who have at last been allowed to mix in the living areas of their messes. These are tiny boxes with beige airport-lounge seating and a television for videos stuck against one wall on which, one afternoon in the Gulf, three off-duty women in combinations of jogging gear and pyjamas were watching *The Jungle Book* again, moaning and filing their nails.

Because they were older, most with a few years' experience before going to sea, the women in some ways had an easier time than the young men, who had to suffer the traditional male initiation

41

ceremonies. The rites of passage are called 'bites', educational japes like being sent on fog watch (impossible) or being asked to be a splash target, supposedly tied in a frogman suit to a target towed behind the ship which is then shot at for practice. New male ratings get their heads shaved and are dunked in a barrel of water the first time they cross the Equator. Rating Joe Jones, a seventeen-year-old with a skinhead, explained the rules below deck. 'See those arrows,' he said, pointing to some yellow ones on the floor. 'They told me I had to go round shining a big torch on them so they would glow in the dark. Took me a while to work out it was a joke.'

This was the navy Sense of Humour, issued with the unisex blue shirt and trousers of the number-eight work uniform. Like soldiers, nearly everybody mentioned how they could not cope without a sense of humour and most had the same jolly-but-not-ironic model. Perhaps it is part of the recruitment test. The captain explained, sitting under a photograph of the Princess of Wales in a white Wren's hat: 'The thing I notice most of all is that this ship is an extremely giggly ship, with a good sense of humour and women have made the men take a look at themselves and laugh. The girls were thrown pell-mell into war along with the chaps and, well, after three months they are frightfully confident. There are one or two men on board who are still resentful, but most realise the girls are here to stay and this is not an experiment. I sit here and watch the whole thing with a degree of amusement. For instance, when all the other ships in the area are fighting to be heard over the radio, and suddenly a lone woman's voice comes over the radio and says, "This is *Brilliant*", the whole network falls silent because they just can't believe it.'

When women came on board, with their high voices and hair-driers, they also destroyed a culture built up over hundreds of years – not exactly Winston Churchill's 'rum, sodomy and the lash' – but certainly one built on traditional roots. Men had learned to be alone together for long periods of time, far more than any military landlubber with his weekends off, and had relationships which were fatherly, brotherly or occasionally more intimate. They had been used to strutting around the mess naked after a shower, but the women forced them to take to towels and modesty. The men talked in their own language, a mess-deck teasing banter laced with swear-words, and had their own codes: what you did off ship was your own business and your fellow sailors would not mention it to their wife or yours.

Naturally, to begin with, they had little respect for women with whom they had never worked before as colleagues or bosses. The fact that women could indeed lift heavy hatches, work in the heat of the engine room and load the stores was emasculating. And some men on *Brilliant* in their forties with half a lifetime at sea understandably found it hard to take orders from twenty-five-year-old 'wee lassies' who had just about learned to cope with being seasick.

'The navy isn't like the army. We don't go in for shouting at people because we've all got to live together for months. You just say, "This needs doing",' said Sub-Lieutenant Alison Trehearne as she sat sipping tea in the officers' wardroom (mess). 'But if push comes to shove,' said Sub-Lieutenant Kathy Green, 'you know when to ask, when to tell and when to give an order.' She admitted her old Wrens officers' training, before sea-going was possible, lacked relevance to her present job as a weapons engineer. They taught her deportment, how to wear stockings and eyeliner, and a bit of naval history, when she really wanted to know how to service Exocet missile systems.

The Exocets never left their casings in the Gulf, except in the nightmares of the crew. HMS *Brilliant* went through a war where something was always about to happen, but never did. There were chemical alerts, people in gasmasks scrambling up and down ladders in a blacked-out ship, and mine scares. Two other ships in the allied fleet, the *Princeton* and the *Tripoli*, were hit by mines. Wren Stores Accountant Ruth Langdon said, 'We were apprehensive about the war but being on ship you are in your own little world and morale stays quite high.'

Captain Elliott thought the war made integration easier; no one was going to make mistakes or waste time teasing if their lives depended on the efficiency of the ship. But the sailors could only imagine, and never see, the 75,000 or so Iraqi corpses that had littered the desert only a few miles across the sea. It was as though the ship was one of those plastic bubbles filled with detergent stuck in the drum of a washing machine. The dirty laundry is all around, but the bubble does its job, and remains unchanged and separate. The only indication of the carnage on land was the odd piece of detritus which floated by, inconvenient fluff in the drain of the washing machine – up-ended palm trees, empty Iraqi army food boxes and the occasional abandoned boat.

Combat at sea has a distancing effect. There is something very clinical about sending out a Lynx helicopter to destroy a ship or submarine far away; you are quickly gone and do not have to observe or bury the results. Long-range missiles, with over-the-horizon targeting systems, are the same. They eliminate the physical proximity of the enemy. It is more machine against machine at sea, rather than man hand-to-hand against man, or woman. So the sheer aggression required to destroy another ship need not be as strong as on land. Sue Bradbury, a former WRNS officer, weapons analyst and mother-of-two, wrote in the *Daily Mail* when the women-at-sea issue was being debated that she believed unequivocally that female sailors would be able to kill as ruthlessly as men when the need arose.

> I know what it is like to stand in the operations room and to fire real missiles, to face a bank of radar screens, and to know that the blip on the horizon is the enemy that will blow you and your mates out of the water. We're not talking about cold-bloodedly running a bayonet through a fellow human being, which is why the question of women in the front line of the army is a different matter. No, combat in the navy is more impersonal, remote and anonymous. The fact is that when people on your ship are under threat I can't see why a woman would have any more qualms than a man about pushing the relevant buttons – or feel any more emotional about it afterwards.

Perhaps that was why the British found it easier, back in 1990, to put women into combat at sea first, long before they considered the same in the air or on land. Like the present American position, the

Royal Navy at first discussed only allowing women on non-combat hospital and supply ships, and a 1989 report on the Wrens suggested that. But following pressure from politicians, largely the Conservative Armed Forces Minister, Archie Hamilton, the British went the whole way. Mr Hamilton said at the time, 'We have concluded that to attempt to categorise ships into "combat" and "non-combat" would be artificial and misleading ... when all ships will be liable to serve in potentially dangerous waters.'

Wrens – who are in fact now regular members of the navy rather than a separate female branch – are employed on most ships, from aircraft carriers to destroyers, and may in future serve on submarines when new or adapted ones can accommodate both sexes. Not every ship has its contingent of women, because the navy decided that it was best to ensure ten to fifteen per cent of some ships were female rather than send a tiny number to each one without the support of colleagues. Women presently make up about six per cent of the navy and that percentage is expected to increase, even taking into account the NATO defence cuts. Day by day, the presence of women at sea is becoming ordinary rather than extraordinary. But as the Americans hold out against women on combat ships, it is worth looking at the debate which resulted in British female sailors being taken on board.

The British navy is not usually there at the front line pushing for women's rights, so it was a surprise that out of the three forces the navy should be the first to send women into combat, and train them to fly fighter helicopters and fire missiles. But it was not, initially, a desire for equality that drove the navy to send women to sea, but a combination of demographics and economics. There was a huge shortfall of young men joining up – the UK population of sixteen to nineteen-year-olds of 2.33 million in 1985 will fall to a low of 1.73 million in 1994, down by a fifth. Coupled with that, expensively trained Wrens were leaving in droves after a few years when they saw their landlocked careers going nowhere. And at the top, politicians were pointing to the social changes for working women in the outside world and wondering loudly when the navy was going to catch up. Like any institution under siege, the navy did the sensible thing – it commissioned a report.

Captain Alan West, DSC, a Falklands veteran who had led the

victory parade and whose ship HMS *Ardent* was sunk in that conflict, was sent for six months to investigate sending women to sea. Perhaps some more traditional admirals secretly hoped that a solid navy man, with twenty-six years' service, would come up with a convenient conclusion of 'No', or 'Maybe later'. Instead he came up with 'Why not?'

Captain West, who by 1991 was working in maritime intelligence, was to be found deep in the grey-green painted intestines of the 1930s-designed Ministry of Defence building in London. By his desk lay a bowler hat and a rolled umbrella; due to terrorism nobody wears military uniform in London. For his study into the employment of women, he had gone to America, Denmark and the Netherlands, all of which already had women at sea, interviewed dozens of Wrens and visited large civilian companies to look at their female employment policies. The findings of his report are significant, first from the point of view of the Americans, who had had women on tender ships since 1978 but still ban them from warships; and second, for the British army, which still has many combat-related jobs closed to women.

Captain West said the navy, like the other services, was not using the enormous potential of women. 'Those applying generally had higher IQs than the men we were taking on, but despite all the verbiage about equal opportunities, there were not equal opportunities for women. Far fewer jobs were open for them,' he said. Because of the combat restriction, the forces were exempt from civilian equal opportunities' legislation. 'If you wanted a ship's writer [administrator] you'd get a man without a single GCSE, but you could get a woman with an A-level. The women were much better trained, much better behaved, they could concentrate and would not arrive for work half-paralytic from the night before.' He concluded, then, that the navy needed to 'get the best value for money from this high-grade commodity'.

There were other solutions to the navy's manpower crisis. One was to increase pay dramatically, but defence-budget cuts made that quite impossible. Another was to recruit ethnic minorities more effectively, but that was already happening without huge success. A third was to bring back limited conscription – which is how the French navy avoided the demographic trough – but that was politically unthinkable in Britain. So recruitment and retention of women was a cheap and convenient solution.

But although women were clearly intelligent enough for the job, with over half having three GCSEs or more, compared to under a third of men, there were other questions. Were women physically capable of all the jobs on a ship? Were they aggressive enough? Would menstruation affect their skills? Would a mixed ship be a happy one? Would pregnancy become a problem? In searching for answers to all these questions, Captain West also found there were many lies and set beliefs about women at sea, or in combat. An issue that constantly arose was that women should not go into battle because when they did so in the 1948 Israeli War of Independence, three men turned back to aid each woman that was hurt. But the Israelis had no evidence to confirm the myth. 'This story that women will hold men back gets huge credibility, and it's not true,' Captain West said. 'You are dealing with an ingrained thing between the sexes. It is so fundamental to society that people completely convince themselves into believing untruths.'

Despite the fact that the difference between the average upper-body strength of a man and a woman is thirty per cent, Captain West could find no job on a ship that a woman was physically incapable of doing, including lifting heavy metal hatches. Some tasks that were too much for a woman working alone were also beyond the capability of many men. The Health and Safety at Work Act prevents anyone from lifting over-heavy weights; as the integrated Canadian and Dutch navies discovered, a job like loading stores was often done more safely and efficiently by a team, and the men suddenly experienced fewer back injuries. They also found that in the initial stages of integration, men had a tendency to be chivalrous and undertake the dirty, heavy tasks, but after a while they respected women's capabilities and left them to it.

But what of emergencies, when part of the team may be injured and a woman has to do heavy work by herself? During accidents and fires the Dutch, who have had women at sea since 1981, saw no difference. Captain West admitted there was a possibility of problems in a high-damage situation when the ship was hit by a mine or missile, 'but when people are scared stiff they get this amazing surge of adrenalin, so it is very difficult to gauge'. In the same way, he found that although men tended to be more aggressive than women, there was no conclusive evidence that they would perform worse during a battle at sea.

A second physical question was menstruation, but medical research shows only eight to ten per cent of women as a whole suffer adversely and even that can be reduced by taking light pain-killers. The symptoms range from slight loss of coordination to severe pain and nausea, but those with the severest attacks tend not to take up strenuous jobs, like those in the military. There are occasionally cases of synchronicity, when a group of women living in close quarters find their menstrual cycles start to coincide, but this does not affect everyone. Studies of women in the police and fire services showed that periods did not have a significant effect on efficiency. 'Anyway, a chap with a raging hangover from getting jugged up the night before is probably in worse shape and less coordinated than a woman with PMT. Men have rhythmic cycles too; they work better at certain times of day,' said Captain West. Seasickness was equally bad for both sexes.

Then there was pregnancy and the point constantly made by detractors, that women used it in other navies as an escape route. 'There was an element of that. It's bloody hard work at sea and it is an easy way out which men don't have, especially if the ship is deploying for a long time.' But those taking advantage of pregnancy were outweighed by those experienced women remaining in the forces after giving birth. What annoyed him about all the complaints of large numbers of women getting pregnant on ships was that the women were at the peak of their sexual activity and their childbearing years. 'They are no different from the outside population and there is no tutting when a bloke is having his fourth child.' He was, however, slightly worried that a navy of British size might find it hard economically to allow its women sailors long breaks for pregnancy.

From pregnancy Captain West digressed on to the subject of wives, in particular the protesting British sort, and mentioned that during his travels he had discovered the opposite problem: American servicewomen complaining that their husbands had joined the wives' club back at the Norfolk naval base in Virginia and were worried about their forty-two husbands being left with 600 lonely wives. He had also made some interesting discoveries about what happened on board mixed ships, despite their no-fraternisation, no-touching rules. Having captained three ships himself, he found he could tell within a day or so of being on board whether the crew were happy and whether the ship was being properly run. Often ships' own captains had no idea what was really going on, but simply by examining the stores log, Captain West could see how many condoms were being bought. If purchases went up just before a shore visit, that meant discipline was good on the ship and there was little or no sexual activity among crew members. If purchases were constant, he drew the obvious conclusion. He also found lesbian and homosexual sex was present on badly run ships.

Often, when discussing the issue of women at sea with those opposed to it, he found 'people were convinced they were *all* going to be lesbians, or there was going to be an orgy and they would *all* get pregnant. Well, it can't be both.' He found going to sea made no difference to the sort of women recruited. There was every degree of femininity, just as in civilian life, and he said a few more masculine girls were attracted to more masculine jobs. 'We rather turned a blind eye to lesbianism in the past unless we caught them at it. We were less hard on that than homosexuality. If a ring formed and younger girls who normally wouldn't be lesbians were being forced into it, then we would put a stop to it straightaway.'

British ships have separate accommodation for men and women, which means female sailors can only be replaced by females and vice versa. In Swedish and Danish ships, the messes are mixed. 'In one Danish ship I found a man and a woman both stark naked washing together, but their society is different. I don't think that would work here.' He asked his assistant at the time, a petty officer, what he thought. 'He said, "I don't think I could hold my stomach in for that long."' Although two beautiful eighteen-year-olds might be a pleasant enough sight in the morning, decided Captain West, for most privacy was a better idea. The Canadian and Scandinavian navies also discovered the presence of women had a beneficial effect. There was a reduction in alcohol consumption, improved standards of behaviour, fewer serious disciplinary offences, improved cleanliness and a more natural atmosphere.

Had it not been for the decision to send the Wrens to sea, women might have died out almost completely in the British navy. The government was pressuring for some of the land-based posts, mostly done by Wrens, to be civilianised and the Wrens themselves were leaving after only a few years, disenchanted by the unstimulating nature of the work. The 3,000 or so ratings and 300–plus officers were known as 'Admin Annies' and treated as 'a sort of protected species, cosseted, charming and delightful', said Captain West. 'If a Wren was working for me I'd probably call her Susie, but if it was a man I'd call him Able Seaman or Petty Officer.' Even Commandant Anne Spencer, the Wrens' Director, said her top-level job was 'rather like being a masonic wife'. She was aware of a lot that was going on, but there was always something she just didn't know.

Women had to put up with a lot of abuse from older men who had come through single-sex schools into a largely single-sex force and whose attitudes had solidified for ever somewhere in the mid-fifties. A good example was the splendidly-named Rear-Admiral Sir Morgan Morgan-Giles who told the *Sunday Times* in 1990: 'Women's eternal role is to create life and nurture it; a fighting man must be prepared to kill.' Warming to the subject, he continued, 'Women do wonderful things for men, but combat duty to defend us should not be one of them.'

Of course, women had always been close to combat in the navy. Many sailors on Nelson's ships had their wives with them. It was normal practice for senior officers to bring their wives, if they wished. But when two of them applied for the Navy General Service medal because they had been in battles on the Nile and at Trafalgar, they were refused on the grounds it would encourage 'innumerable applications'. The Wrens were founded in 1917 to replace men in shore-based work during the war and were disbanded in 1919. When necessity called again in the Second World War, 74,600 women were recruited and by the end of the war some were even piloting small ships across to the invasion beaches. They suffered casualties at sea en route to foreign drafts, the worst being when twenty-two communicators sailing to Gibraltar died when their ship was torpedoed in 1941. Now, the demographic shortage, not war, means women are once again useful commodities.

Wrens' jobs *had* to change, because female ratings were staying an average of six years compared to the men's ten. In particular, new technology had made communications jobs too easy to be challenging and retention was at an all-time low. From the American point of view, where women are still excluded from permanent employment on a large number of ships, a 1985 navy survey of reasons why women were leaving made grim reading – sixty-nine per cent felt the job did not use their ability, sixty-seven per cent found advancement poor, sixty-four per cent found the work boring and twenty per cent complained they spent hardly any time at sea (women were allowed short sea trips and temporary jobs on ships). Forty-two per cent said they would have stayed if there had been improved promotion prospects – women constantly found themselves moving sideways rather than up the ladder, because there were so few jobs for high-ranking females. Similar frustrations are still felt now by women in the British and American armies, who leave after finding many senior posts closed to them because of their lack of combat experience.

Despite Wren ratings being trained with the men since 1981 at HMS *Raleigh*, officers combining at HMS *Dartmouth* since 1976 and firearms lessons starting in 1989, job prospects without sea-going experience were dismal. They were not even awarded the same ranks as men, but had a separate female system. A Wrens officer with fourteen years' service who answered the survey said her career had not developed at all to her satisfaction. 'In recent years any form of career structure has totally disappeared. I am presently doing virtually the same job as I did twelve years ago as a junior Wrens officer. My staff course training has not been used at all.' A direct-entry secretarial officer with eleven years' service said, 'The girls we recruit are already changing and we will have to face the fact that an integrated service will attract a different type. They are already more assertive, pushy and street-wise. We simply have to move with the times and accept that the "nice young lady" image may fade slightly as a result.' And a radio operator added, 'Apart from the training aspect I feel I've gained nothing in the past four years. Work-wise, I struggle only with trying to keep awake. The brain very rarely gets taxed.'

Lightly taxing the brain was part of the Royal Navy's subconscious plot to keep women as outer-office ornaments. Everything pointed to it. Take their uniforms before sea-going was allowed: tight little skirts and jackets in which it was impossible to run, let alone breathe easily, and black patent high-heeled court shoes, which would have been a joke on narrow metal ladders inside ships. Just as the Victorians restricted women with corsets, the navy (and until recently the other services) restrained them with uniforms, which were usually selected by a committee largely consisting of men, who viewed the possible suits on pretty models. Even the women's ranks were denoted in baby blue, while the men got gold braid.

By not allowing pregnant women, until 1990, to remain in the service, the navy also ensured its female workers were mostly young girls, or older spinsters. Men were never challenged by mature, worldly women; instead they were sex objects (young) or sexless, headmistress figures (old). Unlike men, who could have children and a career, a successful female career in the navy had to be a barren one.

Lastly, by making everything more mysterious and complicated than it was, some thought the female tide could be stemmed. Engine rooms were too hot, hatches too heavy and ropes too long for women. That may have been the case in the past, but with air-conditioning, mechanical lifts, light synthetic ropes and computer-operated weapons, brawn was relegated to the second league. Even the height restrictions for men fell to five feet, so claims that women were not physically capable became more unconvincing. Going to sea was not quite so macho.

Integration in the British navy has begun well with the wartime baptism in 1991, but the future will not be trouble-free, as those on the other side of the Atlantic have discovered. The US Navy, which has had women on tender ships since 1978, and the Canadians with women on all ships since 1987, are now going through a difficult teenage patch, as unisex ships get used to their new identity. They have discovered it is necessary to take positive steps to encourage integration and continuing efficiency; male sailors do not instinctively throw away hundred-year-old naval traditions and ingrained opinions the second a woman steps on board. Female sailors expect equality, but often secretly still hope it will be tempered with gallantry; some are not above having their cake as professionals and eating it using feminine wiles.

The greatest problem to emerge in countries which have been sending women to sea for some time is, without doubt, pregnancy. Lieutenant Roberta Spillane, who studied the American Women in Ships programme, said at first pregnant women were treated like 'victims of the bubonic plague' and were immediately offered shore duty or a discharge from the navy. No one knew how many women used this to escape sea duty or get an early release from an enlistment contract. There was one report in 1979 of a generous and enterprising pregnant sailor on an East Coast tender ship who shared her urine sample with several women who were not pregnant to provide them with a means of escape.

When the USS *Arcadia* arrived in San Diego after seven months of Gulf duty, in April 1991, the US Navy admitted that thirty-six crew members, one tenth of its female crew, had become pregnant during the deployment. Newspapers referred to it as the 'Love Boat' and the most senior woman in the navy, Rear-Admiral Roberta Hazard, said the attention focussed on *Arcadia* had detracted from the otherwise superb performance of women in the Gulf. She was in charge of a study group on women at sea which reported there was 'a perception among male and female sailors that some junior enlisted women become pregnant primarily to get out of sea duty or an unpleasant situation'. The suspicion hurt morale because it was directed at all pregnant women, regardless of rank or performance.

Pregnancy can have a quite devastating effect on the operational readiness of a ship. Because it usually happens without notice, there is often no time, or resources, to find a replacement, so the rest of that department must do extra hours to cover for the woman. Understandably, this causes resentment, particularly among men who do not have that escape route. Lieutenant Spillane cited the case of a West Coast tender which reported that more than forty per cent of its female enlisted seamen became pregnant during the work-up to deployment and no replacements were authorised. Sailors can remain on board for up to five months into their pregnancies, but that still left five more months without a full crew.

Some of these cases of widespread pregnancy are ten years old and coincided with the first batch of American women sent to sea, who in terms of non-acceptance had an appalling time by all accounts. Now, the need to escape is much less pressing. Lieutenant Spillane said, 'Unfortunately it seems that many women assigned to ships lack maturity, good judgement and the sense of responsibility required for sea duty. The same is true for men, of course, but men do not have the option of becoming pregnant.' As a solution, she suggests that women sailors should sign a voluntary contract before going to sea, acknowledging their responsibilities not to get pregnant during the sea tour. Breach of contract would result in disciplinary or administrative action, including, but not limited to, discharge. Such a contract might be approved by some women, but for most it seems too draconian and unfair when men can sow their seed without a worry.

Another difficulty on some American ships was sexual harassment, often worse than on land, because at sea there is only one chain of command and if the person harassing is very senior there is no method of appeal. Obviously small-scale harassment goes on all the time, just as it does in civilian work. But one case in America showed how the problem could overtake a whole ship if crew members passively condoned the actions by their silence. In 1987, Lieutenant-Commander Kenneth Harvey of USS *Safeguard* was charged for sexually harassing the eighteen female members of his crew. An investigation showed he had offered, for fun, to sell them over the radio to other ships. He also verbally abused the women, gave them lower performance ratings when pregnant and told them sexual favours 'would make life easier for them'. Parties were tolerated at clubs on bases in the Philippines where there was 'a liberal and routine "use" of local females', who also participated in noontime ship shows called 'dining-ins'. The report found that 'the encouragement of a macho image contributed to behaviour that was at least inappropriate and at worst morally repugnant'.

Of course there are regulations to prevent that happening: the British have the widely-interpretable no-touching rule; the Canadians and Americans have rules against fraternisation and preferential treatment. This is the definition of fraternisation from the US *Manual for Courts Martial*:

Any behavior that compromises the chain of command,

results in the appearance of partiality, or undermines good order and discipline or morale – whether behavior occurs between an officer and an enlisted professional, two officers, or two enlisted sailors – degrades readiness and, therefore, should not be tolerated.

But such a rule can be imbued with many different shades of meaning, from showing favouritism, to having a private drink with someone or putting an arm round someone: when are these parts of normal social life and when do they become offences? And when does what happens during shore leave start to affect discipline on board?

Some have attempted to solve the problem by not becoming involved with any of their colleagues. Sub-Lieutenant Kathie Waltenbury, a twenty-three-year-old watch-keeper on the Canadian tender HMCS *Protecteur*, said, 'My cardinal rule when I joined was to never to date anyone on the same ship as me.' But unwelcome attention or unfairness is not preventable if you are an obvious minority. There were thirty-five women and 260 men on the ship, a giant tanker which smelled of old cabbage and new paint, and was berthed for repairs in Halifax, Nova Scotia.

Women only make up 3.1 per cent of the regular Canadian navy but thirty-eight per cent of the naval reserves. In the last five years they have turned in their skirts for trousers, and started entering combat related and hard sea jobs, like weapons control and marine engineering. It will be a long haul. Lieutenant-Commander Anne Gourlay-Langlois, aged forty and in charge of the supply department on the *Protecteur*, remembered a remark made by one of her previous bosses. 'He was running the Fleet School and he insisted all the women wore skirts. Well, you can't crawl round a submarine wearing a skirt, but he said, "If you're going to steal men's jobs, the least you could do is show a bit of leg and give us a thrill in the office".' Other female officers found the ordinary sailors saluted the male officers, but would walk past women, until they were threatened with disciplinary action.

Along with either degrading or preferential treatment because of their sex, the women on the *Protecteur* also described suffering from the 'goldfish-bowl' syndrome throughout their careers. Because there were so few of them and they were breaking into traditionally male areas, they were carefully observed by everyone – sailors, officers, the press and the public. The stress of being pioneers had worn them down – almost all of them smoked while talking. 'You knew the chances of other women following depended on your performance,' said Lieutenant-Commander Gourlay-Langlois. 'Women behind us have now got the freedom to fail.' Sub-Lieutenant Waltenbury added, 'Our jobs are challenging enough without the added weight of being a pioneer.'

She was in the process of becoming fully qualified as a maritime surface (MARS) officer, getting her 'driving licence' to navigate the ship. Three other female MARS officers who had just qualified had featured in a large photograph in *Sentinel*, the Canadian forces magazine. 'That really annoys the men. There is never a photograph when they qualify. They should only single us out when we do something amazing that a guy wouldn't have done.' The hassles of being a pioneer were cited as one of the reasons why female attrition is very high in the navy. A survey of fifty-eight women on the ship HMCS *Nipigon* in 1990 showed that seventy per cent intended to leave after their basic three-year engagement period. The most common reason – also cited by men – was that they did not want a navy career, but the second was that they were tired of being pioneers. The third reason many left was that their career advancement was slowed by *Nipigon* – the only mixed ship at the time – going in for a long refit, during which time they were not allowed, as the men were, to transfer to male-only ships.

Until recently, career advancement without combat-ship experience was difficult. Lieutenant-Commander Gourlay-Langlois said, 'It wasn't exactly that you didn't have a tick in some fictional combat-experience box.' But in reports they would get eight out of ten for the personal assessment and two for future potential, because they could never take as wide a range of jobs as men. This is exactly the problem women in the US Navy are still suffering.

Although Canada has had trial integration since 1987 and has allowed women to go into combat jobs in any of the three services, following a ruling by its Human Rights Tribunal in 1989, there are still pockets of resistance. Even at the top, in the personnel department, a senior male officer advising on women in the navy had decided, with scientific proof to the contrary, that women were less able to deal with sleep deprivation on ships than men. Yet Sub-Lieutenant Waltenbury was working shifts as watch-keeper, four hours on and four hours off, managing to grab a little sleep in the night; her body just got used to it after a couple of days. For some women, sleep was even difficult before they got to sea. During the MARS course, they had to lock their doors when they went out, or they would come back to find men waiting in the dark in their beds. Other rumours, that women were more prone to seasickness, circulated too, but there are now skin patches with anti-sickness drugs which sailors can put on when they start to feel nauseous. At least ninety per cent of the crew of the *Protecteur* got sick in the North Atlantic on the way to the Gulf. The only advantage for men was that they were in the habit of walking with their legs wider apart, balanced better and so felt less queasy. The women were considering taking up this tip.

In general, the Canadian military scores high on equality. Rather than throwing women into non-traditional areas and then praying that somehow it will work, it has anticipated some of the difficulties and embarked on a mixed-gender integration programme. That may sound aggressively prescriptive and might be expected to irritate rather than educate, but its content is both simple and sensible. Instead of talking about putting women into an all-male environment and assessing how they perform with the spotlight beaming on them, it looks at the result of mixed-gender groups. Integration has become a question of good leadership, rather than gender. If male officers want to succeed, they have to make sure their subordinates work as a team, and do not divide along male and female lines.

Acceptance of women by all-male groups, who in the military are likely to be instinctively conservative in outlook, is far from simple. A lesson in feminism is a bad idea; it merely raises the hackles. A Canadian study on male-female integration found that before the arrival of women, men talked with growing trepidation and negativity about the idea, and referred to women as 'they', the outsiders. Immediately after the arrival of women, the men's attitude became favourable – they discovered that women were ordinary people, the ship did not change, jobs got done and there were no disasters. One or two months later, their attitude became slightly negative again –

there had been friction between the two groups, differences had been noted and not fully accepted, and there had been changes in the way of doing things. Finally, after six months to a year, the attitude became more favourable again; there was group cohesion and acceptance of women as part of normal life on board.

To encourage that process, the military arranged seminars and lecture notes as part of the general officers' leadership programme which showed that the people at the top supported integration, set common goals and emphasised cooperation rather than competition. The seminars discussed policies on harassment, male-female relationships, pregnancy and single parenthood for men and women. The packages were tailored on a sophisticated level for captains and senior officers, and at a simpler level for trainees. For those on the MARS officer-training course, the discussion handouts were almost as entertaining as a Mills and Boon: 'Sub-Lieutenant West had not intended for it to end this way. She was a Radar Plotter in his division and one of the best. There seemed to be a natural attraction between them from the beginning. At first the advances were resisted, but after a while she began to look forward to the special attention . . .' The results of this relationship were then to be analysed in terms of the effect on that department's morale, the participants' careers, resentment in others, the extent to which the sub-lieutenant had abused his rank to get the girl and the best way of dealing with the problem.

Such discussions are a far, far thing from the old-fashioned military leadership techniques, which often consisted of creating an atmosphere of fear through shouting, punishment and boot polishing. But as Major Cheryl Lamerson, who monitored the integration, put it, 'In the Canadian Army we've now got male and female, French and English, and black and white soldiers, and you've got to be able to lead them all. The military can no longer be a cookie cutter, fitting everyone into the same mould.'

4

ALWAYS AMAZONS

There have always been stories of women warriors – the Amazons of Greek and Roman myth, and later Boadicea and Joan of Arc. The Romans had a goddess of war and wisdom, Minerva, whose presence meant a conflict would be won by military skill and courage, rather than by animal violence and bloodlust which were represented by the male god of battle, Mars. The Amazons appeared in the writings of Herodotus, and Homer paraded them alongside mythical beasts. For more than 2,000 years, they were assumed to be closer to fantasy than reality. Bloodcurdling tales of thousands of one-breasted female archers on horseback, gaining their name from the Greek *a masos* – without a breast – were thought to be the dreams of the male historians of the time. Later warrior queens who fought the Romans such as Boadicea and Zenobia of Palmyra (now Syria) could be dismissed as one-offs, aberrations who filled their dead husbands' shoes. Even Joan of Arc could be sidelined as a religious fanatic.

There seemed to be no real blood tie joining modern women flying fighter planes and battling in the Gulf to the Amazons of history. There seemed to be no proof that fully-trained large armies of women had existed – until, in the 1950s and 1960s, Soviet archaeologists began to find the skeletons of female soldiers near the Sea of Azov in what is now the Ukraine. This was exactly where Herodotus had located the original Amazon army which came to fight the Greeks, and the skeletons of their descendants were dated back to the third or fourth centuries BC.

In the first grave shaft by the sea, a woman had been buried with the traditional accoutrements of the privileged class, bronze and silver bracelets, a necklace of glass beads, a bronze mirror and a Greek amphora. But according to Tim Newark's book, *Women Warlords*, two iron lance blades had also been placed by her head, and a quiver of twenty arrows and a woman-sized suit of iron-scale armour lay beside her. In barrow graves in the Ukrainian steppes, other female skeletons were found, one crouching, surrounded by weapons, others with swords and quivers. (There was no sign, incidentally, in the design of the chain mail that the women had really been in the habit of lopping off one breast to make archery more convenient.) Other objects proved, however, that all the women belonged to the Sarmatian Amazon culture described by Herodotus and Hippocrates, and all appeared to be soldiers.

Hippocrates wrote in the fifth century BC:

> There is a Scythian race dwelling around Lake Maeotis [the Sea of Azov] which differs from other races. Their name is Sauromatae [Sarmatians]. Their women ride, shoot and throw javelins while mounted. They remain virgins until they have killed three of their enemies and only then may they marry once they have performed the traditional sacred rites. A woman who takes a husband may no longer ride unless she has to at times of war.

Although Hippocrates may well be exaggerating their skills and, more likely, their chastity, what he describes here and elsewhere does seem to be backed up now by archeological evidence. The fact that he writes in the fifth century BC and the women soldiers' bodies were dated to the third and fourth has been taken to mean that their society lasted for a number of generations.

From that time on, there are mentions almost every century of women going into battle, usually as leaders, Celtic queens or bands of tribeswomen. Many also went to sea and into combat disguised as men – an estimated 400 fought in male uniforms in the American Civil War. But the history of women as officially accepted members of national armies is more recent. The experience of female soldiers within militaries is of more relevance to this book than well-known tales of individual heroism. Even the participation of over half a million women in the Auxiliary Territorial Service, the Women's Auxiliary Air Force and the Women's Royal Naval Service in the Second World War is familiar, and need not be repeated.

What is of interest here is not the phenomenon of women freeing men to fight by taking on auxiliary roles, but the female soldiers who took up weapons and fought themselves. Three fairly recent and well-documented cases are of particular relevance: the Dahomeyan Amazons of West Africa in the nineteenth century; the British female soldiers of the Special Operations Executive who were parachuted into occupied territory to organise armed resistance in the Second World War; and the 800,000 Soviet women who fought against Hitler, in every combat role from sniper to fighter pilot.

The presence of Amazons in the Kingdom of Dahomey, now in Benin, was first confirmed by British slave traders in the eighteenth century. Reports filtered out of a bloodthirsty king, who was usually portrayed as fond of displaying piles of the severed heads of his enemies, and accompanied by ferocious female bodyguards. But by 1850, under King Gezo, the bodyguard had become an army of around 4,000 women, a central rather than ornamental part of the Dahomeyan military. They were of equal status to the male warriors and were recruited every three years when the citizens were forced to bring their teenage daughters forward for selection by the king. The strongest and most intelligent girls were chosen as officers, and the rest were either rejected or became footsoldiers.

In *A Mission to Gelele, King of Dahome*, the explorer Sir Richard Burton wrote, 'The origin of this somewhat exceptional organisation is, I have said, the masculine *physique* of the women, enabling them to compete with men in enduring toil, hardships and privations.' If a girl particularly pleased King Gezo, she became part of his harem, the Leopard Wives, or was taken by his son, Gelele. When Burton arrived in 1863, he had missed the Amazons' heyday and Gelele had become king. The new ruler emphasised to him that although in the Dahomeyan army female soldiers were officially superior, 'a woman is still a woman'.

Those she-soldiers who did not tickle the royal fancy and join the harem were expected to remain celibate on pain of death. Burton thought this increased their ferocity, since their energies were not depleted elsewhere. 'They are as savage as wounded gorillas, more cruel by far than their brethren in arms.' The Amazons often went bare-chested and would train – much to the delight of passing British adventurers – by leaping over burning barriers and running barefoot through thorn thickets.

In very early photographs, the Amazons appear in cloth sarongs, holding spears and wearing halter tops of white beads which left their arms free for archery or shooting. Some wore white headbands, sewn with the shapes of blue crocodiles. Burton describes the five Amazon arms in detail:

> 1. The Agbarya or blunderbuss-women, who may be considered the grenadiers. They are the biggest and strongest of the force, and each is accompanied by an attendant carrying ammunition. With the blunderbuss-women rank the Zo-hu-nun, or carbineers, the Gan'u-nlan, or Sure-to-kill Company, and then the Achi, or bayoneteers.
> 2. The elephant-huntresses, who are held to be braver. Of these women, twenty have been known to bring down, at one volley, with their rude appliances, seven animals out of a herd.
> 3. The Nyekplo-he-to, or razor-women, who seem to be simply an *épouvantail* [object of baseless fear].
> 4. The infantry ... are armed with Tower muskets, and are well-supplied with bad ammunition; bamboo fibre, for instance, being the only wadding ... personally, they are cleanly made without much muscle.
> 5. The Go-hen-to, or archeresses ... are armed with the peculiar Dahoman bow, a quiver of poisoned light cane shafts – mere birdbolts, with hooked heads, spiny as sticklebacks – and a small knife lashed with a lanyard to the wrist.

The archeresses had fallen in esteem with the advance of weaponry, but in King Gezo's day, they were the pride of the army. Before they indulged regularly in slave wars, but by 1863 they were used more as scouts than leaders and indeed Burton considered the Amazons to be in decline. Their days of trying to equal and beat the male soldiers in battles appeared to be over. Some were overweight and grumpy-looking, and he was not convinced quite so many as claimed were virgins. However, he did write, 'The women are as brave as, if not braver than, their male counterparts, who certainly do not shine in that department of manliness.' He felt the term 'weaker sex' was not apt here.

Almost thirty years later, in 1892, the Amazons were to have their swansong. The latest king (turnover was fast) was called Behanzin and he went to war with the French colonialists over trading rights. King Behanzin invaded the Porto Novo area, with 12,000 troops, including 2,000 Amazons and 5,000 armed slaves. He was opposed by a better-equipped but smaller French and Senegalese army of 3,500. Its commander, a Colonel Dodds, had machine guns and French Legionnaires to add to his power. The Dahomeyans, male and female, had rifles.

The French advanced into the interior of bush and mosquito-ridden swamp, in humid rain, with the intention of wiping out the Dahomeyan kingdom once and for all. They travelled for two months until they were within sight of the king's palace. As the French tried to make a secret crossing of the nearby river, they were set upon by the Amazons who were, wrote Newark, 'armed with the finest breech-loading rifles and began to pick off the Frenchmen as they descended into the tangled foliage beside the river. Many of the Amazons were expert hunters and to their deadly accuracy they added the frightening power of exploding bullets, usually reserved for shooting elephants.' Colonel Dodds' men were forced back and the Amazons then advanced from above using giant ant-hills as cover, and tried to attack the French at close quarters, until the foreigners were forced to retreat to their camp.

The French were victorious in a second attack, using a bridge over the river, when they rushed the male and female Dahomeyans with their bayonets and fought from trench to trench, and the tide of the battle slowly turned in their favour. King Behanzin burned his city down rather than allow foreigners to take it, but Dahomey was soon to become part of the French Empire and the Amazons faded into the bush, never to return.

For at least 200 years, there had been a culture in this part of West Africa which fêted and made constant use of women warriors, in tribal slave wars and other close combat. It was not until better equipped and trained soldiers came from outside their culture that they – and their male compatriots – were finally vanquished. To the colonial explorers and slave traders in the eighteenth and nineteenth centuries, the Amazons seemed not only a different and strange race, but almost a different sex from the British women awaiting them at home. Yet less than a hundred years later, Britain started sending armed and combat-trained women into enemy territory to fight behind the lines in the Second World War. Although trained to use Sten guns and grenades, rather than spears and muskets, the British women showed appropriately Amazonic qualities and won various medals for bravery, including the George Cross.

While all eyes were directed on the home front and the ATS, munitions workers and land girls of the war, a small group of women were about to fight quite a different war. It was only afterwards that their role was made public – they were members of the Special Operations Executive which worked with the resistance sabotaging the German hold on occupied territory. There were 430 men in the French Section and thirty-nine women, but only 375 of the total survived and many of those had been tortured or interned in con-centration camps. It was a high-risk enterprise being parachuted, or brought by boat or train, into a strange area, finding resistance groups, and organising their attacks and communications. Because the Germans would send any healthy-looking man to work in a factory, women were ideal secret agents, drawing little attention to themselves. But of the British women sent, twelve were killed by the Germans, and three of those returning had survived Ravensbrück concentration camp.

From 1942 to late 1944, British female agents were mostly used as mobile wireless operators, sending coded signals back home with information on troop movements, munitions factories to be bombed, or times and places for Allied ammunition drops to supply the resistance. Other women, working alongside the men of the SOE, led bands of the Maquis in guerrilla warfare and sabotage, or organised safe-escape routes for those at risk in France. When there was time, the women agents-to-be were sent to train at military bases in the wilds of Scotland, enduring forced marches and daily cross-country runs, as well as learning the basics of guerrilla warfare.

They were taught how to use plastic explosive, which destroyed hundreds of French railway lines, as well as Bren and Sten guns, rifles, pistols and grenades. (It was not until the 1980s that British female soldiers were again considered capable of using weapons and fully trained.) All the women trained by the Ministry of Defence were already bilingual and officially part of the mainstream First Aid Nursing Yeomanry or FANY, which is all that even their closest relatives knew of their activities. After training, they were supplied with forged French papers, clothes with suitable foreign labels and left to fend for themselves.

Nancy Wake was a twenty-six-year-old Australian who had been living in France and brought herself to the attention of the SOE when she helped some British prisoners-of-war in Marseilles to return home. Later, she went for training in Scotland and was parachuted back into France on her first official mission in February 1944. According to James Gleeson's book, *They Feared No Evil*, when Ms Wake landed at 1 am – in a hedge – she was carrying high-heeled shoes which she refused to leave behind, a million francs and had a revolver in each pocket.

She had been sent to organise bands of the Maquis hiding out in the mountains of central France, fixing ammunition and arms drops, and arranging wireless communication with England. In the area there were 22,000 German troops and 7,000 in the resistance, but the Maquis inflicted damage which outstripped its numbers. At first, Wake had a hard time finding acceptance among the men, but when her wireless operator was forced to destroy his codes in a skirmish with the enemy, she cycled a hundred miles through German check-points to get replacements and returned safely. She led a daring raid on the Gestapo headquarters in Montluçon, where she ran in and threw grenades into the hall and up the stairs, while the rest of her group threw explosives in windows. On a raid on a German-run factory, she killed a sentry with her bare hands. Her citation afterwards for the George Medal praised her bravery under fire and her leadership, and said, 'The Maquis troop, most of them rough and difficult to handle, treated her as one of their own male officers'.

After the war, the work of those in the SOE along with the resistance was considered to have sapped the confidence of the enemy, diverted large numbers of troops to internal security, destroyed railways and power lines at the most inconvenient moments, and on D-Day delayed movement of German reinforcements by a useful forty-eight hours. Once the Germans had been routed, Wake and her band took up residence in an abandoned château, and lived in style for a few weeks.

Other women in the SOE were not so lucky. Many were informed on, or discovered when other members of the resistance were tortured. Others were caught by German detection machines as they broadcasted wireless messages, for unless they moved constantly, the enemy could get a fix on them within minutes. Four women were shot after being interned at Dachau and another three were given lethal injections. Three were also shot after imprisonment at Ravensbrück and one died of malnutrition in Belsen. For men and women, being in the SOE meant they had a one-in-four chance of being killed. As the war drew to a close and the Germans grew increasingly desperate, punishing whole villages for the acts of the resistance, the likelihood of being informed on increased. For however well the man or woman managed to take on a new identity and blend into the town or village, the necessity of working with others meant constant risk.

It was not just young single women who were sent. A French widow, Odette Sansom, who lived in Essex with her three young daughters, was discovered to be bilingual and agreed to leave her family and go to set up a resistance cell in Auxerre. On the journey, she met a Captain Peter Churchill and was told to stay with his resistance group. They worked together very effectively in both senses and got married out there. Mrs Churchill was in charge of the group when he was away. After many successful attacks on the enemy and various installations, the Churchills were caught by a German officer. She was sent to the notorious Fresnes prison in Paris and tortured. The Germans suspected (wrongly) that she might be a relation of Winston Churchill, and put a red-hot poker on her back and tore out her toenails. She refused to talk and merely tore up strips of clothing to bandage her feet.

The Nazis then told her, 'You are condemned to die, first because you are a British spy, and second because you are a Frenchwoman.' Then they tried to persuade her to save herself by becoming a double agent. When that failed, they sent her to the womens' concentration camp at Ravensbrück. She was there for over a year, including three months in solitary confinement on the usual rations of one bowl of soup and a piece of bread each day. According to Gleeson, the Germans cut off her food and turned the heating full up in her underground cell as a 'punishment' when British Forces landed in the south of France. This nearly killed her, but at least got her moved to an upstairs cell, where she recovered slightly.

In April 1945, by which time she was thirty-three, the camp commandant took her out of her cell and handed her over to American officers at the camp gates. He said, 'This is Frau Churchill. She has been a prisoner. She is a relative of Winston Churchill, the Prime Minister of England.' Mrs Churchill said, 'And this is Fritz Suhren, Commandant of Ravensbrück Concentration Camp. Please make him your prisoner.' She asked Suhren for his revolver and walked away.

Had it not been for her name, Mrs Churchill might have been shot along with the other members of the SOE. She was sent straight to England, distressed and still in her prison clothes, and the first person she saw was an army doctor. 'I could yet hardly believe I was free,' she said. 'The doctor glanced at me and said, "I have heard you have been a prisoner of war. How tiresome for a woman." Then I knew I was back in England and I could have hugged him. "Tiresome!"'

Odette Churchill was awarded the George Cross. So was Violet Szabo, another SOE member, but her four-year-old daughter had to collect it from the king, since her mother had been shot in Ravensbrück. Like many of the women of the SOE, Mrs Szabo had no particular experience in anything military, but relied on guts and instinct. She wanted to fight in the war after her husband, a member of the Free French whom she had met in London, was killed by the Nazis when he was on a secret mission in France. She was reported to have said, 'I just want to have some Germans to fight and I will be happy to die if I can take some of them with me.'

The bilingual shopgirl who had worked in Woolworth's in Brixton was sent to train in Scotland and as a former gymnast performed well in the physical aspects of the course. She was flown into a secret airfield near Paris in a light Lysander aircraft and travelled by train to the Cherbourg peninsula, sharing a carriage with German soldiers and smoking their cigarettes. On arrival, she had to rebuild a resistance circuit which had just been smashed, report on conditions and memorise information for the Ministry of Defence. She then returned safely to England.

Mrs Szabo's second mission was to Limoges in south-west France where she had to work with the Maquis, sabotaging lines of communication to coincide with D-Day. But on one trip, she and her male colleague found themselves driving towards an advance party of thirty German infantrymen. The two agents abandoned the car, and she was shot in the arm and injured her ankle as they ran into the surrounding woods. She told the man to run on and emptied the magazine of her Sten gun on the German troops, who took her prisoner while the other agent escaped and hid. She too was taken to Fresnes prison and tortured, and then sent on the train to Ravensbrück on which she met two other SOE agents who survived the war and told her story. She died, aged twenty-three, in Ravensbrück, shot through the back of the neck by the cremator in the cemetery yard.

Women like Mrs Szabo and Mrs Churchill knew exactly what they were letting themselves in for, since many other SOE agents were known to have been tortured or killed by the Nazis. They had more to lose than most, since they were leaving children behind, but they clearly felt fighting the Nazis mattered most. There must also have been something in them that wanted to be daring, that wanted risk and excitement, in the same way as the men who went. They lived on their wits and were their own bosses in the field. When missions were successful, like Mrs Szabo's first one, the urge to go back was strong.

The Ministry of Defence used women out of necessity, since in some occupied areas they were the only people who could move about freely. Officials were surprised at how well the women coped, and handled weapons and explosives. The main qualification required of potential SOE agents was complete fluency in French and those who mentioned this when applying to join the ordinary forces on the home front were sent for special interviews. What the SOE proved was that seemingly ordinary women were capable of extraordinary bravery.

While the British were forced into using a few women in combat out of necessity, the Soviets were so desperate they called on 800,000 in the Second World War. After millions of young men died at the front and the Nazi advance continued, single women started to volunteer or be conscripted, and seventy per cent of those fought in the field. Some joined when the enemy was only a day or two away, ransacking their lands and homes, and killing their families. It was better to fight than wait to be raped or burned alive. Others who joined earlier in the war went to men's training camps and were taught to be snipers, fighter pilots, drivers in tank batallions, sub-machine gunners in the infantry and medical orderlies, even though the Russian vocabulary lacked a female form for all these titles.

Most of the women and girls came from the Communist youth organisation Komsomol, which mobilised 500,000, of whom 200,000 were their members. Little was known of the activities of these women until after the war – the Russians wanted the Germans to think they were fighting an army of men. Even after the war, a few photographs were released, but it took until the 1980s for extensive first-hand accounts of the survivors to be published in the West.

The women of the Red Army forces trained in all-female groups, but once posted, they usually worked as ordinary soldiers among the men. Soviet writer Svetlana Alexiyevich visited hundreds of female veterans over four years in the 1980s and tape-recorded accounts of what they called the Great Patriotic War. For those who say women cannot and should not fight in wars, these lifestories are an object lesson. For the battles in which they fought were some of the bloodiest.

These are the words of a young female signaller, Antonia Fydo-rovna Valeszhaninova, who fought in the battle of Stalingrad. 'One battle stands out in my memory. There were scores of the dead. They were scattered over a huge field like potatoes brought to the surface by a plough. They lay in the positions in which they had moved ... like potatoes ... Even horses, such sensitive animals, who walk in fear of stepping on a man, even they were no longer afraid of the dead.'

Many of the women were trained as snipers, hiding out in the field just in front of the German lines and picking off stray soldiers. One of these snipers was Lance Corporal Maria Ivanova Morozova, who won eleven combat decorations and worked until she retired as a senior accountant at a machine plant in Minsk. She tried to join up after completing a military rifle-shooting course at seventeen, but because she worked on a collective farm, she was refused. She went to the central office of the Young Communist League and demanded to be sent to war. She got her call-up papers a few days later and went to the enlistment office. 'We were immediately taken in one door and out the other; I had a very beautiful braid that I was so proud of and I had no braid when I left that place.' She was issued with a high-collared field shirt, a cap and a knapsack, and put in a freight car to the women's sniper school.

There, along with dozens of other women, she learned about shooting, garrison duty, discipline, camouflage and chemical-warfare precautions. Each woman was taught to mount and demount her rifle in the dark, and how to evaluate distance and wind speed, as well as shooting when crouching or crawling. Lance Corporal Morozova was sent to join the 62nd Rifle Batalion near Orsha. When her first German soldier came in sight, she was seized with fear and her hands shook. 'I could not bring myself to take a shot at a human after a plywood target. Nevertheless I braced myself and pulled the trigger. He swung his arms and fell. I began to shiver even more.' By the end of the war, she had killed seventy-five.

Once the women snipers had seen burned-out houses full of bones and the red metal stars which was all that remained of their fellow soldiers after the Germans had passed through, they had no qualms about killing. They would advance, in camouflage, to within 500 metres of the enemy trenches. At one stage they were killing ten men a day and when the Red Army scouts captured a German officer, he asked to see the accurate marksman who had killed so many of his men, exclusively with shots to the head. They were unable to show him the marksman, a woman, as she had died in a sniper battle the day before.

At least snipers worked at a distance. For women in the very heart of the battle, working as medical orderlies, the sights were horrifying. Maria Seliverstroma Bozhek found dealing with amputations the worst. 'Sometimes they amputated as much as a whole leg and I could barely take it to the basin. I remember the limbs being very heavy. I would take it as noiselessly as possible so that the wounded did not notice and carry it like a baby... I used to have dreams that I was carrying a leg.'

The orderlies working with tank regiments found extraordinary reserves of strength. Girls weighing forty-eight kilogrammes described dragging injured men weighing seventy-kilogrammes off the battlefield, five or six times in a row, under enemy fire. Nina Yakorlevna Vishnevskaya, who was with the 32nd Tank Brigade at the battle of Prokhorovka, was at first refused enlistment because she was thought to be too young, at seventeen, and too small. But she inveigled her way into the army, and found herself pulling injured men and women out of burning tanks. 'It was difficult to drag out a man, especially a turret gunner ... you had to keep your feet clear of the caterpillars so you wouldn't get dragged in.' She was the only survivor out of the five girls she joined up with. In the 1980s, she still kept a tankman's helmet in her living room.

Medical orderlies and snipers, despite the harshness of their work, did not earn the same fame as the Soviet women fighter pilots. The supposed glamour and danger of that skill meant their stories reached the West far more easily. Bruce Myles' *Night Witches* is one of the few books in English chronicling the lives of the women of the Red Air Force.

About 1,000 women started training as fighter and transport pilots in 1941 and 1942. All had already learned the basics at civilian flying schools, and the Russians decided it was more sensible to use their skills, rather than training men from scratch. The girls, many hardly out of school, were sent to train at the Engels air-force base near Stalingrad. In six months, working fourteen hours a day, they learned flying skills that normally took two years to gain in peacetime. At first they wore huge men's uniforms and oversized boots, but later uniforms were specially made for them in smaller sizes. They practised night flying, flying without radio contact, or with the minimum instruments, as well as bombing and dogfighting. On graduation, the pilots, along with female women mechanics and engineers, were assigned to one of three regiments – the 586th Women's Fighter Regiment, the 587th Women's Bomber Regiment and the 588th Women's Night Bomber Regiment.

Myles said that the main role of the women's regiments was to protect installations like railways and munitions factories, and to chase away enemy planes before they reached their targets, as well as bombing the Germans on the ground. But two of the women showed themselves to be so skilled at aerobatics after five months at the front that they were sent in 1942 to join the men. Lily Litvak and Katya Budanova became the first women in the 73rd Fighter Regiment, which was defending the skies above Stalingrad.

The pilots were known as the Free Hunters of Stalingrad, an élite who flew in pairs of Yak-9 fighters, the leader on the attack and the wingman on the lookout and defending behind, seeking the enemy in the air, and engaging in dogfights. When the two women – both in their early twenties – flew in to the airstrip, the male pilots thought they were just transporting the fighters and never considered they might go into battle. But good fighter pilots were desperately needed, since the Germans had 600 aircraft bombarding Stalingrad and the Russian army was surrounded. The air was full of Junkers 88s, Messerschmitts, Heinkels and black Stukas, and within days the Russians had flattened fifty airfields in the area and prepared to fight back.

That fight was not going to involve women pilots, according to the commander of the 73rd Fighter Regiment, Colonel Nikolai Baranov. 'I will not have girls flying with me,' he told Lieutenant Litvak. 'No arguments about it. You'll be transferred out of here within two days.' The colonel thought that any man who had to depend completely on his wingman for defence would refuse to put his trust in a woman. However, one of his pilots, Alexei Salomaten, decided to make a test flight with Lieutenant Litvak in her Yak behind him. He performed aerobatics and dives which made her vision redden with the G-Forces (the pull of gravity), but stuck close to his tail, mirroring every move. Thereafter, his confidence won, they worked in a pair, according to Mylles' interview.

Lily Litvak, just five feet tall, slight and with blonde hair, looked most unlike a fighter, but her small size was useful in the cramped cockpit and she had 'the reaction speed of a cat'. Each day she and Lieutenant Salomaten would get into their Yak-9s, which had a top speed of 400 mph. Although that was slower than many German planes, the Russian fighters made up for it in manoeuvrability. The planes had a 37mm cannon and two 12.7mm machine guns. The pilots would spot the Germans and wait for their most vulnerable moment when they changed direction after dropping their first load of bombs. Using cloud cover, the Russians would wipe them out from above.

After a series of spectacular kills, Lieutenant Litvak soon gained a reputation and the Germans could be heard shouting '*Achtung, Litvak*' over their radios as she approached. As she grew in confidence, she had a white rose painted on the fuselage of her fighter and was given the nickname, The White Rose of Stalingrad. There was also a down side – every few weeks, one of her fellow pilots would be shot down and few survived. Once, she had to listen on the radio as one of her fellow pilots screamed as he burned to death in his plane. Then her partner in the air, Lieutenant Salomaten, whom she had fallen in love with, was killed in a dogfight. His death, followed by that of her fellow female pilot, Katya Budanova, made her even more desperate to beat the Germans. She took increasing risks.

Soon after Lieutenant Litvak had destroyed her ninth German aircraft, she was shot down herself by a Heinkel III bomber, which raked her engine with machine-gun fire and also hit her leg. She crash-landed in a field, climbed out and fainted. Within weeks, however, she had recovered and was back in the cockpit, and brought down her tenth plane, a German ace pilot, in a dogfight which lasted for fifteen minutes. To encourage herself, she imagined he was responsible for the death of her friends. She aimed her guns and the Messerschmitt burst into flames as the pilot parachuted out. The German ace was captured by Soviet soldiers as he landed and brought to the airfield. He was in his forties, with grey hair, and had shot down twenty Russian planes. He was asked if he wanted to meet the pilot who brought him down and he answered, 'Yes. Whoever it was, it must be one of your top men.' He refused to believe a woman had been his assailant, until Lieutenant Litvak described the dogfight to him, move by painful move.

Soon after that, with one year's combat experience behind her, she dictated a letter home, unable to write because her hand had been grazed by a bullet, although she continued to fly. She said, 'Battle life has swallowed me completely. I can't seem to think of anything but the fighting. I'm burning to chase the Germans from our country so we can lead a normal happy life together again.' A day later, eight Messerschmitts came towards her in the sky. They had spotted the white rose on her fuselage – and the fact she was alone. Lieutenant Litvak turned her plane to meet them and was gunned down. Her aircraft and body were never found.

5

THE BODY OF A WEAK AND FEEBLE WOMAN...

'You're gonna drop out. You're gonna drop out. Go on. You're tired. You wanna get in the truck and stop walking. Get in. We'll get you hot coffee and doughnuts...' That was how the warrant officer baited the two artillery-officer cadets, in the early stage of their training as they marched for days in the snow with huge backpacks. After weeks of the most gruelling expeditions and sleepless nights in the permafrost, Second Lieutenants Ann Procter and Holly Brown-Malanka were almost on the point of taking up his offer and dropping out of combat-arms training in the Canadian Army. Just for a second, they let the doughnuts and warmth cross their minds, and then marched on with the rest of the men, whose strength and longer strides made their ordeal just a little easier.

In August 1991, Second Lieutenant Procter graduated as the top officer cadet in the Gagetown artillery school in New Brunswick. She was the parade commander on graduation day, shouting the drill instructions in her rich voice, as the lines of infantry, armour and artillery cadets saluted and stood to attention. Her family watched the graduation, along with Lieutenant Brown-Malanka's husband and her four-year-old daughter Stevie who stood proudly in the stand. The women had become members of a rare species. There are perhaps five female artillery officers scattered in a few armies around the world, and they got there against huge odds.

Canada opened the combat arms to women for a trial period in 1987, which became permanent following a Human Rights Tribunal on equality in 1989. Other countries, including Belgium, Denmark and Norway, have successfully integrated men and women in front-line fighting units; Spain and Portugal are in the early stages of recruiting women for newly opened combat jobs. But Canada, with 86,000 troops, is the largest country to test women in combat, and training has begun in the infantry, artillery and armoured corps, as

74

well as on fighter jets and warships. The standards were not altered at all to accommodate women, although gender differences in physical training were allowed for at the recruitment stage. The lessons from and successes of the Canadian experience – the only comparable volunteer force – can now be applied to the British and American armies still pondering the female-combat question on the sidelines.

Two facts about combat training immediately became apparent in the barracks room shared by Second Lieutenants Procter and Brown-Malanka: it was dirty and it was exhausting. They lay near-dead on their beds, drinking Coke and Kiwi-fruit-flavoured mineral water, eating tortilla chips, and luxuriating in comfort and the possibility of a hot shower after four days in the field. They were in their final week of training and they were deeply happy it was almost over. Even that night, there were still boots to polish, and packs and webbing to be cleaned; the next day it was up at six or seven again to wash down the armoured guns and trucks. Second Lieutenant Procter thought she might see her infantry-officer boyfriend for perhaps an hour before they were separated at different bases for nearly two months.

The last four days had consisted of a mock battle, using live ammunition, for the infantry, armour and artillery cadets. They rolled in tracked vehicles over 750 square miles of scrub- and mountain-covered New Brunswick, and got almost no sleep at all. Second Lieutenant Procter, aged twenty-five, had been safety officer in the field, a real job among live explosives, not just a test of leadership potential. There were three huge M109 guns the size of tanks, their barrels aiming across and beyond the pine trees. She stood wearing ear protectors over her mop of blonde hair and floppy hat, checking the elevation and coordinates of each gun before shouting it was safe. 'This is awesome,' she said, 'I love it out here.' The ninety-eight-pound shells ripped deafeningly into the air and landed about three miles away. The sun was setting red in the distance and the mosquitoes started to buzz. That night the twelve trainee officers were drenched, lying under trucks and guns in a huge summer thunderstorm, but three hours' sleep was normal for them.

That was nothing compared to Phase Two of artillery-officer training – basically the infantry section. Second Lieutenant Brown-Malanka, aged twenty-eight, had photographs of five-day marches in snow shoes in sub-zero conditions, which she displayed as though they were holiday snaps. 'We dragged toboggans behind us. We did what dogs do on Arctic expeditions. They sometimes set up tents where we could get warm for an hour or two, but sleeping, no,' she said. Sleep deprivation was used to test the combat cadets' capacity for mental and physical stress. 'By the end we had all started to hallucinate. We were having conversations with people who weren't even there.' One infantryman in Phase Two recalled coming across a fully operational washing machine in the jungly bushes during an equivalent exercise in the summer and taking off his jacket to clean it, only then discovering his mistake.

So why did two clearly sensible women like these put themselves through such unpleasant training? Neither suffered from a crazy bloodlust. They wanted to be close to the action and excitement, liked the technical and logistical skills involved in understanding artillery, and found leadership as an officer in the field mattered far more than it did in the safety of an office. Combat-trained officers also tend to be promoted more quickly. During the infantry part of their training, which every artillery officer must do, they also used live ammunition. 'Once you ran out it was so frustrating. They told you to keep going and say bang, bang, bang, but it sounded really dumb,' said Second Lieutenant Brown-Malanka. 'I wanted to do it properly.' They both knew that if it came to it, they would be some of the people closest to the front ordering the killing and pointing the guns. That was part of the job and it was a job they wanted to do as well as any man.

Second Lieutenant Procter studied geology and maths at university, skills which were useful in the artillery field, and was in the army cadets from the age of thirteen, so this was a natural progression and she was serious about success. Rumour had it among her friends that she practised drill commands while driving her car, shouting with the radio turned up full as a cover. 'Men, if asked, would prefer we weren't there, but once we are, they don't mind. When you've been told to take command, they tend to question you more and argue the point. If it takes ten minutes to argue over a five-minute job, then I say, "OK, I'll do it myself", and usually they or someone else come to help you. The thing about leading is you've got to show you're confident, even if half the time you're not quite sure what you're doing. But if you take no shit, you don't get it. I tell people if they're getting on my nerves and usually we work together OK after that', said Second Lieutenant Procter.

The women's only complaints were about a non-commissioned officer who constantly criticised them and gave them an unfair share of the work. After he persisted in this, it was noticed, and he was 'promoted sideways and away'. As for the physical aspect of the training, they gave everything, and made it. Second Lieutenant Brown-Malanka said she lost fifty pounds after joining the army over a year before, and had to have all her clothes taken in. The only difference they noticed between themselves and men was that they tended to dehydrate quicker – which often means women are more prone to urinary-tract diseases than men – but they just made sure they filled their water bottles.

The major worry cited by men about women in the field, menstruation, proved to be no problem, despite the lack of showers. Often women's periods stop altogether in military training, as athletes' do, because of constant physical exercise and stress. The artillery cadets survived on a combination of babywipes and Tampax, which they buried. But the process caused no end of consternation for their male tutors who would gather a mixed group together and say nervously, 'Have you *all* had enough private time during this exercise to wash your genitals?' The women discovered that provision had been made for them to go back to base if they wished for a quick shower during exercises lasting more than a couple of days, but they thought that was quite unnecessary and would be felt unfair by their colleagues. 'How did Chinese peasant women manage working in the fields all day before this?' they pointed out.

In the combat arms, women have emerged as most successful in the artillery – to date, two officers have passed and about twenty enlisted women have qualified as field-artillery gunners, and perhaps ten as air-defence artillery gunners. In combat support, which opened at the same time, seventy-five women soldiers have qualified as front-line radio operators and three as linemen (signal-mast erectors). Three women are serving as armoured crew in tanks and other vehicles. One tank driver was found to have such a good aim in training she was nicknamed the highly complimentary 'Deadeye Dickless' by her unit. Field engineers have started training too.

Armour, artillery and engineering, although slow to begin, are starting to see women coming through after two years' full participation and two of trials. It is only the infantry which has been an initial disaster.

Out of 102 women who started the first infantry trials, only one succeeded. Almost half pulled out, or failed initial general-recruit training, which is not so physically demanding. Only fifty-three started the gruelling infantry course and although a few made it to the second and third phases, most transferred to other army occupations. By the fourth phase only one woman was left, Private Heather Erxleben, a twenty-five-year-old former lumberjack of about five foot nine inches. She served three years in the infantry and then left the army. As Chief Warrant Officer Jim Hickson, a former infantryman in the personnel department, put it, 'The gals just ran out of gas.'

Although the male attrition rate in the infantry is high with perhaps five or six failing out of a platoon of forty, the female score of one out of fifty-three in the first trials took some explaining. The Canadian forces' first mistake was to allow women into the infantry with 'gender-normed' entrance standards – which meant women could qualify with a far lower level of physical training and strength than men, but get the same performance rating. The lesser qualified women were then expected to be able to keep up on a course designed for men. 'You had 110-pound girls of five foot three inches carrying seventy-five-pound packs. It's obvious the equation isn't going to work,' said one sergeant out in the field. 'The packs were so long they bumped against the back of their knees when they were marching and the sleeping bag on top banged them incessantly on the back of the head. The ones who had any sort of chest found the backpack straps cut right across them. It was ridiculous.'

While men worked at perhaps seventy-five per cent of their possible physical capacity at the beginning of an exercise, straight-away women used ninety to 100 per cent of their strength and stamina, so at the end of a week in the field, they had no reserves to draw on. They also found it hard to recover overnight. Private Erxleben admitted she only managed to cope by going to the gym to work out every time the mostly teenage men went to the bar to pass out, and she had been weight training and running for eight months before she joined up.

Brigadier-General Dan Munro, director of personnel policy in the Canadian Army, said, 'We allowed women to attempt the infantry training who couldn't have passed it in 1,000 years. That was unfair on the system, on instructors and candidates.' The average-height woman will still be weaker than the average man; upper body strength is usually lower, and cardiovascular capacity is smaller too. Physiologically, equality is impossible, but that did not stop the army. It tried to force large numbers of clearly unsuited women to join the infantry, because of the critical-mass theory – there had to be at least twenty per cent women, or else they would fail due to lack of peer support. The recruiters grabbed anyone. 'They thought they wanted to be in the infantry, but they had absolutely no idea what that meant. Some of them couldn't even *spell* infantry,' he said.

But the assembled collection of undersized, unfit infantrywomen, who only had to pass the basic-fitness test, had the added difficulty of instructors who had no idea how to motivate a mixed group. If a traditional drill sergeant's abuse of recruits centred round calling the men 'cissies', 'poofs' and 'women' to encourage them to greater macho feats, how was he going to deal with live women in the ranks? Brigadier-General Munro had to go out to military bases to explain the new policy allowing women into combat. 'It was bloody,' he said. Senior non-commissioned officers were constantly coming up to him saying, 'How do I get a load of hostile privates who don't want anything to *do* with women actually to work with them, when I'm not even convinced myself?'

Most women signing up had no idea that the ordinary infantry is often a haven for the bloodthirsty and a dumping ground for soldiers not smart enough to get into other branches, where they could at least learn a technical skill useful in later civilian life. Although recruitment in the Canadian military is down to almost nil following NATO defence cuts, the combat arms remain open. They are always open, because not many men want a 'dirty, muddy, rotten' job so close to the front, said the general. The nickname for infantrymen, Grunts, is not undeserved. 'The sort of eighteen-year-old boys we get joining up are unemployed and want a job straightaway. Their Dad's probably tired of them hanging round the house and is thinking, "What this kid needs is a good, swift kick on the butt. He could do with a bit of discipline." The kid's choices are narrow, so he goes for it. After doing their three years very few young men want to stay in the infantry.'

These were the sort of young men Private Erxleben was thrown in among; and she survived. Infantry officers are generally more civilised, although while the women were training at Gagetown their male colleagues poured milkshakes all over a new pool table, smashed cues, abused waitresses and broke each other's noses on an average night in one of the officers' messes. Private Erxleben also had the problem of the age gap. She was twenty-two when she joined, and the men were mostly eighteen. She managed to work with them in the field, indeed was carrying their machine guns when they were exhausted, but they had no outside interests in common. She told the general, 'All these kids are only interested in ass, tit, beer, the sports page and their cars.' Her interests did not overlap. 'When 4.30 pm comes, I work. I go to the gymnasium and that's why I'm able to keep up with them next day. There's no way I'm going to spend time in the mess with them. I don't mix and I don't want to mix.' Although she decided (understandably) to isolate herself, she did prove it could be done and although many women may not want to be Grunts, they have the leadership skills to be infantry officers, and her example has encouraged them to fight the physical battle.

Learning from the mistakes of that initial trial, the Canadian forces have created one infantry performance standard for women and men. Fewer women are coming forward, but at least they are physically capable and have a good chance of passing. At the time of writing, four women had finished Phase Two, the battleschool section of the infantry officers' training and physically the most demanding. They were out in the field for four days, covered in camouflage paint and living in trenches or under armoured personnel carriers. The top performer in the whole class was female, Captain Sandy Perron, aged twenty-five.

She and the other female infanteers were deadly serious about the course, and knew beforehand exactly what they were letting themselves in for. 'We all trained before we came up here. Some of us did judo, swimming or running, and we all did weightlifting so we could carry the loads. I went on a three-week hiking march, twenty miles a day, carrying a big pack to get in shape,' she said. Despite that, one of the other female trainees pulled her back and another came down with glandular fever through stress and exhaustion. Women tend to get slightly more injuries than men in military training, in particular stress fractures in the feet and legs from running in heavy boots. This is often because they were not in the habit of playing sport at school; that too is changing. Most armies have now moved over to training shoes for long runs and men now get fewer injuries too. The Canadian Army has also found it necessary to redesign its boots, made for the broader feet of men.

It was clear, however, that physical difficulties were not going to hold Captain Perron back. She looked thin but muscular, and was bursting with good health and intelligence. She was bilingual in French and English, and had transferred from her job as an officer in a transport-service battalion to train for infantry. She knew she needed combat experience to ensure the best chances of promotion and had already come top of a previous parachute course. Traditionally the best parachute student was sent to America to do the tough Airborne Ranger combat course, but she missed out because they refused to take women. Like Private Erxleben, she was by no means ordinary. They were both in the superwoman category and had to be, to keep up with the averagely strong man. Although there are few women with those capabilities, to deprive the army of their maturity and leadership skills by a gender rather than size- and strength-based rule would be wasteful.

'This course is so physically demanding,' said Captain Perron, stretched out in her camouflage uniform and boots on the airport-lounge-style armchairs in the grim barracks sitting room. 'We all keep up but we have to try twice as hard to do the same thing as the men, and we are too tired to do any extra workouts, but so are they.' The base commander, Brigadier-General Maurice Baril, said the soldiers who arrived every few weeks for courses had no idea what they were letting themselves in for, and they only stayed in out of sheer pride. It was not that their instructors took malicious pleasure in sending them out for days without enough food in the permafrost or the boiling summer heat. The training had to be agonising because real combat was much, much worse.

The day started between 5.30 and 6 am with a three-mile run, push-ups and chin-ups on metal bars on the lawn outside the barracks, and it could end as late as midnight if there was studying, and an inspection with boots and kit to clean. Apart from forced marches, the infantry class had been getting weapons training on 50-calibre rifles, C9 machine guns, M62 rocket launchers and grenades. The women said they had no problem throwing the grenade the required twenty metres – the U S Marines still ban women from throwing grenades, even defensively, because they claim they cannot make the distance.

As for accuracy and reaction times, a study done at the U S Army's Aberdeen Proving Ground compared three groups: women, women on the pill and men. In visual-reaction times, women on the pill scored highest, followed by women and then men. The same result appeared in reactions to hearing instructions. In speed of hand-eye coordination, in the first trial, men scored best, followed by women on the pill. But in a repeat of the video-game-style experiment, when women became more familiar with it, the ones on the pill again scored higher than the men. Having a steady set of hormones obviously kept the hands steady too, eliminating the slight pre-menstrual clumsiness experienced by some, so women tend to be able to push buttons and plot coordinates better than men. Some women also find the pill increases emotional stability, lessening pre-menstrual tension.

Captain Perron had no problem with the accuracy or aggressive aspects of shooting her rifle. 'I think women can be more aggressive than men.' During 'Oka Crisis', a dispute in 1990 with native Canadian Indians over a piece of land just outside Montreal, when bridges and roads were barricaded and a policeman was killed, the military was called in. 'The native women were throwing rocks at the army, and the men ignored it, but a lot of the girls I know would have been fuming. You have to be aggressive to be here. Most women are who join the infantry.'

The qualities that women would traditionally be expected to lack are aggression and physical stamina. These turned out to be the least of the problems for the four female trainee infantry officers. Like the trainees who had survived before them, what they found most difficult was keeping up their morale. The four were billeted in a separate room away from the men, so although they got on in the field and classroom, there was no real camaraderie. 'There is no privacy on this course anyway – we sleep together in foxholes on exercise, and wear boxer shorts and T-shirts when changing – so we could be in the same rooms as the men. Then at least we would know what was going on.' The infantrywomen found the men were friendly in groups of one or two, but when more came together there was a sense of male pride and exclusion. They would not, for instance, consider inviting the women to go with them downtown in the evenings. 'Perhaps it's because we've got hair down to our butts' – Captain Perron had an impeccable blonde French pleat – 'and aren't really ugly and manly that we challenge them more. We are women and we can't really hide it, but even in our own time we can't really act like women because they don't approve.'

The performance of mixed-sex units was tested by the US Army Research Institute for the Behavioral and Social Sciences in 1976 and 1977, in the MAXWAC (Maximum Women Army Content) Study. Units in the field were composed of between fifteen and thirty-five per cent women during a three-day exercise, and officers were asked to say whether the percentage of women influenced each company's ability to perform. Results of three sets of analyses provided 'no evidence that companies' performance during the exercise suffered as a result of having women assigned'.

The Canadian women believed that integration and bonding in the field would have been even better if there had not been so much attention focussed on them, and they had been allowed to share the same accommodation in the barracks. It was not that men and women could not work well together as a small military unit – mixed guerrilla armies and terrorists are loyal, often to the point of death. The attitude of their instructors also did not particularly aid integration. When the women surpassed some of the men in physical training one day, their warrant officers said, 'Guys, the girls deserve a good round of applause.' But they had only done what the men did each day and naturally it was resented. The men then clapped the women every time they went to the bathroom and so on.

The army found that over-focus on the attributes of women and close scrutiny of the detachments they were employed in often made integration difficult. When a woman made a mistake, everyone knew it and everyone also knew her name. Men who were bad leaders as officers could also get away with it for longer than the women, because they could always be physically strong enough to go back and help the person lagging behind, and appeared to have a robust attitude. A woman, however strong, still had the problems of a small presence in terms of size and a smaller voice.

The recognition that Captain Perron got for being top of the class *and a woman* made everyone touchy in a way they would not be had a man done the same. There were also things women just could not do. On an exercise, they all lay on the ground ready to fire. The sergeant told them not to move and to eat their lunch there. If you want to pee, he ordered, roll on your side – an impossibility with female apparatus. Such differences were few, but the men made much of them. Because so much of being in the infantry, even as an officer, involves putting your life in your colleagues' hands, it was essential that each platoon bonded together. Eventually, with time and usage, the women thought their acceptance by men would change. Until then, they were coping with a little less support from their supposed buddies than they needed.

These, then, are the results of the Canadian women-in-combat policy. Their military is a good test sample from the British point of view, since there is the same regimental system, volunteer force and similarly high standards. The Canadian recruiters' initial mistake was allowing women into the infantry who were physically nowhere near the men's standard; but they have learned from it and the few women who attempt the training now succeed more often. The recruiters' desperation to prove women could succeed outweighed the practicalities, resulting in a set of statistics for women's attrition from the infantry which, General Munro said, 'You might as well throw away.' On average, the top twenty per cent of women are as strong as the bottom twenty per cent of men, but since infantrymen are probably among the strongest in the military, to expect that more than a few women will be able to compete with them is ridiculous. Infantrywomen will always be in the minority, but that does not mean the option should be closed to them altogether, particularly as it results in the respect of colleagues and faster promotion. A spell as an infantry officer is also seen as one of the very best tests of leadership against the odds.

The physical aspect is of real significance only in the infantry. Despite a US Army survey which showed that only eighteen per cent of women could lift weights between fifty and 100 pounds, the

Canadian Army has found no significant difficulties with women's lifting strength in the armour, artillery and engineers. A little weight training does wonders, so from the American and British points of view what is the hold-up in allowing women full access to the combat arms – artillery, engineering, and armour – which are more about machine than muscle? Is it not more emotional than practical?

Take the artillery: new weapons are being designed to be lighter and more efficient, and with either weight training or practice, a woman can lift a ninety-eight-pound shell – and besides, this work is done by a gun crew of two or three, not a person alone. Artillery is on treads, and the military has now discovered the fork-lift truck and the hoist. Gun positions do get attacked in battle and women would have to defend themselves in close combat, but this happens rarely and a long-distance strike is much more likely. The British and Americans already allow women into the air-defence section of the artillery, but not field artillery at the front.

For combat engineers, who clear minefields, razor wire, obstacles and create roads, landing strips and gun emplacements, there are fears that opening up the way to the artillery may bring them into heavy fire. On the other hand, armoured diggers and personnel carriers are used, and the heaviness of the work is no different from that which a civilian female engineer or roadworker meets every day.

In armour, there is also proximity to the front, but again, tank crews are more likely to die in shelling, long before hand-to-hand combat arises. The shells in tanks weigh only fifty pounds on average and again there is team loading. Tanks and armoured personnel carriers have to be repaired on the go, but again teamwork and good equipment helps, and replacing a tank track will only require huge effort once, not repeatedly. There is no privacy in a tank and under chemical alerts the crew can be sealed in for days or even weeks. At that point, though, privacy will be taking second place to pure survival. A trial in the Danish Army with women in mixed companies on Leopard and Centurion tanks 'turned out very satisfactorily and showed that women can be trained to work on equal terms with men without weakening the combat capability of the unit'. The Canadians have female officers in the armoured corps and enlisted women gunners. The Israelis, however, have put themselves in a rather ridiculous position: women are fully qualified instructors of male soldiers in the combat arms, including sharpshooting, use of explosives, chemical warfare and driving tanks, but they are not allowed to go to war themselves. The image of the Israeli fighting woman is based on myth going back to the days of guerrilla wars and not on modern reality. If war looks likely, Israeli women are immediately sent back from anywhere near the front and replaced by men.

Of course, a major argument against allowing women into the combat arms is that everyone in those units may be called on as infantry – and Vietnam and the trenches of the First World War are still uppermost in people's minds. But a modern war, like the Gulf War with its 'smart' weapons, showed that most of the damage in future will be done by bombers and missiles, and the infantry will be sent in afterwards to clear up the remaining pockets of resistance. It will rarely be the first thrust. Until the Gulf, people did not understand the modern battlefield. Now they are beginning to realise, as Western armies shrink, that they will need the most intelligent and motivated personnel to work highly complicated equipment. To lose the skills of fifty-one per cent of the population in a gender bar is somewhat inefficient.

The Gulf War also showed that being outside the officially designated combat zone made little difference to survival. The worst single scud attack, with twenty deaths and ninety-eight injuries, was on a support unit at least a hundred miles from the front. Also, talking to women soldiers supposedly miles from the action on the British second echelon revealed some had been close enough to the front to see Iraqi tanks. Women were as close to the danger as most men, yet often they had not been trained as thoroughly in the use of firearms and hand-to-hand combat. Army Specialist Melissa Coleman, who was taken prisoner by the Iraqis only a few miles from the border, might have found additional combat training useful. As many women in the military complain, they can go to *be* killed, but they are not allowed to do any killing themselves.

Women themselves are not, on the whole, madly clamouring to join the infantry and the other combat arms. Nor are most men, for they too prefer a career with good prospects of survival and choose the majority of military jobs which are in the support rather than combat areas. There are also suggestions that fewer women will join up if they know they are liable for combat, as are all men, but since 1987 the Canadian military has made all women agree to combat work if they join and there has been no fall-off in applications. The British navy found women's applications went up by thirty per cent after they were allowed to go to sea. In America, the pressure to open more jobs to women comes mostly from officers frustrated in their careers. At the moment, all air-force jobs are open, including fighter pilot, but the percentage of jobs available to women in the navy is fifty-nine per cent, in the army fifty-one per cent and in the Marine Corps twenty per cent, according to a Department of Defense survey.

Enlisted women show little interest in expanding prospects, but officers find that lack of combat experience is the equivalent of the glass ceiling barring the way to the top for female managers in civilian companies. It is a bit like expecting to become the head of a bank without being able to add up; the army's business is combat, so its leaders have to know what it is like on the killing edge.

Understandably, perhaps, some American and British generals, facing large-scale NATO defence cuts, are just not interested in the extra organisation involved in opening up combat occupations to women. Those unreconstructed men, who would not know feminine mystique or a female eunuch if it bit them, find women fighters quite repulsive on moral and traditional grounds. Take former US Marine Corps commandant, General Robert Barrow, a man strongly of the view that women should stay at home and nurture. These were his words in 1990: 'Clearly we are moving toward women on the battlefield. As a combat commander in three wars, I can tell you that that would be a serious mistake. Strangely, women who advocate sending their younger sisters into the bloody hell of combat have never seen combat themselves, nor will they ever see it. The rest of us have either been duped or intimidated.'

Only retired generals dare to speak out so strongly; those still in the military find it is impolitic not to pay court to the equality lobby at least in public. The service chiefs couch their opposition more delicately. 'We don't find that our women wanted a change,' said General Alfred Gray, the Marine Corps commandant, at a similar Senate hearing. 'They seem to be satisfied with what they do. They like the assignments.' The Army Chief of Staff General Carl Vuono said he had not seen or heard a major groundswell demanding alteration of the policy. The navy and the air force were more luke warm, saying they preferred the status quo, but they could understand why women wanted changes. Following that particular hearing, the Senate voted in August 1991 to allow women to fly combat aircraft, in the air force, navy and army. It is probably the thin end of the wedge.

The Canadian experience shows that almost anything is possible for women in the military. So long as strict physical standards are maintained for the infantry, for both sexes, there need be no job closed to a woman by reason of her sex alone in the artillery, armoured and frontline engineering corps. The British and American military are left in the anomalous position where they argue that women should be banned from combat, while other arms of their forces – the Royal Navy and the US and British air force – send women into battle.

Carolyn Becraft, a former US Army officer and now director of the independent Women's Research and Education Institute in Washington, believes it is now only a matter of time before the other American services cave in. 'It isn't logical that female fighter pilots will be able to land on aircraft carriers, yet women mechanics will not be allowed at sea to carry out the maintenance on them.' She is part of an increasingly successful lobby in America, which includes Democratic Congresswoman Patricia Schroeder, who, since women were under fire during the invasion of Panama in 1989, has been campaigning for a four-year combat trial for women. As a member of the House Armed Services Committee, she helped engineer the advances for women pilots. She works alongside the Government-funded Defense Advisory Committee on Women in the Services, or DACOWITS, which visits bases gathering information on women, and has direct access to the Secretary of State for Defense.

No law actually bans women in the US Army from combat. Like the British military, the exclusion is a matter of custom and practice. But a remaining American law, Title 10, U.S.C. 6015 of the 1948 Combat Exclusion Act, applies to the navy and the Marine Corps, and bans women from combat missions. 'The services all interpret the meaning of "combat" differently,' said Becraft. Direct combat is defined as 'engaging an enemy with individual or crew-served weapons while being exposed to direct enemy fire, a high probability of direct physical contact with the enemy's personnel and a substantial risk of capture'. But the exclusion was not exactly foolproof in Desert Shield. There were two female prisoners-of-war, supposedly in jobs that did not involve 'a substantial risk of capture' and there were women working on Patriot missile batteries 'engaging an enemy with crew-served weapons', and there were women exposed to the 'direct enemy fire' of the Scuds. The law on women in combat is riddled with holes. It may not hold together for much longer.

6

. . . THE HEART AND STOMACH OF A KING

As Simone De Beauvoir said, 'One is not born a woman, one becomes one.' It is the same with soldiers. The military mindset is artificially grafted on to the civilian one and only after a while does it begin to look natural. If armies train men in the art of controlled aggression, is there any reason why they cannot train women too?

As with all indoctrination, it is best to get the victims at an early age. The Marine Corps boot camp at Parris Island in South Carolina is, as it says over the gates, 'Where It All Begins'. This is where they take fresh-faced girls of seventeen or eighteen, who have only just discarded the pink and pale blue bouffant dresses of their high-school proms, and in eleven weeks turn them into Leathernecks.

'We're not going to cheeseball this out. We're going to kick him hard enough to send his nose through the back of his fucking head. And I want his heart busted,' advised an instructor in a black T-shirt featuring a red skull and crossbones. Thirty sweat-soaked female recruits laid into their companions, roaring and finishing off by almost crunching their boots into the bridge of their noses, clearly imagining the victims were men. Girls' khaki T-shirt sleeves slid up, and showed their tattoos and muscles. The women Marines' close-combat class was going nicely. It was rather a new innovation, a mixture of martial arts designed with medical advice so that each move breaks a bone in the victim's body, if he is still alive.

Male and female Marines are trained separately, largely because of physical differences, although otherwise, apart from some extra battle training, the course is the same: slobs are moulded into soldiers. Women are more mature at that age and tend to learn quicker than men, so male recruits are constantly yelled at, while women pick the rules up after the first reprimand. The mental assault is far worse than the physical one. The pack of female drill sergeants break the teenagers' fragile, half-formed egos into smithereens, stomp on them for good measure and then build the fawning, thankful victims back up in their own image. 'When they come here, their thinking process is a mess,' said one instructor ominously. 'It's like taking a bag of marbles and throwing them in the air. By the time they finish, they pick up the marbles they want back and leave the rest.'

At fifteen days into what were to be the worst eleven weeks of her life at boot camp, recruit Ricquel Adams, an eighteen-year-old from Oklahoma, was stroking the butt of her M16 rifle padlocked to her bunk. 'I can't wait to learn to shoot this thing,' she said. 'We're desperate to get to the rifle range on Saturday. At first carrying the rifle all the time felt really heavy, but then it becomes part of your body.' Another recruit looked up, sounding like a religious convert, and said, 'We've got rifles now instead of boyfriends.' Boyfriends only remained as faded images in prom photographs, since most of the thirty-four new recruits of platoon 4034 had left high school only a few months before and were not allowed to telephone home during their training. Already the schoolgirls in the pictures looked flabbier and less directed than the recruits with neat bobbed haircuts, khaki shorts and T-shirts. Two weeks of abuse, humiliation and rigorous physical workout had done a great deal for them.

The misery and total exhaustion among the platoon was military-manual perfect. That evening, after a 4.45 am start, they were sweating and pallid, on their hands and knees on the linoleum floor of their fifty-bunk squad bay, and cleaning it inch by inch with undersized scrubbing brushes issued to each on arrival. 'As you know, the US Marine is never without his scrubbing brush in battle,' said one, risking speech. 'Why are you talking? There ain't nothin' to talk about,' barked the drill instructor. Indeed, talking about the situation only made it more depressing. Improving notices on the wall and even on the mirrors explained what bulkheads were or asked 'When should deadly force be used? Only as a last resort.' The air conditioning had failed in the barracks and the temperature was in the 80s, compounded by the exertions of the recruits who were also being forced to do sit-ups, press-ups and arm-pulls on the iron wall bars, the only ornamentation in the room. As it got dark, the mosquitoes moved in from the swamp.

'It's not supposed to be fun,' said the instructor. 'If they want fun they can join the army or the navy. Everyone who comes here knows that.' She smiled. 'They just don't know how bad it's going to be.' Like anyone wanting to have adventures and travel, the recruits should have read the brochure first. It clearly advertises the 'indoctrination of the Marine recruit in the fundamentals of service life, the development of discipline ... and love of corps and country'.

The women find it harder to acquire the team mentality, because they have usually been less involved in high-school sports. A twenty-five-year-old drill instructor, Sergeant Antoinette Pugilese said, 'Men have been taking part in little-league baseball since they could walk, whereas women are socialised individuals, daughters nurtured by mothers as someone special, so they find working as a unit harder to handle. Also men are taught that if it hurts, it's not OK, but it's manly. Women think when it hurts they should stop.' Some do stop – twenty per cent of women recruits usually drop out, around twice the rate for men. Physical injury accounts for some of the losses, but most leave because of the psychological stress. Occasionally recruits attempt suicide, and physical and mental stress causes nine out of ten women to have disrupted periods. Some lose them altogether for a while; others bleed twice a month instead.

A few manage to subvert the system just enough to stay sane. One recruit put on make-up at night and slept red-lipped because she had no time to do it in the morning with only a few minutes to make her bed and get dressed. Others wear lacy underwear or camisoles, the only clothing permitted which is not Marine issue, but they still have to magic-marker their names in huge black letters on each pair of knickers. But it is the idiosyncrasies of Marine life that bring them closer to the edge. These petty peculiarities have more to do with the warped sense of humour of someone who has spent too long in the military for her own good than common sense. There are rules that women can shave their armpits but not their legs. They can shower but have to ask permission to wash their hair. They can jog past the Baskin and Robbins thirty-one-flavours ice-cream shop on the compound but they cannot go in until they graduate. They can write home, but they are not allowed to telephone.

Although there is no leave during the eleven weeks of boot camp, recruits are banned from phoning on pain of punishment on barracks called 'office hours'. They quickly forget to compare their boot-camp experiences with the values of their previous non-militarised life. Within weeks, they are obeying first and thinking later. Writing is their only contact with the outside world, apart from newspapers and 'instructional' television. Indeed, writing is their only contact with men who are not instructors, since male and female recruits are strictly segregated until graduation. Besides, they are too exhausted to have sex – with either sex. They have one hour's free time every day before lights out at 8.45 pm and four hours on Sunday during which it is suggested they go to church.

Like many things military, receiving letters is far from simple. The recruits line up, after their cleanliness inspection, respond 'Yes, Ma'am' when their names are read out, sandwich the letter exactly between two flat palms, and say, 'Mail received, Ma'am.'

Recruit Adams opened hers as they stood in line. She looked as if she might cry. 'It's my Mom,' she whispered. 'It's my prom picture.' The recruit from the bunk below, Pauline Zukowski, aged seventeen from Michigan, had her prom picture too and showed it to the sergeant under the rules in case of pornographic content. 'This is my fiancé. I've asked him to write to me every other day, but I don't always have enough time to write back.' There were other voices. 'My boyfriend's been sent to another base.' 'It's my Granma . . . How are you hope you're doing pretty good the weather here is 105F . . . He bought a Mustang but it'll need a lot of fixing.'

It is only at moments like these, when the recruits have time to think, that they question why on earth they are here, ask exactly what psychological games are being played on them and remember the privations involved.

'I crave junk food and chocolate,' said Recruit Zukowski. 'I crave my Mom,' said Recruit Adams. Both joined the Marines for the usual reasons – they wanted to travel and to serve their country. Many of the recruits come from small-town America and are often those whose families could not afford a college education. 'My Dad was in the military. He keeps writing to me to say he's so proud of me, that I'm doing real good. I'm going on to study aviation electronics. I know if I can get through this, I can get through anything,' said Recruit Zukowski.

There were one or two older enlistees, including a former accountant from Boston who needed a change, a challenge, and woke up one morning and dialled 1-800-MARINES. That was why she had spent the whole night on her belly, dug in a six-inch trench in an ant- and snake-infested forest, machine gun ready to shoot blanks at the fictional enemy which was attacking Combat Town, a sort of mini-Beirut designed for wargames, but used mainly by rats. The recruit used to earn $30,000 a year and wear power suits. Now she was on $800 a month, wore Marine-issue brown spectacles, camouflage paint, insect repellent and was utterly convinced by the whole package – and almost keen to die for her country.

The drill instructors looked rather more stylish than the recruits who wilted in holes in the dust. Sergeant Pugilese even had designer warpaint, camouflage cream in green, brown and orange, carefully applied. She worked sixteen-hour days, seven days a week, for eleven-week stretches. She marched by a line of recruits in full kit who had been standing in the midday midsummer sun for about half an hour. 'Are you sweating?' she asked. 'Yes, Ma'am,' they answered. 'Outstanding,' she said. She was married to another drill sergeant, but both did such long hours that their six-year-old daughter lived with her grandmother in Pennsylvania. She put everything into her job, so when a recruit made a mistake, she took it personally. This explained why she gave a fairly innocent-looking girl, with 'LOMBARDO' written on her helmet, more abuse than she had ever had in her life.

She started like this: 'Get your kit off, Lombardo. Get over to that grass.' The little blonde recruit started hopping, as instructed, doing press-ups and running on the spot. 'You know I taught you not to eyeball the area weeks ago. You were looking round. Don't lie to me. Say: "This recruit is not putting forward a reasonable effort."' The recruit said it. She was streaked with dirt and tears. 'See. You admitted it. Do some sit-ups.' Sergeant Pugilese's deep and rather attractive voice cracked with anger – or acting. 'Who is the commander of the Marine Corps? You don't know. Twenty days until you graduate and you don't know? You don't deserve to be here. Get in that truck, Lombardo. Just go.' About a second later, Sergeant Pugilese was smiling. 'It's OK, so long as you don't confuse responsibility with power. Sometimes you yell out of frustration and disappointment. She *knows* her eyes should be front, so you think:

How did I lose her? If my yelling for ten minutes and making her cry keeps her alive one day then it'll be worth it.'

In their final weeks, indoctrinated to saturation, the recruits have two things in common – they all want to be Marines and they all want to escape boot camp. At this stage they will do almost anything to acquire banned pleasures like a cigarette, a Hershey Bar, or a man. Graffiti on the field-toilet door details these desires poignantly: '17 DAYS TO GO TO A BOWL OF FRUIT LOOPS'.

Those teenage Marine recruits are like little pieces of clay in their drill instructors' hands, there to be moulded and melded until their individual identities and desires are subsumed under their uniforms. The raw material is deprived of contact with the outside world, harassed, bullied and degraded in every waking moment, and kept close to exhaustion. It is not surprising the brainwashing is successful. The prom queens shed their girly femininity within a few weeks, though whether it is replaced by strong womanhood or a sort of perverted imitation of a male soldier is another question.

Military psychology was designed with men in mind and old-fashioned men at that, so in many ways cannot be applied so successfully to the female soldier. As John Fowles said in *The Magus*, 'Men love war because it allows them to look serious. Because it is the one thing that stops women laughing at them.' Although the seventeen-year-old recruits are not laughing yet, more experienced mid-career army women are finding it hard to take the butchness myth seriously. War itself they know is serious, but the posturing of peacetime soldiers, many of whom have never seen a corpse, is taken with a large pinch of salt.

Some of the techniques for building a soldier will have to go. The traditions that women are a treat to look forward to after a hard day's killing, either as whores for recreation or mothers for procreation, are hard ones to shake off. But if a mother-whore-soldier is standing right next to you in line holding a sub-machine gun, who and what are you fighting for? When the drill sergeant is in the habit of accusing his soldiers of looking like wimps or girls when their shoulders droop, what does he say to the private who cannot help looking like a girl, because she is one? And what about bonding? To have a cohesive group, to be an 'us' you need a 'them'. In the first place 'them' represents the enemy, but in peacetime when soldiers have no real conception of who the enemy might be, they differentiate themselves from the surrounding society. The 'us' were once tough soldiers, and the 'them' were women and wimps. But now the outsiders are the insiders.

There are, among other factors, psychological motives for taking up an army career. The types of men attracted are often those who want to prove their masculinity because they fear they are not 'real men', and those who think they are already rather manly and wish to celebrate the fact. The army has always been a refuge for closet wimps and Rambos. But with the giant feminine spanner now deep in the works, these reasons wear thin. This is also perhaps why the US Marine Corps, whose tough reputation is well-known, finds it hardest to accept women and has only opened twenty per cent of jobs to them. As Marine Lance Corporal Jimmy Pitman, who had just come out of battle in Kuwait, put it, 'You've busted your ass to get up there and get that uniform, and you see a woman wearing it and you think: what's it worth now? You earned that, you're wearing it with pride because it took everything you've got and you wonder how *she* got it.'

Militarism serves to reduce men's anxieties about their own effeminacy. Dr Norman Dixon, a former army officer and psychologist, writes in *On the Psychology of Military Incompetence*, that this results in great importance being attached to outward signs of sex-role identification, like hair length and moustaches, coupled with taboos (greater than those for civilian men) on certain topics and pastimes – football scores are in at mess dinners, analysing works of art is out. 'By being admitted into a society of men bent upon the most primitive manifestations of maleness – violence and aggression – the individual achieves the reassurance he requires.' Added to this is a deep-rooted prejudice towards women who try to adopt male roles, so the addition of women soldiers to this society has a somewhat emasculating effect.

In many ways the ideals of the military are falling behind its function. Dixon says that in military establishments 'size, muscle and prowess at games' are still the main criteria by which a man may be judged. There is a deliberate cult of anti-intellectualism: 'A lifetime of having to curb the expression of original thought culminates so often in there being nothing left to express.' Now, when missiles, spying, intelligence and sophisticated weapons systems have in large part overtaken the suicidal act of 'going over the top', anti-intellectualism is the last thing an army needs, yet its traditional social structures and rules, designed perhaps 200 years ago for men without machines, still attempt to foster that.

Aggression and sheer brute strength, except for a tiny minority in the infantry, are going out of fashion. Military structures in some ways recognise that themselves. It is difficult to feel really hostile towards an enemy which is an over-the-horizon blip on the radar. The soldier's survival instincts will not immediately get the fight-or-flight adrenalin flowing. In fact his flight instincts may outweigh his desire to fight, so some other imperative is necessary to make him press the button. For the lower ranks, it is fear of discipline or court martial and for officers it is more a sense of honour. 'The social consequences of flight are rather more unpleasant than the physical consequences of fight,' says Dixon. The group will reject a soldier who lets them down; he would rather risk death than public shame. So the system of reward and punishment, rank and medals, coupled with enforced habits like obedience to order and ingrained, over-practised drills, makes a man overcome his fear and go into battle. Success does not depend on the individual mind, but the group mind. The soldier is not operating on aggression and instincts alone. Instead, he has been trained to follow a certain pattern of behaviour. Group aggression succeeds where individual aggression fails. And if men believe it, why not women?

Group dynamics work, but they have to be of the right kind and, to convince women of their worth, they may have to be more emotionally subtle, less basic. Dixon explains, 'Since men are not by nature all that well equipped for aggression on a grand scale, they have to develop a complex of rules, conventions and ways of thinking which in the course of time ossify into outmoded tradition, curious ritual, inappropriate dogma, and the bane of some military organisations, irrelevant bullshit.'

Fear of going into battle, and shock afterwards, is natural, yet somehow men are supposed to cope with this trauma better than women. There is no scientific proof of that. If, for instance, male and female victims of concentration camps, who have seen a similar sort of death and violence, are compared, the level of trauma is the same in both sexes. The stiff-upper-lipped suppression of emotion and fear by the military may lead to individual breakdown rather than comfort. Many military men, particularly the older ones sent to single-sex boarding schools and colleges, learned not to cry at an early age and expected to find nothing else in later life, having spent so much time with their own sex. Not discussing fear does not mean it disappears. The advantage of having even a few women among troops near the front is that women tend to express fears and emotions publicly far more than men, but that does not mean they are unable to do their jobs. That became clear during the Scud attacks of the Gulf War – women admitted their fear and encouraged men to do the same, to talk rather than bottle-up, and the men said it did relieve tension and aid sanity.

Groups can be used to support and encourage members, as well as to create joint aggression. But the soldier may not always be able to rely on group strength and aggression. If a woman has to lead men into battle, or has to fight on her own, is she aggressive enough to do it? Certainly, women have shown immense courage alone as guerrillas, terrorists and resistance fighters. Fanaticism can create aggression. Whatever their politics, the female members of the IRA and the Baader Meinhof Gang, the Sandinista guerrillas, and the suicide bombers in Beirut have been central to their organisations and often inspiring leaders. If women believe in their cause – be it anti-fascism in the Second World War or terrorism now – they find the courage.

The wider question of aggression is an almost impossible one to answer, because at root exists the huge scientific debate on nature versus nurture. There is no room for more that a cursory look at the subject here, since aggression can be moderated by biological, psychological, group and societal factors, and one factor alone is not enough to explain the differences and similarities between women and men.

There are various well-rehearsed themes. Men's behaviour is more aggressive. Male monkeys are more violent. Men are hunters, women nurturers. There are far more men in prison for violent crime than women. Males have more testosterone and so on. As much as possible, women avoid physical confrontation, because they know they will come off worst against a man, but that does not mean that as a last resort, when completely cornered, they will not resort to violence, and often effective violence. Pause to consider the number of battered wives who have one day suddenly had enough and murdered their husbands, often in cold blood or when the husband is drunk or asleep, because that is the only time guile can overcome strength. Or look at the newspaper polls during the Gulf War. Before the air and ground war began, sixty-eight per cent of British men approved of starting the war, compared to forty-one per cent of women. But once the war had begun, seventy-three per cent of women against sixty-seven per cent of men favoured assassinating Saddam Hussein – once war actually began, they were prepared to be very tough. Perhaps, however, they preferred killing one man to thousands.

'It's not that women don't fight. It's just that they fight when there's something to fight about,' says Professor Deborah Tannen, a linguistics specialist and author of *You Just Don't Understand: Women and Men in Conversation*. By contrast, men engage far more in ritual combat in the form of sports, arguments and playfighting. Ashley Montagu, an anthropologist and author of *The Nature of Human Aggression*, was quoted in the *Washington Post*: 'Whatever the factors responsible, it is the males that are the warriors ... who incite conflict, and it is the women who are conciliators and do not believe in confrontation. You can see this in any culture in the world.'

Biologically, however, scientists are discovering there is more to aggression than the direct violence-testosterone link. Even if women are pumped full of testosterone, it has to be converted by the brain to the female hormone oestrogen before it becomes behaviourally active. But it is interesting to note that when women commit most crime, during the pre-menstrual syndrome just before or on the first day of their periods, that is when their hormones are at the closest level to the average man's. Maternal aggressiveness when protecting the young is not dependent on testosterone or oestrogen. Instead oxytocin, a hormone released during milk production, has been shown to induce maternal behaviour after being injected into the brain. Suckling is important not only for inducing maternal responses towards the young but also heightened aggressiveness towards males. And although the average female soldier is most unlikely to be suckling, what this does show is the sources of aggressive behaviour are by no means as simple, or as solely male, as has been assumed.

Obviously a large part of men's aggression and women's submission must come from culture, the socialisation at an early stage into pink and blue, dolls and trucks, English and maths. Of particular importance to a child's future as a soldier is the spirit of competition and aggression inculcated through the more physical sports. Although these were traditionally confined to men, with women on the sidelines as cheerleaders and supporters, sport is now seen as acceptable to everyone, and women's competitive football, baseball and cricket teams have increased dramatically.

Perhaps the military, with its ingrained male structures, will change more slowly than the outside world. On the other hand, there are at last female role models – fighter pilots, infantrywomen, tank drivers – which are encouraging for young women in civilian life. The cultural expectations of women and men are changing quickly. What were seen as admirable traits in a woman in the Victorian age – submissiveness, quietness, passivity, delicacy and lack of aggression – are now often seen as the reverse. According to women's magazines, ideal women are supposed to be emotionally and physically strong with 'well-toned' bodies and at least one course of assertiveness lessons behind them. So 'stereotypically feminine' personality characteristics vary according to the time and the place of the stereotyping. We are also seeing the opposite – men being encouraged to express their emotions, to father their children properly, to care.

That is the better side of male-female cross-fertilisation, but psychology experiments go to show women can be equally, if not more cruel than men, when ordered. In the seventies, the Yale University professor Stanley Milgram conducted a series of now famous experiments on ordinary, law-abiding citizens to see whether their desire to obey orders would outweigh any qualms they had about inflicting pain on other human beings. He was testing what is known as the 'Eichmann syndrome', the Nazi war criminal's defence being that he was only obeying orders. Milgram took forty men who volunteered and invited them to act as 'teachers' in an experiment which was supposed to investigate the extent to which punishment aided learning. Every time the learner made a mistake, the teacher was told to give him an electric shock, increasing in severity with each mistake. The shocks were fake and the learners pretended to be in severe pain, so that the 'teachers'' obedience to authority could be tested.

Although the 'teachers' could either see or hear the victims screaming increasingly loudly through the glass in a separate room, most of them did not hesitate to make the electric shock voltage higher and higher, until it went past the point that said 'Danger 450 Volts'. In one experiment, twenty-six men out of forty were prepared to deliver the maximum voltage shock. Obedience to authority easily outweighed compassion.

The experiment shows how powerful obedience to authority can be. For some soldiers, obedience may overrule fear as well as any sympathy for the suffering of others and make it possible to kill, even in cold blood. But surely women would not allow obedience to authority to override their supposedly higher levels of compassion, and desire to care and nurture?

Although Milgram only experimented on men and with an actor playing the victim, similar tests were repeated on women a few years later by the American psychologists Sheridan and King. Instead of using an actor, the female volunteers were ordered to give genuine electric shocks to a puppy, who gave genuine howls of pain. Every single one of the women in this experiment, when ordered, gave the puppy the maximum shock. It would seem that women's need to obey authority is even stronger than men's.

7

IN THE COCKPIT

'I've been aircrew all my life and one thing I have difficulty with is seeing women go into combat aircraft. They'd have to have G-suits, rubber kit, and wearing that heavy gear is already quite tiring physically before you're in the aircraft and start pulling lots of G. It's damned physical. I can see them flying modern transports in their shirt sleeves, but not fighter jets. There is a place for women aircrew, but they only need to *fall in love* and all sorts of things happen.'

That was the personal opinion of Group Captain David Wilby, director of officer training at the Royal Air Force base at Cranwell, where all British pilots, male and female, begin their careers. He was at pains to make clear his views do not affect his commitment to the RAF policy of opening all flying jobs to women, but such words are not entirely reassuring for the female officers leaving to start their pilot training. At least they learn at an early stage that breaking down the barriers will be a long haul, from their very first day as an officer-to-be. During his twenty-six years in the air force, Group Captain Wilby had seen many men die in flying accidents. 'One day one of those little girls is going to crash, spin and burn, and then there will be a massive reaction.' He had failed to notice that exactly that had happened to one American woman pilot in the Gulf War, Major Marie Rossi, who came home to a burial in Arlington military cemetery alongside the male pilots who had also died. There was no more, and no less, fuss about her.

What the opinions of those like Group Captain Wilby show is that the air force, supposedly billed as the least backward of the services, still has a long way to go to realise its policy of equal opportunity. Its senior officers' private views must in some way affect their public behaviour. It is not surprising it was not until 1989 that air-force women were allowed to fly non-combat transport planes and helicopters – when civilian women had done so for years. The performance and excellent safety record of female transport pilots in the Women's Auxiliary Air Force in the Second World War also seemed to have slipped the military memory.

It took until 1991, and the success of female pilots in the Gulf War for both Britain and America to allow their first female fighter and bomber pilots to start training. The Americans said yes to women in air combat in August 1991 and the British followed four months later. Even then, military leaders expressed their nagging doubts. The US Air Force Chief of Staff, General Merrill McPeak, said at the Congressional hearings on the subject that he preferred women not to be assigned to combat roles. 'I find great comfort in the law. I would like it to stay on the books. I am not eager to increase exposure of our women to additional risk.' General McPeak said his bias towards keeping women out of combat extended to the point where he would prefer to have a less qualified man flying a combat aircraft than a better qualified woman. He admitted his view was 'a little old-fashioned'. At that time, the US Air Force was fourteen per cent female and had 1,100 qualified women pilots.

Britain, by the end of 1991, had precisely two qualified female pilots, both of whom had come out of university air squadrons. Around sixty are now in training, and some of them could go on to fast jets like Tornadoes and Jaguars. Altogether eight per cent of the RAF is female. Although ninety-seven per cent of RAF ground posts are open to enlisted women, the jobs of fireman, aerial erector and gunner are closed, the first two on 'strength grounds' and the last because of combat restrictions, but that will probably change, since it is an anomaly that women can fight in the air but not on the ground.

In the past, the Women's Royal Air Force preferred evolution to revolution and did not push its women into the front line. In the last three years, however, all that has been turned upside down, and there is much talk of progression and opening up female opportunities in the fully integrated RAF. Air Commodore Ruth Montague, the WRAF Director, said, 'I am very pleased we have now opened up the last avenue for our women to fly combat aircraft. It has taken two years for us to get our first woman pilot and first navigator, but we now have dozens more in training.'

Flight Lieutenants Julie Gibson and Sally Cox were the first women to take basic pilot training. Flight Lieutenant Gibson has now passed a multi-engine jet course and is flying the Andover transport aircraft out of 32 Squadron at RAF Northolt; and Flight Lieutenant Cox trained on fast jets and has been flying the Hawk. The first British women fighter pilots will probably not start to appear until after 1993. When the first two pilots joined as officers, their only opportunity to fly was as passengers, although Flight Lieutenant Gibson had taken a course on civilian aircraft when her university air squadron refused to let her train as a pilot. She even wrote – unsuccessfully – to Parliament to demand a change in the rules. But civilian flying at least provided her with a tantalising taste. 'It felt both exhilarating and comfortable which confirmed my deep down feelings. I had to fly,' she told *Aircraft Illustrated*.

But her only choice, until the rules were changed, was to train as an engineering officer and she ended up travelling around Europe for eighteen months with a squadron of Phantom jets. On her last day, she was given a flight as a passenger. 'I had an hour of absolutely fantastic supersonic runs and high-level practice intercepts. I was madly in love with the Phantom as it was an amazing machine, with seemingly little dynamic ability, just brute power, and a beauty in a different way. It was probably one of the best days of my life.' Clearly, Flight Lieutenant Gibson was serious about flying, but she did further penance as an armament engineering officer before she got her hands on the joystick. 'I had been considering my future very carefully before the female aircrew opportunity came along... My future in the RAF would not have allowed me to be a pilot and with the commercial market as it is now, there are vacancies for female pilots, including instructors on a wide variety of aircraft.' The rules changed just in time to stop her defection to the civilian world. She had joined the RAF in the first place because she thought it gave women the best deal and offered them exactly the same training as men. She was positive about the air force and said she enjoyed working with men and felt very comfortable in a largely male environment, and had suffered little from chauvinism since joining.

Many women officers were frustrated by the combat ban because traditionally the positions of pilot and navigator lead to promotion. In the US Air Force, forty-six per cent of all officers were flyers, rising to seventy per cent for colonels. In Britain the average female officer stayed in for nine and a half years, and males for fourteen, according to the latest figures available (those for 1989–90). There were two reasons for women leaving earlier, the first being career frustration because of lack of aircrew experience. The second was that until 1990 pregnant women were discharged from the RAF, so a female graduate joining at the average age of twenty-one would have to leave if she wanted children by the age of thirty.

Flight Lieutenant Sarah King said she would have left her job as an RAF air-traffic controller if piloting had remained closed to women. She was seven weeks into elementary pilot training (preceding basic) on antiquated Chipmunks at RAF Swinderby in Lincolnshire. 'I didn't think I would get in because I'm too old and too short, but I got a good aptitude score in tests which must have swung it for me.' Flight Lieutenant King is almost five foot four inches and the lowest height limit for pilots is five foot five inches; and she was twenty-seven, when recruitment usually stops at twenty-six. About eighty per cent of men fail to pass the tough initial tests. 'They don't tell them why they failed often, apart from the fact their score was too low. So many people want to do it they can afford to be a bit picky. It is a lot easier if you take the trouble to have a few hours of flying lessons in a Cessna.' While working in her previous job at Cranwell she had persuaded pilots of various different fighters and helicopters to take her for flights so she could get the feel of each one. 'I just love flying. That's all there is to it.' She did not find she had to be particularly technically minded, although four years in air-traffic control helped. 'A lot of the guys hadn't a clue how an aeroplane works. Some had come from agricultural college.'

If the pilot option had not come up, she would probably have gone on to be an air-traffic control instructor, before leaving the military. 'I wouldn't have been very good at it, I'd have hated it. I haven't got any patience and I hate other people making mistakes.' These qualities were more useful for her new career out there alone flying aircraft. Although she talked with the assurance of a pilot, she did not look like one, sitting in the officers' mess in a short cream skirt and high heels. The RAF did not yet make aircrew boots or soft leather gloves her size, so she settled for oversized men's. The rickety red-and-white single-propeller Chipmunk she was training on was thirty-five years old and lands on three wheels at once on the windswept airfield. Because the nose is so high the pilots cannot see the ground properly; they have to zigzag when taxiing down the runway, looking out at one side and then the other, so the planes look like crazed chickens as they land. Flight Lieutenant King did her first solo flight after eight and a half hours in the cockpit. 'The Chipmunks are very good training because they're so old and difficult to fly.'

She wanted to fly 'everything' including fighters, having flown in a Jaguar, but expected she would specialise in helicopters, particularly the search-and-rescue Wessex and Sea King, but it would take two years before she was fully qualified. Unlike Group Captain Wilby, she foresaw no difficulty with physical aspects like G-Forces during aerobatics or fast turns. She described it all with relish. 'Your blood goes down to your feet, your vision turns to greys, blacks and whites, and if you pull too much G for too long, you black out. Fortunately, the shorter you are, the better it is for you, because there's less distance for the blood to go.' She had worn a G-suit, which inflates when the pilot turns, squeezing her stomach and legs to prevent the blood running to the feet. 'It's like wearing swimming armbands all over. It doesn't hurt.'

Research from Canada shows that women react no better or worse to G-Forces than men, although the Committee on Women in NATO Forces shows that women who are menstruating are slightly more susceptible than men to altitude chamber decompression sickness, but not to a dangerous degree. Women's susceptibility varies in direct relationship to the hormonal changes in the menstrual cycle. Eight NATO countries now have women pilots, but only seven – Britain, Canada, the USA, Denmark, the Netherlands, Belgium and Spain – allow them into combat in fighters. The position for pregnant women in military aircraft varies from country to country. Denmark has banned all pregnant women from fighter aircraft 'or any environment which may be detrimental to the welfare of the mother' after one of its F-15 fighter pilots had a miscarriage at between two and three months, two weeks after she had flown. There was no evidence to suggest the events were connected, but the ban went ahead. Women are allowed to fly in civilian aircraft under doctor's orders during the first few months of pregnancy, and the NATO meeting concluded that there must be flexibility on deciding when to ground a pregnant pilot, depending on her type of aircraft and individual health.

Other research presented to the NATO committee – on sexual differences and muscular force, electrocardiograms, and reaction to ejection-seat acceleration and impact – revealed no conclusive evidence against women serving as aircrew. The physical debate is similar to that in other services: the anthropometry – the difference in the length of parts of the body – on the whole favours male pilots. Fewer women have the arm or leg reach, or the distance from hip to knee in a seated position, to fit the average cockpit. Women over five foot five inches do better, but on the other hand many men are too tall for certain aircraft. Again, cockpits and instruments can be adapted – male pilots and female pilots sometimes sit on cushions to give them the right height. Canada has begun computer measurement of cockpits so it can come up with a new unisex size range for each plane.

On the subject of selection tests for pilots, reports to NATO show that women do worse than men in the psycho-motor tests now in use and this has had an adverse effect on the numbers of women getting into flying training. But once in training, women do as well as men. It is suggested that since test results have little correlation with training results, capable women and men might be excluded by them, and perhaps they should be redesigned. The changes in the upbringing of teenagers is also now showing in tests, with the gap between male and female scores closing. In some ways, all these tests and measurements look a little silly, because the experience of 1,000 Soviet women fighter pilots in the Second World War shows both sexes are equally capable.

Not all women can be pilots and even fewer can fly fighter jets, but that is true of men too. Half the world's air forces are probably filled with daring young men hankering after flying machines who are mechanics and air-traffic controllers because they failed the pilot tests. The glamour, heroism and the fact you are in control of your own machine are as attractive as they always were, and technology just adds to the appeal. Women want to be 'top guns' too. They are few and far between, but will start to increase in the next few years as more American women qualify. The Canadian Air Force, which is nearly eleven per cent female, decided to open fighter-pilot training to women in 1987. The next year, Major Deanna Marie (Dee) Brasseur became one of the first female fighter pilots in the world. The story of Major Brasseur gaining and retaining her wings says more than a long argument over the pros and cons of female pilots ever could.

Major Brasseur flew $35-million (Canadian) F-18 fighters, which were used by Canada for missions over Iraq from Qatar during the Gulf War. Now thirty-eight, she never expected to fly at all when she joined the military. Women didn't. The daughter of an air-force officer, she lived on various bases as a child, and remembered parking her bicycle on the approach path to the landing runway at the basic-pilot-training school, watching the planes coming in and thinking 'boys are really lucky that they can fly'.

Major Brasseur was about five foot six inches, slim and neat in her air-force blues, good-looking with short hair. Asked to guess her occupation on appearance alone, fighter pilot would not come to mind. But her conversation was gutsy and snappy. Her enthusiasm for all things mechanical and technical, and the cocky edge in her voice when she talked about the danger, were exactly the same as you would find in a man; it was fighter-speak. 'I'm not a warmonger. I'm not a killer, but I just wanted to fly fighters. In this day and age you're lucky if you're going even to see the plane. It's like playing a big video game, except you're flying a fighter bomber and if you don't do it right, you know that someone else is flying that aeroplane on the screen and it's either him or you. It's going to be your rear end. So you do it.'

Getting her rear end into a position to be shot took Major Brasseur nineteen years of 'battering down brick walls'. With 20/30 vision in her right eye and 'something' – she did not say what – anthro-pometrically too short, the chances of her becoming a fighter pilot were next to nil. When she joined the Canadian forces as an enlisted administrative assistant at nineteen, there was a total of 1,500 women, tied to traditionally female jobs. She intended to serve only six months, as she was engaged to a serviceman. Instead she discovered she liked the camaraderie on her course, decided marriage would cramp her style and called if off. The same thing happened ten years later when she once again got engaged, but decided she would get more out of the air force than the man. Rising thirty-nine, she awaited the next proposal.

After two weeks as an administrative assistant, the then Private Brasseur was bored and about to quit, when her father suggested she apply for officer training; she eventually became an air-weapons controller. 'That was where I first met the male-female monster. As the first woman on my crew I experienced the stares, the snide comments and the questioning of my abilities.' The men could not understand why she wanted to be a member of a previously all-male group, but after she established her credibility as a competent controller and demonstrated that crude language and bad jokes did not bother her, she was accepted. That experience, with the same scene played by different characters, was to occur again and again in her career – when she trained as an ordinary pilot, when she became a flying instructor and when she became a fighter pilot.

Major Brasseur was one of the four women who were given pilot training as part of the Canadian SWINTER trials – the Study of Women in Non-Traditional Environments and Roles – which started in 1979. Naturally, the media was fascinated, and the female pilots were interviewed at selection, at the beginning and end of basic training, after land- and sea-survival training, and during basic jet training. The male trainee pilots were covetous of their traditional prestige and jealous of the interest shown in the women, who were mostly embarrassed by it all. When one failed the course, the whole nation knew her as 'the girl who didn't make it'. 'From then on we were aware that we could be national failures and our progress was being strictly monitored.'

She believed that for the first few years, the Americans and Britons starting fighter-pilot training would suffer the same fishbowl experience, and they, rather than the politicians who made the decision, would be blamed by their colleagues for causing the change. Attitudes would remain behind reality even after the first women came through. 'The Americans are still more traditional,' said Major Brasseur. 'They're very homemade apple pie – with women at home making it. They think women can only do certain things, whereas in Canada, there was no public protest. The distances are so great that a pilot flying in Sheerwater, Nova Scotia, isn't going to affect anyone in Vancouver, British Columbia.' But the presence of three women on her course certainly affected their male colleagues. It is probably somewhat deflating when you have struggled to be selected as a pilot your whole life, only to find that girls can do it too. It was during advanced jet training that Major Brasseur came across the male trainees' worst opinions, until then held in check in public. Before then 'we were relatively unaware that we were fat ugly dykes, or looking for husbands, or looking for national acclaim'.

By comparison with the social battles, learning to fly was far less painful, although at any moment the trainees can be thrown off the course if they do not gain certain skills within a number of flying hours – an extra hour on a trainer plane is one thing, but an extra hour on an F-18 fighter costs US $1,500. Out of 1,200 who pass aircrew selection in Canada, an average of 150 get their wings. The rest fail along the way. Fighter-pilot training costs up to £2 million, so it is not wasted on anyone who does not come up to the mark. They have to be in good physical condition to cope with dogfights and aerial combat manoeuvres which go on throughout a thirty- to forty-minute training exercise. The pilots go from minus-G to 7-G. 'Holding the position for thirty seconds to forty-five seconds, and then making another move. It's like doing asymmetrics for forty minutes, tensing all your muscles and then letting them go,' said Major Brasseur. It is two or three times more stomach-churning worse than being on a massive roller-coaster. On top of that, pilots have no real idea of the physiological changes their bodies are going through, since they cannot really feel the effect of changing pressures and altitudes, and the blood coursing to their feet with the pull of G-Forces.

While all that is happening, the pilot has to make split-second decisions based on the information showing on a veritable computer bank before her. In some ways it is more like being a systems manager. 'Although I don't believe in being egotistical, you've got to be good to survive. "Split-second" is not an exaggerated description of the speed of thought necessary.' In the headquarters' canteen, Major Brasseur went into full battle mode for the next few descriptions. 'You're strafing with an F-18 doing 500 miles an hour, pointed at a seventeen-degree angle to the ground, with your nose aimed at a sixteen-by-sixteen feet target a mile and a half away. You have to pull the trigger at 3,200 feet, stop at 2,500 feet and put on four-G in two seconds to miss the ground by 350 feet. The basic time between 3,200 feet and 2,500 feet is three-quarters of a second, in which you have to lock on the target, pull the trigger and get the hell out before you hit the ground.' All around, coffee-drinkers stared wide-eyed. Major Brasseur looked pleased.

As an instructor, she found flying was even more nerve wracking, because the student can make an irrevocable mistake. When the jet is pulling nearly seven-G, it is almost impossible to move. Trying to turn your head to look out of the window to see what is coming up from behind entails grabbing the dashboard of the jet to lever round. When one student did that, his hand slipped and crashed down with huge G-Force on the gear handle, mangling everything, and the only way out was by ejector seat and parachute. This experience is often new to a pilot since they never practise parachuting from ejector seats, because they are too valuable to be injured.

Major Brasseur talked with apparent relish about her near wipe-out when a bird flew into the engine of her Tutor jet, as a student was flying at night. 'The Tutor only has one engine, so that was it. We were too low to bail out, but we were four and a half miles from the airstrip and 1,800 feet off the ground. Well, I took the controls and started thinking to myself that in the books it says you can glide about two and a half miles per 1,000 feet, so if we traded air speed for altitude we might make it . . . but then we had a twenty-five-knot headwind, so I started making these calculations. Your mind goes into hyperspace. It's an incredible phenomenon, called "temporal distortion" – your mind moves so fast, yet it seems to take forever. I transmitted to the tower and they gave me control of landing. I pulled the throttle up a bit but nothing happened. I was just pouring gas and exhaust in there and making a hot fire. It was the most sickening sound I have ever heard in my life, the sound of metal grinding on metal. I'll never forget it. Blades were just eating each other up.

'So I thought, "Why the hell did I take control of this?" And right away a voice in my head said: "Because you're the instructor." I was trying to stay cool. I knew if the runway started coming up in my windscreen I was going to land short, and if it went down, I was going to land too long. But for half the time it stayed right there level in front of me. I put down the gear and the flaps, and managed

111

to turn the engine off. The lights went, and by that stage my knees were doing a little dance I was so terrified. But we landed perfectly and when I opened the canopy, I saw the moon really big, way off to the west and I thought, "Yeah, thanks, that's one for you." '

With that sort of useful experience behind her, Major Brasseur was utterly frustrated during the Gulf War. She had torqued her elbow flying a Cosmo, a big transport plane, and had to have three operations on it and was out of service at that time. Otherwise she would have taken part in the bombing raid on Iraqi positions – it was her previous squadron that was deployed. 'I was dying to go to the Middle East. I felt it was my duty as a member of the air force and my responsibility as a citizen of Canada, and that I have as much right to defend my country as my brother does.' She would not have hesitated to pull the trigger. It is her job, although afterwards when there was time to contemplate death and destruction, she had no doubt it would be a heart-wrenching experience; but the mission itself had to be swiftly and accurately executed.

Even if she were to be shot down over enemy territory and taken prisoner-of-war, she said she would still much rather have been there, fighting on the front, than back home letting someone else do the job for her. It would be much worse awaiting rape and pillage if an enemy army was about to invade than risking worse treatment, as a prisoner-of-war, than a man.

As an instructor, she learned a lot about ways to get the best out of both sexes, discovering that many women – and indeed many men – did not share her tough, tomboyish go-get-'em attitudes. She felt that because traditionally women were never raised in an atmosphere of constructive criticism, they find it hard to take. 'I mean their husbands don't come home and say, "Well, that cake could be better if you added a little less baking soda and a little bit more icing." He says it's good whether it is or not. If you're not used to taking shit, you cry because you think, "Oh my God, someone's screaming at me." ' The male instructors still came up to Major Brasseur, who by this time had been raised to non-gender status, and complained about the 'Goddamn women.' She advised them not to think about male and female, but about what suited each individual student. Having come close to making a number of men cry, she knew that sometimes she had to put her 'suede gloves' on.

'When some cocky egotistical young guy screws up, you tell him, "You fucked that up", and he says, "Yeah, I know", and gets on with it.' But with a woman she suggests they talk about her approach, what was good, what was bad, in a solicitous sort of way, if it looks like the tears are pricking. The different techniques get the same results. Major Brasseur puts it down to women generally being raised in a less aggressive environment, never having been roasted by coaches on the football field, or abused by team-mates. They have never 'rough-housed' (play-fought) and, she said, 'the traditional male skills of challenge and response to a problem should be life skills, and for the moment most women don't have them'. Female attitudes can be changed and in fact are altering as women play more tough sport. Those in the military are often those described as tomboyish when young, or who were involved in school sports. 'They've learned the rules of the game of combat already, they've learned about teamwork and they've also gained physical-mechanical skills, like hand to eye coordination.'

As for that other team-induced skill, male bonding, Major Brasseur thinks mixed bonding can occur. She noticed that the female pilots coming after her were much more part of their group which went to basic military training, and got through selection and flying training together. The women were there from the beginning, so they were not seen as invasive, but judged on their abilities. But she believes there will always be a difference in the way women and men think, and each will always understand the motivations of their own sex best, but that should not preclude men and women doing the same job and having some level of bonding together. 'Now whether we go out and chase women together – or men – is a different thing. That's going to interrupt the bonding process somewhat. If you're prudish, you're not going to make it, but you don't have to swear every second word either.' Social survival is a balancing act between being too laddish, and trying to maintain female differences, without grating on the group.

One problem always cited by detractors talking about mixed groups in combat is that the men's instincts will be to protect the women above all else, destroying their competence and efficiency as fighters. When fighters are flying to battle in a group, those behind are supposed to defend their winger or leader 'but not to the point of being stupid', said Major Brasseur. Chivalry will probably put the whole group in more danger than necessary. 'If your leader's gone, he's gone. Better to get out of the way and come up again and kill the enemy. There's no point in sacrificing yourself uselessly and worthlessly. If a man tried to sacrifice himself for me, I wouldn't want him on my wing.'

Like many other arguments against women in combat, such speculation remains at the level of fiction. Major Brasseur thinks the whole idea is being looked at in the wrong way by the military. 'People keep being negative, saying, "Yeah, but..." instead of "Can do."' Instead of deciding to use the added resource of women in the best possible way, those in power keep digging up more reasons against. Instead of blaming women for getting pregnant for perhaps a few months out of a twenty-year military career, they should consider it a management problem and work out how to cover for those months with other staff. 'The military can accommodate women with a few small changes, but that does not mean it has to compromise any standards.' Besides, it is too late to close the hangar door on the women fighter pilots following in the wake of Major Brasseur. A whole generation wants its wings and to get their hands on the controls of the fastest aircraft in the world, and no wonder. 'When I go flying, I don't really land in my head for an hour after my fighter has touched down,' said Major Brasseur. 'If you had the choice of driving a Greyhound bus or a Porsche, which would you take?'

Above: *Dahomeyan Amazons of west Africa wearing hats with blue cloth crocodile emblems, identifying them as members of the king's bodyguard, in the late nineteenth century.* © Peter Newark's Historical Pictures.

Left: *Soviet air-force fighter pilots in the Second World War study a new battle order. The Yak fighter belongs to twenty-two-year-old pilot Lieutenant Lily Litvak, on the left.* © Imperial War Museum.

Above: *Violette Szabo of the British Special Operations Executive in the Second World War. She was captured on her second secret mission to occupied France and executed in Ravensbrück concentration camp.* © *Imperial War Museum.*

Above right: *Hero of the Soviet Union, Senior Lieutenant of the Guards Rufina Gasheva. During the Second World War she flew 850 missions as a navigator and dropped 170 tons of bombs on the enemy.* © *Imperial War Museum.*

Below: *Mechanics of the Women's Auxiliary Air Force carry out advanced rigging maintenance on a Second World War Lysander light aircraft.* © *The Times.*

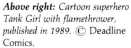

Above: British Women's Auxiliary Air Force advertising poster from the Second World War by Jonathon Foss. © Imperial War Museum.

Above right: Cartoon superhero Tank Girl with flamethrower, published in 1989. © Deadline Comics.

Below: Majors Dee Brasseur (right) and Jane Foster, Canada's first female fighter pilots with a CF-5 Freedom Fighter. © Canadian Forces (photograph by Corporal Joel Weder).

Above: *British Army Lieutenant Wendy Smart of the headquarters' company of The Royal Scots, under camouflage nets in the battlefield in Kuwait.* © Stuart Reed, Ministry of Defence.

Below: *US Army Captain JoAnn Conley in Saudi Arabia, wearing a badge of her two-year-old daughter Stephanie.* © DoD pool, Andy Clarke.

Above: *British women truck drivers with the 68 Squadron Royal Corps of Transport in Al-Jubail, Saudi Arabia.*
© Stuart Reed, Ministry of Defence.

Above: *Women's Royal Naval Service Rating Tanya Luffman aboard HMS* Brilliant, *the first British navy frigate to take women, before it sailed for the Gulf.* © Denzil McNeelance, *The Times.*

Below: *Canada's first infantrywoman, Private Heather Erxleben, preparing to fire a C9 machine gun during training with Princess Patricia's Canadian Light Infantry.* © Canadian Forces (photograph by Sergeant Ed Dixon).

Above: *US Army Specialist Hollie Vallance saying goodbye to her seven-week-old daughter Cheyenne as she leaves Fort Benning, Georgia, for the Middle East.* © The Associated Press.

Above: The British Army launching new uniforms for its women soldiers in 1991. The more practical wardrobe designed by fashion-college students includes parade uniform, barrack dress, temperate and tropical wear, mess dress and sportswear.
© UPPA.

Right: A soldier of the Women's Royal Army Corps passes out during a passing-out parade, due to severe cold. The earlier uniform, with its narrow skirt, was designed by Sir Norman Hartnell.
© Cassidy and Leigh.

8

THE BATTLE OF MOTHERS

There were two ways in which the Gulf War was different from those that had gone before. One was the deployment of smart weapons, like high-technology laser-guided missiles. The other was the deployment of soldier-mothers. Never before had so many military mothers been so close to the combat zone. Never before had there been so many newspaper stories with pictures of tearful women in uniform kissing goodbye to the newborn babies on docksides and airports: the life-bearer was going to face death. Some people found that and the 'Mother Courage' headlines and television pictures very hard to stomach. Soldier-mothers went against every cultural stereotype: woman as giver, woman as nurturer, woman as peacemaker. Often the man – the killer, the warmonger – was left literally holding the baby.

Saddam Hussein's 'Mother of Battles' was also a battle of mothers. The dismantling of the stay-at-home stereotype hurt. There was much railing and debate about the rectitude of it all, which served to show how little the public knew about the make-up of the modern army in America. (The British had only started to allow pregnant women to stay in the forces in 1990, so the problem has yet to arise for them on a large scale.) If eleven per cent of the American military were female and sixty per cent were married, the chances of mothers being sent to the Middle East was high. The US Army sent 2,462 couples with children in the Gulf, and 16,104 single parents, over two-thirds of whom were men. Oddly, no one made a fuss about the 12,379 male soldiers who left their children in the care of grandparents, friends, boarding schools or babysitters. Children in one-parent families losing their fathers for six months must have been just as distressed as those losing their mothers.

But it was the mothers who took all the flak. 'No place for women in the Mother of Battles' went the headlines. British columnist Mary

Kenny wrote in the *Daily Telegraph*: 'Depriving a tiny baby, who so desperately needs those early months of close bonding, of its mother in this way is a barbaric idea. Why applaud it? ... Young children need their mothers more than they need their fathers.' The *Sunday Telegraph* said the unhappy soldier-mothers were at fault and showed not courage but 'the most blameworthy lack of imagination and common sense. Why give birth to children if you are prepared, when so ordered, to abandon them?' And in the *Washington Post*, Sally Quinn added, 'If we can't win a war without our mothers, what kind of sorry fighting force are we?'

That was precisely the point. The American forces had taken integration so far that if mothers were told to stay at home, their specialist jobs in each unit could not be filled instantly by male soldiers. With little time to prepare for deployment, units went as they were, without personnel changes. Over one in ten soldiers were women, and there was no alternative.

It would also have been wrong to deny women the right to fight for their country – they joined the forces in the knowledge they might one day have to go to war, although most were hoping for a quiet peacetime career. They had made child-care arrangements in peacetime long before Saddam had set his sights on Kuwait's oil. Besides, sending women home, who until that moment had been treated as colleagues and equals, would be very unfair on the men who were risking their lives. So the Gulf War was nicknamed the 'Mom's War' by soldiers, and military policies which looked good on paper were tested by the extremes of real life.

The women had no real idea of the effect of their absence on their children, their husbands and themselves until they came home. In discussions with twelve mothers at the Fort Bragg army base in North Carolina on a hot summer's day, after they had returned from the Gulf War, it emerged that none of them regretted doing her job. What they did see, however, was the high emotional cost of serving their countries. They had all learned to be tough and practical, to make sacrifices for their careers. This was just a bigger sacrifice than usual and it showed in their faces. Some had been rejected by their children at what should have been an ecstatic homecoming. Young mothers were handed babies who did nothing but scream in their arms. Older children had done badly at school and become disruptive. Only in some cases was the separation beneficial, making teenagers more responsible and bringing extended families together as they coped with child-care.

For the women at Fort Bragg, 'Home of the Airborne' and America's second largest military base with over 40,000 personnel, there was a contrast between being part of the 'big happy family' on the base, and being left to cope alone all of a sudden when child-care and money problems loomed with the deployment. Despite the family-services centre, the twenty-four-hour helpline, support groups and seventeen churches in the Fort Bragg grounds, parents found the tough part – like persuading relatives to bear the burden at extremely short notice – was something they had to do alone.

The soldier-mothers were keen to talk about the experience, overlapping and interrupting each other. Mostly in their twenties and thirties, it was clear they had not all decided themselves whether the soldier in a woman could take precedence over the mother. The experience had not made any of them decide to leave the army. War was a hazard they accepted and hoped would not recur again during their careers. They saw themselves as little different from civilian mothers – it was just that they had to find childminders for months and not nine to five. In short, necessity had taught them to cope. It was too late to debate and too late to make the choice. Instead, there were flat tones of resignation in their voices.

Specialist Kandy Johnson, a truck driver out in Saudi Arabia for six months, explained some of her anguish on return. 'When I left my one-year-old baby had diapers and a bottle and when I came back she was potty-trained. She was a little person and she could talk real good for her age. It took a few weeks for the baby to get used to me again, she was more attached to her dad. My six-year-old understood what was happening, though. He knew his mom was in Saudi Arabia, I wrote letters and I got to call home once a month, but he's too young to read properly.'

When Specialist Johnson left, her civilian husband had to give up his job to look after the children. He worked nightshifts and they could not find a babysitter to do those hours. Used to relying on two salaries, they had to file for personal bankruptcy when it became one and payments to creditors would be apportioned until her husband got a job again. She was philosophical about it. 'There's nothing else we can do. It's no big deal. Going to war was something I had to do and my husband did a very good job while I was gone.'

During the war, the six pawn shops, including the Park'n'Pawn along the Bragg Boulevard, did well. Many soldiers were away so long their payments lapsed on rented homes in Fort Bragg and the nearby town of Fayetteville. Families found this hardest, since on return from deployment they wanted space and if possible a garden, and there were not enough army houses on the compound with yards and identical whirligig washing lines available when they returned.

Some parents were hurt more by emotions than economics. Specialist Sheila Spencer sat in her camouflage uniform and boots as the hot August rain thudded on the roof, and talked about leaving her baby behind. 'He was five months when I left, and when I came back he was talking, walking and everything. It took him about a week and a half to recognise me again, and that was very difficult to cope with. He wouldn't come to me and once he did, he wouldn't stay long.' Her son went to a babysitter every day from 9 am to 6 pm until he was picked up by his father. 'This is our first child, and I haven't had enough chance to be with him, change him, fix him up, dress him . . .' She faded into silence.

Other mothers had the added agony of a child becoming seriously ill in hospital and not being able to get regular reports or leave to come home. Often they would find out about illnesses or problems at school long after they happened and all they could do was feel guilty. Communications were bad, with letters arriving weeks and even months late, and telephones were available to most only after the war. Specialist Antoinette Sands was told her twin brother had fallen ill and died when she was in Saudi Arabia. It was too late for her to go back for the funeral and it was not considered an emergency. Meanwhile, her ten-year-old daughter had been uprooted and sent to stay with her grandmother in Washington DC. The grandmother had just had a stroke and the daughter, who was used to the relative small-town calm of Fort Bragg, was terrified to go out in that area of Washington, and had difficulties at school.

Many children were moved for six months or more, forced to find new friends in new schools and lose their old familiar ones. For teenagers already burdened with the normal difficulties of that age, seeing parents leave for the Gulf just added to their insecurities. Staff

Sergeant Bennie Bradley was away for six months and her husband for seven. They have a son of thirteen and a daughter of fifteen who were sent to live with her mother in Virginia. 'It affected them a lot. They both went from being honours students to F-grade. They felt we had both abandoned them and they were very hurt. They thought we would die, that neither one of us was coming back, so there was no point in their getting good grades and they stopped going to school. Now they're back to normal in their old school, but I think if we'd been more in contact it would have been better. They got two letters from me and I got one from them, months late. Some must have gone missing. And we didn't get to make many phone-calls.' The psychology and its results are clear to see. Sergeant Bradley said she was just hoping her children never had to go through a separation like that again. The damage was taking a while to repair.

Of course when parents like Sergeant Bradley wrote their Family Care Plans, legal documents nominating an official guardian in the event of deployment, they never expected the arrangements would be used. The US Army, apart from small spates in Grenada and Panama, is a peacetime force and a military job is not impossible to combine with bringing up a family. But when reality thudded down, the call-up papers arrived and soldiers had to write their wills, arrangements made five years before to send children to often aged and ailing parents suddenly fell through. The US Army said only 124 soldiers were not deployed because of faulty or missing Family Care Plans, and most of those made other successful arrangements.

It was not all bad news. Some soldiers who had been ready for the event found their plans worked. Sergeant Carol Sparlin, a confident single parent in her twenties who had been in the army for six years, had been preparing for a year's tour in Korea. She was sent to Saudi Arabia instead, but the arrangement she had made for her four-year-old son to stay with his aunt and uncle was successful. Also her ex-husband, although not looking after the child, was at least able to visit. 'The army looks at it this way – they didn't *issue* it, so they're not responsible for it,' she said. 'That's fair enough.'

Sergeant Sparlin's (relatively) high army pay and benefits compared to those of a single mother in civilian life mean she can afford to send her son to a private school. 'I've got standards,' she said. But money was still not quite enough. When she went with her ex-husband to pick up their son after the war, he ran to his father first. Then when she got home he followed her constantly round the house. The boy behaved the same way after she went away for a month on a primary leadership course. Every time she left to go to work, he thought she was leaving again permanently and would throw a tantrum. The only advantage of her absence was that it brought her entire family together because they all had to be responsible for the child.

The military itself has had to do the same. Day centres, on-base nurseries and schools have had to become part of the deal if it wants to attract the right calibre of soldier, and not lose the investment in her training and experience when she becomes pregnant. Fort Bragg has a family-services centre, eight schools, day-care centres and a child-development programme. A mother in combats putting aubergines and washing powder into a shopping trolley with a toddler in the seat is a common sight on the base supermarket. At the Smoke Bomb Hill Shopette and Tire Center, the uniforms were Ninja Turtle T-shirts for the children and khaki for the adults. The once low-priority concerns of officer's wives' clubs are now central to the smooth running of the military.

Soldiers returning from the Gulf to Fort Bragg were each given an advice booklet, *About Reunion*, also used for peacetime separations. Relations had not only to be rebuilt with children, but with partners too. The booklet is simplistic and filled with rather hammy cartoons of a soldier and his wife sitting far apart on a sofa, but the message is there. 'Your joy at reunion is powerful and exciting – and disappointments can be extra strong too,' it warns. 'Separation and reunion can be challenging – but there's a chance for families to grow too,' it continues with hectoring jolliness. The booklet includes questions for both partners to ask themselves, such as 'Did I do OK with the kids?' They are told communication will be difficult at first, to 'expect some sexual tension' and that readjustment will take up to eight weeks.

The Marines, appropriately enough, issued a rather raunchier reunion booklet, directed more at the single than family man or woman. 'Re-establish your sexual relationship slowly. You can't make up for lost time in a single night.' On experimentation and new positions it advises, 'Give it time, she may be suspicious of where you learned about these ideas! (Ha, ha.)' The boys-only tone of some of these statements reflects an older-fashioned service. Section headings in some of the new, more family-orientated booklets are just as fascinating, including 'Infidelity – Truth or Fiction?', 'Roadblocks to Satisfying Sex' and 'Language ... Those Little Four-Letter Words'. But compared to the real experiences of most of the women in the Gulf, these pamphlets and their advice seem thin and trite. Often the damage, to both children and relationships has already been done.

So it was not surprising that business was booming after the war for Renee Rothrock, a divorce lawyer in the nearby town of Fayetteville. She estimated applications for divorces and separations tripled in the months after the war, and ninety per cent of her work is with couples where one or both partners are in the military. Many of the divorcing couples had children.

A former army lieutenant for three years and daughter of a military man, Rothrock knew more than most about the effect on families of separations in the line of duty. She talked in her Southern-style office, with a glass and brass table, and plush, pink velvet armchairs. 'I didn't get this number of cases following Grenada and Panama, even though some troops went for two or three months. I think Desert Storm was somehow different and if there was anything wrong with a marriage the separation served to intensify it.' After the deployment, as soon as she came back from court each morning, Rothrock found she had clients booked every fifteen minutes, until five o'clock. There were divorce and separation cases, involving financial arguments, child-custody fights and even dog-custody fights.

'Some soldiers came back and found their civilian husband or wife had found themselves a new civilian partner. The marriage often hadn't been good and this was just the opportunity they needed to lead a normal life, away from the military.' One army husband was met by his wife at the airport. She handed him their child and said, 'I'm outta here.' She had run up credit-card bills, spent his pay and his house was about to be foreclosed on. More often it was the other way round, with men and women in the desert having to contemplate their own mortality. 'They would do some soul searching out there, realise their life was not complete and decide to separate when they got home.' Mostly it was couples that had been together for two or three years that split, but she did have one case of a sergeant who had been married for twenty years and his wife had written to him in the Middle East to say she wanted a divorce. He came to Rothrock, incredulous. She discovered he had been running his home, and the lives of his wife and children, as though they were soldiers in a barracks. He was authoritarian, meticulous and restrictive, and without him the tension in the household suddenly melted, and the family became relaxed and comfortable.

Learning more about someone through their absence was common. For men left home alone holding the baby, or the teenager, there were disturbing discoveries to be made about the amount of work involved in child rearing. There was a new home front, made up of previously domestically innocent husbands, who had inadvertently become part-time house-husbands. Despite being dual-career families and used to shared parenting, they realised often how inequitably the burden had been distributed.

The new generation of apron-wearers was far greater in number than that of any previous war. Many men had no idea that their wives had actually *volunteered* to go to fight – most implied that they were forced to go in case their husbands tried to stop them. Eric Laver, a civilian accountant with two children from San Leandro, California, only found out his wife Carmen had volunteered and not been sent when she wrote to him from the hospital ship USS *Mercy* in the Middle East, where she was a medical corpswoman. In an interview with the *New York Times* he said he had been wrestling with feelings of 'How could you do this to me?' since he realised his wife had volunteered. 'It's my selfish heart but inside it hurts to know she had a choice.'

Laver was left looking after his three-year-old daughter, Tara Lynn, and son David, six months. He learned how to plait his daughter's long hair, how to make dinner one-handed with a child on his hip and how to decide whether a squealing baby was wet or hungry. He no longer dawdled after work, since he had to pick up the children from the babysitter. 'There are nights when you want to collapse, but you can't ... I talked real big when I married into this situation and told everybody I could handle it. Well, now I know the responsibilities aren't just to love, honour and cherish. You may also have to be Mr Mom.' He gained a new respect for his wife and working mothers in general. 'When that woman comes home, I'll treat her like a queen.'

Since both parents were working, they already had a babysitter, and Laver knew how to cook and clean, but like most fathers, he still spent less time with the children than his wife. Now his children know him better than ever before. Each afternoon during the war he went to pick them up from the babysitter's house. 'When the baby hears me, he's out of the door, coming at me,' Laver said. 'Before, it was only Carmen's voice he responded to.'

The Lavers were lucky – at least one of them could stay at home without totally disrupting their lives. But for families where both parents were called up there were tougher decisions to be made. Staff Sergeant Carrie McNamara and her husband Chuck Sanders were both in the Reserves, and the army also employed her full-time as the civilian manager of the Reserve centre in Greenbay, Wisconsin. Her two children from a previous marriage (her first husband had died) were supposed to stay – according to her army child-care plan – with their paternal grandparents. 'We stopped by at the in-laws' house when all this mess started, but talking to them I just didn't get that warm fuzzy feeling,' said Sergeant McNamara. 'They just laughed and said, "Look after the kids? No way."'

Sanders, a forty-three-year-old Vietnam veteran, decided he would get out of the Reserves and stay at home to look after Kirk, aged eight, and Kimberly, eleven. Sergeant McNamara, who is thirty-five, went to Kuwait with her Greenbay Reserve unit hoping to serve her country. On arrival, she found three people assigned to the same job she had done by herself at home. By the end of the war, her section was vastly over-manned for the light paperwork it was doing. 'I am trying to think of it as a vacation away from work. I expected to be handing out emergency-food parcels, or something more useful than this.'

Spare time meant time to worry about her children, but there was little else to do in the Civil Affairs Unit stationed in sprawling warehouses just outside Kuwait City. Sergeant McNamara said she expected her daughter to get her first period soon and although they had discussed it together, she was worried about not being there when it happened. 'Kimberly was a real daddy's girl and when he died a few years ago, she went to counselling. Recently, she'd been fine, stopped going, was doing well at school and had taken up a musical instrument. But now she's back in counselling again and she won't do her homework.' Sergeant McNamara looked pained.

Her first husband had been in the air force, but had become a house-husband when their daughter was born, leaving her mother in the army. He looked after the children and even went to evening classes with all the other army 'wives' in Germany. Sergeant McNamara worked right up until both her children were born and she wore civilian clothes when khaki no longer fitted. She took just six weeks off after the birth and refused to breast-feed because she thought giving it up would be too painful. So Kimberly's father was the one who was always there when cut knees or upsets at school arose and was very important to her. The disappearance now of a second parent to war had put the child off balance, despite the presence of a loving stepfather.

Sanders was still holding down his job as a highway patrolman, which involved working nine nights every month, so he had to take the children to in-laws, both in their seventies, miles away in Milwaukee. 'He's had a rude awakening,' said Sergeant McNamara. 'My husband was not real good about cleaning the house, but he was real good at leaving the clothes in the washer – for me to do. Now he's having to get the groceries, buy them shoes and take them to music lessons, but at least his mother, and his grown-up daughter and the neighbors, are all helping.'

Role-reversals experienced by hundreds of couples during the war may be beneficial in the long run, according to Democratic Congresswoman Pat Schroeder. 'The men are finding out that it is easier to be a brave soul than a tender of the hearth,' she said. 'The devaluation of women's work in this society – maybe this will help change that. And child care – maybe it will stop just being a women's issue.' Schroeder is also campaigning to have maternity leave in the army and air force increased from the present six weeks to the four months already given by the navy.

During the war, several other members of Congress were so disturbed by stories of dual-career military couples having to leave their children in boarding schools and single parents risking death that they introduced a bill to exempt one parent from being in a combat or 'imminent danger' zone. The forces could have chosen which parent to exempt and could also add the time out of combat onto their length of service. The bill failed, because the military said it would hamper effectiveness and would be unfair to soldiers who were not parents. The Pentagon pointed out that its soldiers were all volunteers and had known the risk before joining. Defence Secretary Dick Cheney said in a letter opposing the changes that they 'would weaken our combat capability by removing key personnel from our deployed units and by undermining unit cohesion and *esprit de corps*'.

A *Newsweek* survey conducted after the war which asked what the public's greatest concerns would be if women were allowed into combat showed that eighty-nine per cent were worried about mothers leaving small children at home, seventy-six per cent about women becoming pregnant and putting the unborn child at risk, and sixty-four per cent about pregnant women having to be replaced. The questions were constructed in such a way that respondents could agree with a number of options; and they were biased, so that the similar question of, say, single fathers leaving small children at home was not mentioned. But the survey also showed that fifty-four per cent of people thought mothers on active duty should be able to refuse assignments, compared to forty per cent who thought they should have no special treatment.

The American military played down child-care problems during the Gulf War. At the post-war NATO conference on women in the military, Brigadier General Patricia Hickerson said, 'What Desert Shield and Desert Storm showed us was that the numbers who experienced dependent-care problems were very small. In addition, for those cases where problems did develop, most were resolved by delaying the members' deployment or returning them for a short period of time to make new arrangements.'

Most soldiers are in exactly the age group which, in civilian life, produces the largest number of children, so as more women join up the compromise between parenthood and military duty will increasingly occur. Over seven per cent of them will get pregnant each year, the same as civilians. The average soldier in his or her early twenties is not always the most responsible of individuals.

Teenage single mothers are a new phenomenon in what used to be bachelor-boy forces.

Single fathers can be just as irresponsible, even when they are experienced as soldiers. When Staff Sergeant Faagalo Savaiki was called up for Gulf duty, he ended up being charged with failing to provide for his children properly. He left them, aged nine, twelve and thirteen, alone in their house in Clarkesville, Tennessee. He had taped a notice on the kitchen wall with instructions on how to use his bank cash-machine card to withdraw money for food. They were discovered and placed in a foster home, and Sergeant Savaiki was recalled to be sentenced.

Many women had the opposite reaction and also found themselves breaking military law for quite different reasons. They could just not bring themselves to leave their children, particularly those still breast-feeding. Army Specialist Melinda Davis had a sixteen-month-old daughter and was arrested in Massachusetts after she failed to report for Reserve duty. She claimed she had no one to care for her child and was held for twenty-four hours. The child was placed with her mother and she was sent to work at an army base until her case was decided. As a Reservist, Davis had never expected her child-care plan to be put into action and could not deal with it when the worst happened. Many Reservists like her discovered they had parents who were willing to take their children in theory but not in practice and they could not afford the sort of child-care they wanted. With many full-time career soldiers sitting around in the States, the Reservist's reaction was 'Why me?'

Out of wartime, a pregnant enlisted woman in America can get a discharge and serve the rest of her obligation in the ready Reserves, who do not take part in monthly exercises. But many of those who thought they had escaped deployment found themselves caught up again when the Reserves began to be called up. Army Specialist Faith Stewart told the *Washington Post* that she went into labour on 22 January 1991, the same day that the papers arrived from the army telling her to report for Gulf duty. She was at her parents' home in Pennsylvania, as her husband Jack was already in Saudi Arabia. As a member of the ready Reserves, she was due to join him after the six weeks allowed for pregnancy leave. Aged twenty-one, Stewart had hardly finished coping with the trauma of birth and was just getting to know her child before she had to hand him over, for God knew how many months, to her elderly in-laws in Florida. 'He's only two weeks old and there's no one here to take care of him.' So much for early bonding.

There is little specifically war-related information on the effect separation has on children. But well-documented psychological research shows that the lack of one parent due to divorce, imprisonment, and even other less traumatic separations causes insecurities and behavioural problems in most children, which can persist into adulthood. How much more frightening is a war, with no return date, no visiting rights and constant horrifying sights available every family dinner-time on CNN or the BBC news? How disturbing is it when your seven-year-old sends you a crayon picture he did in school of a firing tank?

The soldier-mother's dilemma is no worse in some ways than that of civilian mothers, most of whom work. Young children are often looked after by people other than their family for twelve hours a day, whether they are nannies, childminders or after-school schemes. Children learn to attach themselves to the nearest adult, paid or unpaid, and of either sex. What is happening to women in the military only magnifies the values of society outside, which deem that it is possible and often economically necessary to work full-time, and have a family. The needs of children are well-known, but socially inconvenient. Psychologists say we have invented 'the competent child' which has no needs. Until the situation is considered by governments and employers to be a problem for *parents* and not just mothers, change is unlikely. Soldiers, like civilians, will just have to cope.

Pregnancy has its uses too. A number of women got pregnant to avoid deployment in the Gulf, because although the military will send new mothers to war six weeks after birth and still lactating, it keeps pregnant women in less strenuous posts at home. For some, pregnancy was the female equivalent of the traditional bad back or fallen arches – a way out. There were reports of whole outbreaks of pregnancy in certain units, as word spread, but almost nothing could be confirmed. Rumour was rife. But newspaper reports turned out to be exaggerated – only seventy US Army soldiers out of 30,000 were sent home due to pregnancy during Deserts Shield and Storm.

The British said they had two pregnancies out of 1,000 or so women deployed. Obviously a minority of women were pregnant by their partners at home. There is no doubt that some less courageous women, who had not joined the army intending to go to war, took the easy way out by getting pregnant. But pregnancy was unfairly latched on to as the one fault that women could really be criticised for as soldiers, since in other areas they were performing as well as men. But if pregnancy rates are compared to men's sports injury rates during the war, there are similar losses. Women were less reckless and had negligible injuries.

Peacetime pregnancy rates are much higher among enlisted American women, at ten to fifteen per cent, than officers. Pregnant women only stopped being discharged from the US forces in 1978. Since then numbers have grown exponentially and that is not taking into account the numbers who have abortions. With the political sensitivity over abortion in the States and the banning of Federally-funded operations from 1978 onwards, military hospitals refused to perform terminations for their own personnel, except when the mother's life was in danger, so soldiers were forced to find a hospital off base. This made it difficult for women stationed in foreign countries or states with anti-abortion laws, who were forced to travel elsewhere or take risks in badly equipped hospitals. The British military will perform properly sanctioned abortions in its hospitals and women are given sick leave.

Until 1990, the British military discharged all pregnant women at about four months when their uniforms no longer fitted, and those wishing to resume their careers had to rejoin and be retrained. There was no guarantee, as there is now, of a similar job at the same rank. Those who rose to high positions had, until recently, to be dedicated to childlessness or spinsterhood. Now about one-third of women in the UK forces are married and most of those to other soldiers.

The British military used to give twenty-nine weeks' maternity leave, in common with civilian law, consisting of eighteen weeks' full pay before the birth and six afterwards at ninety per cent pay, and the rest at social-services rates. But in December 1991, an RAF and an army nurse – who had been dismissed under the old rules for becoming pregnant – took the Ministry of Defence to the High Court and won £25,000 between them in compensation. The MOD said that the case was 'a catalyst' which caused them to change their rules. Women now qualify after birth for fourteen weeks on full pay, instead of ninety per cent, and they can take unpaid leave of up to forty-eight weeks. So soldiers now have better maternity rules than British civilians.

The Americans give six weeks' paid leave, which assumes expectant mothers remain at work in their camouflage maternity uniforms almost until contractions start. (It remains a mystery why the maternity uniform is a variant of field battle-dress; battle is where a nine months' pregnant woman is unlikely to be.) A new Department of Defense policy will prevent mothers from being sent to an unaccompanied tour location for four months after birth. The policy also applies to single parents and one member of dual-career military couples.

European countries are generally more lavish with military maternity leave, following civilian practice. The Belgians give fifteen weeks' paid leave and an additional optional three months' unpaid leave for breast-feeding, and a further three months' unpaid paternity or maternity leave. The Greeks – who have just under three per cent women in their forces – can afford to give a year's paid leave. The Dutch give six months' unpaid parental leave and six months on half-pay. Norwegian maternity leave has been lengthened from twenty-six weeks to thirty-two with pay, or thirty-eight without. The Israeli Defence Force still conscripts women, but exempts pregnant or married women with children from the draft.

Part of the reason why the American forces are not keen on making life any easier for pregnant women and mothers by increasing leave is that men very much resent watching women work short days and refuse heavy assignments. Also, with 47,000 military couples with children and 67,000 single parents (although two-thirds of those are male), maternity leave takes an increasing swathe out of working hours. Often, mothers are not replaced during their short time off, so others in the unit – male and female – must bear the extra burden for no extra pay.

The peacetime parent, however, is a less disturbed and unhappy soul than the wartime one. If couples can get joint assignments and a place in the child-care centre available on about half the American military bases (there are none in Britain), the parenthood is fairly painless. Captain Clare Jenkins, aged thirty-two, is a tutor in environmental engineering at the West Point Military Academy, where her husband is also a lecturer. They have two children under five. 'We can go over to the day center at lunchtimes or at breaks to see Catherine and Matthew, although I don't go too often because they always want me to stay.' She met her husband when they were cadets at West Point, and thinks the dual assignments mean they can both have careers and probably see a lot more of their children close by on the base than they would in civilian working life.

Parenting is easier the higher you go up the ranks, where life becomes more predictable and some can find a cushy nine-to-five job. This is what soldiers call RHIP – Rank Has Its Privileges. Women pilots with officer husbands, for instance, can talk about hiring a live-in nanny for a year. Enlisted unmarried mothers on low salaries rely on *ad hoc* childminders, or the civilian wives of military men who will take in an extra child during the day, along with their own. But it is at night or on exercise that problems arise. Who can find a babysitter when the call of duty comes at 4 am?

For women in the navy, away for six-month tours, motherhood becomes largely a postal affair, but some manage it with remarkable equanimity. Corporal Barbara Reddick, a cook on the Canadian ship HMCS *Protecteur*, has been in the navy for eleven years, and has two sons aged nine and four. She was given land postings as soon as possible after she discovered she was pregnant, had three months off and then went back on board. Corporal Reddick, now thirty, decided to join when her civilian jobs were badly paid and going nowhere. 'Suddenly I was doing something for myself and getting all this money. When I look at my friends back home, nothing has happened to them, and I've been to Boston and Puerto Rico, St John's and the Persian Gulf. If I had worked on land I couldn't afford to go to all those places and I wouldn't have enough money on my own to give my children a good life.'

Although she is a single mother, the navy gives her an apartment in the married quarters in the port of Halifax, Nova Scotia, and she pays her live-in babysitter to look after her children there, or sometimes they stay with another family. During Reddick's first eight years in the navy she had shore-based jobs and saw more of her sons. Since 1989 she has been on the supply ship *Protecteur*, sometimes in port for repairs, but mostly at sea. With her ship berthed in Halifax, she seemed calm and relaxed in her cook's uniform. She believes being away from her children for some of the year is good for both sides; her eldest son, Michael, is doing very well at school and her youngest, Patrick is happy, she claimed.

She made it sound impossibly simple. 'They see me go to sea, but I just tell them I'm coming back soon and if I'm not back exactly on time, they know they'll get a message.' She misses them, but she also enjoys the break and believes her children have learned to be more independent and less clinging. Her four-year-old washes, dresses and bathes himself, puts a hotdog in the microwave and goes to the local shop. 'Other people explain to them that Mommy has to go away so she can get money to buy them clothes and toys. They've been on the ship umpteen times and they love it. My oldest wants to go to sea when he grows up.'

There is a down side too. The youngest boy took an overdose of pills thinking they were sweets and had to have his stomach pumped while Corporal Reddick was at sea. 'When I got back he said, "Mommy, I won't do that no more." ' She tries not to worry. 'There's no point in jumping the gun unless you're sure something serious has happened.' By talking to the ship's padre and confiding in others, Reddick managed not to bottle up her anxieties. 'I found it hard when I first went to sea, leaving the kids and just seeing water, water, water, every day. I wanted to holler and screech, but I had to put my family first, stay close and provide for them.' By concentrating on economic responsibility, she blocked out some of the doubts and guilt about her responsibility as a mother.

There is something depressing about the idea of a four-year-old microwaving his own hotdog. Childless women and men may find it acceptable; mothers and fathers may find it inexcusable. Nevertheless, it is part of the reality the American and Canadian military has to deal with, and the army of mothers will soon spread to Britain and the Continent.

Few military mothers, whether at war or in peacetime, are satisfied with the arrangements made for their children. But wars are the exception in the Western military, and when they do come they are now expected to be short and sharp. In general the soldier-mother's relationship with her child is probably not much worse than the average civilian working mother's. It is strange that there is something admiring in the tones of people who discuss, say, the lives of glossy-magazine editors: 'She worked to the last day, took two weeks off after the birth and was back at her desk wearing her size-10 Chanel suit within the month.' Yet when it comes to an enlisted woman going back to work after six weeks to keep her job, and pay for good clothes and school fees for her child, there is much indrawing of breath.

Part of this argument is about economics, and those rich enough to afford a good full-time nanny suffer less guilt and disapprobation, in either military or civilian life. Black women make up forty-seven per cent of enlisted females in the US military. They often join the army to escape bias or bad educational opportunities in their home towns and to find a good career, yet they are still disapproved of as irresponsible in some way if they get pregnant.

Military mothers merely reflect the trend towards working mothers generally. In time of war, however, the reflection becomes magnified and it is easy for the outside world to assuage its guilt over part-time parenting by attacking soldier-mothers in public.

It is not really the damage – if any – done to children that is the worry; after all, Victorian nannies and boarding schools have been paid child-separators for years. What upsets the public is that the traditions of soldiering are being turned on their heads. The whole point of going to war was to protect the women and children at home; they were the reward the soldier returned to if he survived the battlefield. If mothers are operating Patriot missiles on the front and fathers buying Pampers, chivalry is somehow undermined.

The other argument is about time lost due to pregnancy, but it must be remembered those months off are added to the length of the service commitment in Britain and considered as six weeks' sick leave in America. Yes, it would be easier to have a men-only army who would not need, say, six months to a year off if they were to have two children in Britain, or twelve weeks off in America. But the reality is that unless armies go back to conscription, they will not get the quality of men they need, in terms of education, maturity and intelligence. Volunteer armies need women to keep their averages up. To lose fully-trained pilots, intelligence officers and ship's navigators the minute they become pregnant is a waste of millions of pounds.

In terms of value for money, women were absent less for sports injuries and disciplinary offences related to drugs and alcohol. Physically, depending on morning sickness and whether the job is a heavy one, a pregnant woman will have to be helped. But there are plenty of desk jobs in the military, which can be easily rotated. Some women keep quiet about it for as long as possible and admit they are still parachuting in the first few months of pregnancy. Others keep up physical training and running until the sixth month, and performance afterwards sometimes can be better – witness Liz McColgan, the British 10,000-metres runner, who won a Gold medal at the 1991 World Athletics Championships *after* she had two children.

Western militaries are faced with something of a *fait accompli* on the motherhood front. By allowing pregnant soldiers to remain in their jobs, they have unleashed a concomitant trail of problems which men schooled in discipline and boot-polishing are at a loss to deal with. In Britain, the problem is in its infancy, but in the States, seventeen per cent of bases with nurseries already have a night-time child-care system, to suit military working hours. This does not necessarily encourage pregnancy, but it means mothers can be called on at any time to be soldiers. A survey for an independent American think-tank financed by the Rand Corporation showed that motherhood did indeed affect national security, in terms of retention of personnel and military readiness. 'If the army ignores these social issues, it may find itself unable to retain enough of the qualified people it wants to keep, and the people it thinks are ready to go to war may be too torn by conflicting loyalties to make good soldiers.'

The fact still remains that thousands of women want to combine having children and soldiering, just as thousands of men have always done. Indeed, many American mothers actually volunteered to go to the Gulf War. And not every woman in the forces wants to or can have children – often women join because they know they are not maternal types and the military can provide a substitute family. Soldier-mothers have also had a positive effect on real families, making men take their responsibilities as fathers more seriously, until eventually parenting will take an equal place in the public's mind with mothering. The fact is that the Gulf War took the lives of 138 fathers and one mother. Why should her family's loss be considered any greater than theirs?

9

AN OFFICER, NOT A GENTLEMAN

The cavernous dining hall of America's finest shrine to masculinity roared with the sound of nearly 4,000 men eating Sloppy Joes – a sort of ill-constructed hamburger – and having 2,000 conversations about the next college football game against Holy Cross. They were identically dressed in black shirts and grey trousers with a black stripe down the leg, part of the 200-year-old 'Long Grey Line' of officer cadets issuing out of the United States Military Academy at West Point, New York State.

Until the sixties when the academy was opened to blacks, West Point was the ultimate WASP experience; a West Point class ring outdid most old college ties, both within and outside the military. Then in 1976 came the final sacrilege – the government forced the academy to take women students. Honour, tradition and the spirit of muscular Christianity were assumed to be in jeopardy; in fact, little changed. Even now, the female presence is hardly noticeable. In the lunch formation marching to the dining hall, there were 400 women dotted among the 4,000 men, identifiable only occasionally by hair protruding beneath their hats or a sudden dip in the height of a line of soldiers. They too talked about football and attended the near-compulsory army games, as part of West Point's encouragement of team spirit. They too greeted every passing superior – upperclassmen and officers – with a salute and the team chants 'Beat Holy Cross', 'Go Moose' or 'Beat Navy', as well as the traditional 'Good morning, Sir'.

West Point's method of turning teenage school-leavers into army officers over four years involved those in the final year being hard on the third years and so on down the line to the first years or Plebes, who were pulled up for tiny misdemeanours constantly, by everyone, and duly punished. Back in the all-boys' days, this involved severe 'hazing' – harassment and verbal abuse of the youngest boys which came close to bullying. They were treated like fags at a bad English public school. Often punishments administered by the senior cadets were physical, most popularly 'bracing', in which a cadet was forced to stand against a wall, chin down on chest and neck sweating on a nickel until it supposedly stuck to the wall. But when women arrived, all perfume and long hair, such punishments were deemed inappropriate for them. Despite the fact that they were to take the same academic and military classes, and only separate for physical training, the techniques that had built the leaders of the past were not to be used on them. The men were deeply resentful of the intrusion which seemed suddenly to water down years of tradition, diluting their macho achievements, and they took it out on the women verbally.

Captain Carol Barkalow was in that first intake of women, which graduated as the class of 1980, and wrote *In the Men's House*, a book about her experiences, many of which only differed in severity from those of female cadets now. She found the minority of women became a target for special 'hazing': 'Men had to prove themselves weak before they became the subject of this kind of harassment; women had to prove themselves strong before they were spared it.' She compared the mental and emotional pressure to the constant threat of terrorism. She never knew when it was going to happen or why.

'Even the simplest social exchange could become an occasion for contempt. If a female new cadet passed an upperclassman in the hall and said, "Good morning, Sir", she might be greeted in return with cool civility. Then again, she might hear back, "Good morning, bitch". Or, "It was a good morning until you got here, whore." ' Not surprisingly, such added harassment to the disturbance of mixing resulted in an attrition rate for the class of 1980 of fifty-one per cent for women and an unprecedented forty per cent for men. Most women dropped out in the first year. Now the aggression has been toned down and for the class of 1992, the expected attrition is thirty-one per cent for women and twenty-four per cent for men, with more women dropping out due to 'lack of motivation'.

In academic and military-theory classes, the first women were very successful, and dealings with tutors and senior officers were less fraught than those with other students. A survey of the eighties showed only fifteen per cent of women left because of academic problems, compared to nearly a quarter of men. Physically, women performed to a much lower standard, are still allowed to do so and do not take boxing or wrestling classes. Women running in ill-fitting boots had constant injuries, but all cadets now use running shoes which has eliminated the problem. The present physical entrance requirement at the end of the pre-West Point summer camp called 'Beast Barracks' is a minimum of forty-two push-ups, fifty-two sit-ups and a two-mile run in 15.54 minutes for men, compared to eighteen push-ups, fifty sit-ups and an 18.54 minute-run for women – not exactly tough going. On the other hand, one former cadet-turned-tutor remembered that fitness scores read out at a reunion for men who had attended the academy twenty years before drew expressions of amazement, because they were so much higher than in the past. 'And those were only the female cadets' scores,' said the announcer, doubly wounding them. Both male and female fitness levels are improving, but women, as is the trend in professional athletics, are closing the gap at a faster rate.

But West Point is there not mainly for fitness, but to build leaders of men, or now, leaders of people. Women do well, being selected at a slightly higher rate than male graduates for promotion to captain and major, but when it comes to long careers in the army, they show less interest, and their numbers begin to drop off around the six-year mark – when most are in their late twenties and getting broody.

Again, this is the stage at which the promotion pyramid begins to narrow and having around half of all jobs closed due to combat restrictions may account for some of the fall-out. Those who do stay often sacrifice the family part of their lives: a male senior officer is twice as likely to be married compared to a woman and only half of married women officers have children. A new pattern is emerging, however, among junior female officers which allows for a family and a career. They aim to be a company commander, an important tick in the promotion box, six or seven years on when they are captains. Company command is a tough, full-time post, but is often followed by an easier desk job, a staff position in headquarters, say, and the regular hours mean these years are a good time to have a child.

Captain Robin Carrington, also a graduate from the class of 1980 and now working in the West Point Admissions Directorate, said,

'These cadets tend to be from very traditional backgrounds and their views reflect that, so for the women there is eventually a difficult conflict between being an old-fashioned wife and mother, and the utterly non-traditional role they have chosen for themselves.' Small and red-haired, Captain Carrington strode across the college quadrangles, through a sea of salutes. Like many of her students, she had married a classmate, and they now have a three-year-old daughter and an eleven-year-old dual career.

Like most men at West Point, her husband joined the combat arms. Like most women, she went into the combat-support services. When they were posted to Germany in the days before unification, she was a quartermaster and he went to the front line with the artillery. 'The funny thing was, although I was in the beans-and-bullets department, I spent about twice as long out in the field as my husband.' She was given two light M60 machine guns to defend six petrol tankers and other supply vehicles, 'but in classic Clausewitzean theory we would have been attacked first – hit the soft underbelly of the enemy by cutting his line of supply'. Carrington concluded that training women to be offensive as well as defensive was no bad thing. 'I'm five foot three inches and 105 pounds, and I can drive a tank and fire a weapon as well as any guy, and I wouldn't hesitate to use it.'

Her former classmate, Captain Barkalow, had a similar experience in the Gulf War, in a support unit attached to the 24th Infantry Division, the unit which spearheaded the final ground attack. She told *Newsweek*, 'Our support outfit was in just as much danger as the combat element. The Iraqi weapons had just as much capability of hitting us as the men in the front. The difference was we didn't have the ability to defend ourselves like the combat troops.' Both women are in their thirties and clearly frustrated by the barriers they see in between their present positions and the mainstream male track to high command. West Point men expect to go right to the top, they reason, so why should the country's top tactical and military minds be solely male?

But following the acceptance of women in combat in the air force, perhaps these barriers will fall, as attitudes slowly change across the military and women officers gain wider opportunities. Certainly the cadets of the nineties are getting used to having a woman in charge at a very early age. Back at the lunch table, female Cadet Robin Schuck was carrying on the tradition of keeping the Plebes in line. 'What's there to drink?' she asked sitting down and eyeballing a small male Plebe with a cruelly short haircut who was on lunch duty. 'Ma'am, the cold beverage for today is lemonade. Does anyone not wish lemonade, Ma'am?' he said nervously, and then ate in mechanical silence for the rest of the meal.

'It's a humbling experience for them, but it's good to learn what the lowest ranking person must feel,' observed Cadet Schuck, who was all-powerful, being in her final year and aged twenty-one. She explained why she had decided on West Point. 'I wanted to travel, and I'm majoring in French and Russian which should be useful, and I thought I had the potential to be a good leader, and I'd have a good job guaranteed for life.' No worries about having children or the glass ceiling on career there. She was confident about herself as a quality resource, since competition is much greater for the small number of female places at West Point. The academy could take more, but it tries to keep female officers to ten to fifteen per cent, since presently enlisted women make up eleven per cent of the army. The men around Cadet Schuck, at least on the surface, seemed comfortable with female command. 'I don't mind taking orders from a woman,' said Cadet Drew Marshall, looking ironic. 'It's much the same as being told what to do by your mom.'

His views are an aberration among the traditional American values espoused by the male cadets. After all, they are here ultimately to lay down their lives for those values and the values of their fathers who often also are part of the Long Grey Line, so changes are unlikely to be swift. Cadet Shaun Greene, a final-year student, claimed nearly all the cadets were Republicans. They must swear to keep the honour code of the academy which says, 'A cadet shall not lie, cheat or steal, nor tolerate those who do.' That means, in theory, cadets have to turn in their classmates if they catch them sneaking back into their rooms after an illegal late-night drink off campus. Somehow the presence of women, the cause of increased sneaking and lying in forbidden relationships, has soiled that code. 'If I had to turn in my best friend because he broke that code, I hope I would be able to do the right thing,' said Cadet Greene. 'Everything here is done for a purpose. What we do to the Plebes is part of their initiation, but it's nothing like as bad as what goes on in fraternities. There is a lot of tradition, but people come here because they want to be a part of that.'

But the statistics – and West Point is keen on statistics – show a less pretty picture of tradition. A 1990 survey showed all sorts of holes in the surface impression of equality. Racial integration was fairly successful – nearly seventy per cent thought it was working. But when it came to the integration of women, a telling forty per cent of men thought it was successful compared to sixty-four per cent of women. Nobody would ever guess that underlying hostility from the sight of the fresh-faced cadets, rendered almost-but-not-quite sexless in their grey uniforms, walking with their arms swinging smartly between the grey stone buildings and parapets overlooking the trees running down to the banks of the Hudson River. It would be hard to discover that even from talking to them. But when it came to surveys filled in anonymously, the female cadets also let go.

Delving further into the statistical pile showed most women thought they were being treated unfavourably. To the question 'Are you treated exactly the same by the corps of cadets, regardless of sex?', only forty per cent said yes, although most thought academic professors and tactical officers treated them fairly. Perhaps this shows that the rigid rank structure helps to protect women actually working as soldiers from unfair attention. Of course, women also experienced favouritism because of their sex. Sometimes, however, this went too far and became sexual harassment. Almost a third of women cadets had experienced pressure for sexual favours, nearly half complained of touching, cornering, pinching, or suggestive looks, and sixty per cent of sexual teasing and jokes. One in five said male cadets had come into their rooms at night and touched them while they were sleeping. Some of this has to be put down to immaturity and student jokes; the rest is a worrying indictment of the attitudes of young officers being groomed for some of the most senior posts in the US Army.

Early behavioural experiments at West Point showed groups of traditionally minded men, who were given a female leader and completed a task successfully, would attribute that to the 'cohesiveness' of the group, not to her leadership as an officer. But when the men failed in the task, they would blame the female leader roundly. Captain Carrington thought the present-day cadets had improved: 'Familiarity breeds acceptance,' she said.

Surviving West Point, or the navy and air-force academies, is just the beginning, and those women who do graduate after four years tend on average to have higher academic scores than their male counterparts and are assessed as equally good potential leaders. There is no problem, then, with the female product of the academies. It is just that too large a number of talented women are lost along the way due to the hothouse atmosphere of harassment and discrimination, which does not bring out the best in them. Accepting put-downs and contempt, and not being equally appreciated for similar effort, do not train a person to be a better officer. It makes cadets, both male and female, bitter. The American academies cannot expect to be successful in teaching modern warfare while trapped in the straitjacket of ancient social prejudices.

Once out in the wider world of the working military, women's ability to do the job and manage troops matters more than their image or ability to withstand constant 'hazing'. As young officers, they tend to be promoted faster than men, due in part to the military trying to improve its record for equality. Women make up 15.5 per cent of lieutenants and thirteen per cent of captains and majors, more than their eleven per cent overall showing in the forces. But when it comes to the higher ranks, like lieutenant-colonel and colonel, they fall to 5.4 per cent, and for generals and admirals it is under one per cent. It takes twenty years on average to make colonel and thirty to make general, so not surprisingly there are hardly any women around long enough to reach those positions. Also, because senior-officer positions are easier to reach with combat experience, female officers tend on the whole to support the opening of front-line branches, while enlisted women, who have little to gain from it, take much less interest.

The British military can boast of no female generals or admirals at all and the highest women are at brigadier level – one for each service. Although women constitute under five per cent of the army, they make up nearly seven per cent of lieutenants and second-lieutenants, and a creditable nine per cent of captains; for major and above, it falls to two per cent. The removal in August 1990 of the rule requiring discharge on pregnancy may change that, since a choice will no longer have to be made between career and family. Until the disbandment of the Women's Royal Army Corps in early 1992, only a limited number of senior posts were open to women, but now the only units not employing them are armour and infantry.

Also in 1992, the Royal Military Academy which trains officers at Sandhurst finally did what West Point had in 1976. It mixed. For although women had been in a separate building in the grounds of Sandhurst since 1984, they had been on a largely segregated course, which originally concentrated more on military administration and less on exercises in the field. It began to evolve with women doing more traditionally 'male' subjects, such as tactics and target practice, and now, apart from physical training, the female platoons do exactly the same as the male ones. There are thirty women in each intake, and three intakes a year, out of a total of about 900, so the course is ten per cent female. There is no shortage of qualified officer applicants, but because enlisted women presently make up only four per cent of army ranks, the military does not want the forces to be top-heavy with female officers.

The Royal Military Academy, for all its 250 years of tradition and equally effective old school tie, is rather different from West Point. Around sixty-five per cent of its female trainee officers and thirty-seven per cent of the entire intake are graduates. They are more likely to be twenty-one or twenty-two than the average eighteen at West Point. The course lasts twenty-eight weeks, rather than the American four years, and the indoctrination is less violent, relying more on the services of non-commissioned officers to knock the intellectually and physically flabby intake into shape, rather than harassment by fellow students.

The site of the Military Academy at Sandhurst, in Surrey, is equally beautiful as the American one, with tree-lined drives, lakes and old buildings in neo-classical white stone and Edwardian yellow-red brick. It is spoiled only by Victory College and the academy head-quarters, a modern concrete mistake in which Sandhurst's Commandant, Major-General Tim Toyne Sewell, was to be found. He is an unlikely-looking radical in the tartan trousers of his Scots regiment, with a more positive attitude towards expanding the opportunities of army women than many senior members of the former WRAC. He thought mixing the officers' course would have a civilising effect on both sides. Women would bring an intellectual edge to the course and competition with men would be good for them. His talk tended in the direction of first Sandhurst, then the world. He saw absolutely no reason why women should not become fighter pilots or tank drivers. 'There have been 250 years of traditional inertia at the academy and a change of attitude is needed. What's surprising is when you actually go ahead with the changes, there's not a lot of opposition.'

The three separate non-graduate, graduate and women's courses will be combined into one, so women will be spending longer in the field, and learning more weapons training and tactics. They will not, however, do full army drill, for the somewhat unconvincing reason that the SA-80 rifles are too heavy to hold for extended periods – and some movements are allegedly tricky with large breasts. Drilling and yelling are seen as less useful than previously – the course was, after all, designed for young boys straight out of public school, who are now in the minority. General Toyne Sewell still remembers his first day when he walked up the college steps and a bawling sergeant looked *down* on him. He is six foot four inches. The sergeant was six foot eight inches. 'Of course we still want the short sharp shock so they know they're in the army now, but I want to confine that mostly to the first term. The colour-sergeants always had an enormous impact here and I think that needs a change of emphasis, so in the second and third parts of the course I want young officers, the platoon commanders in their late twenties, to take over. The slight change of emphasis will make the point to the cadet as well. We've got to start treating them as grown-ups.'

The politics behind making such changes are Byzantine. Major concerns include: who will win the Sovereign's Banner Competition? Previously, companies of men competed on shooting, military knowledge, orienteering and so on, as well as forcing a team holding a log round an obstacle course. Since physically women stood no chance of winning, there would have to be some sort of handicap system, so that equal effort rather than strength was rewarded. But would there be a riot if women won and how could such a competition be fair? Next there was the Sword of Honour, awarded to the 'best leader' and 'rounded character', but women officers do not presently carry swords, so exactly how would a female winner collect her prize? Discussion immediately began on the pros and cons of women carrying ceremonial swords. Such problems, in microcosm, are symbols of how great the imagined divide still is.

At Cranwell, the college in Lincolnshire for Royal Air Force officers, the course has been mixed for all subjects, including physical education for some time, as is the Naval college at Dartmouth. One of the RAF officer cadets, Kirsty Innes, said, 'When we played Sandhurst at sports we ran at the men's pace and the Sandhurst women ran at the women's pace. Afterwards, they wouldn't sit with the men, but we did. I found them a bit girly. We're more modern.' But the army is catching up, and the general said Cranwell's mixed physical training was only possible because the RAF was dealing largely with machines and not expected to lead a platoon in the field for days on end. The atmospheres at the two colleges are very different, reflecting their respective services. Sandhurst is slightly more formal.

General Toyne Sewell thought the navy and air force were right to open ninety-nine per cent of jobs to women. The army, he added, could open a great deal more, although being an infantryman he drew the line at the infantry, because of physical difficulties. 'We have some extremely fit women officers here and we sent them with the men on the Brecon Beacons to see how they would perform. They kept up, but they said that they weren't able to do anything at all afterwards, whereas the men had a little reserve. That will always be a limiting factor on their employment.'

He had also considered the effect on morale of men being led by a woman if she died in battle. 'Seeing a woman's body or severed limbs lying around would have an appalling effect on the men she'd been leading and was close to.' For that reason, he thought using women bombers or fighter helicopter pilots was acceptable, because the impact of their deaths, often far away, was less direct. Unfortunately, there is no research on whether the death of a male or female leader is more devastating to troops, but it would be reasonable to assume that often it would depend on each individual and not necessarily on his or her sex.

Certainly, there was no more fuss about the American women sent back in bodybags from the Gulf than there was about the men. 'People have been terribly blinkered about this,' said the general. 'Women died in the Second World War. Nurses were shelled in hospitals in the First World War and women will probably die in the next war. It is just when they are directly leading men in the field that I think it may be much harder.' He had no reservations about a woman running a gun position, especially with increasing mechanisation, and thought tanks were a possible future option. 'People make too much of the toiletry business,' he said. 'If you're stuck in a tank for four days that's the last thing you're going to worry about. They manage in mixed crews on the space programme, so why not on the ground?' He also pointed out that an increasing number of officers coming to Sandhurst had lived in mixed colleges or houses at university and were unlikely to be petrified by the sight of a box of Tampax.

The younger boys straight from school still fear the unknown female and thus are more scathing about her, alleging all that women are taught at Sandhurst is flower arranging and typing. So it came as rather a shock in a recent rifle shooting competition that three out of the four teams in the final were female. The older generation heading towards retirement also has less confidence in the abilities of women – having worked in an all-male organisation for most of their lives, they have never really dealt with women as colleagues and equals.

But the general talked about the capabilities of women as though he had made an amazing new discovery. 'Spunky' is the masculine adjective he used. He found the women were much better motivated, since unlike the men – for whom Sandhurst was an acceptable tradition – they often had to get over a number of mental and domestic hurdles before arriving at the academy. 'They are more mature and more balanced in outlook than the men. The men here also have no conception of what a physical struggle it is for the girls sometimes. I was up watching an exercise in North Wales in foul weather, blustery and cold with heavy rain, and two companies of boys passed me with their chins down, griping. Then I found the girls sitting in a filthy wet wood, on tremendous form, and their leader gave the best set of orders I have heard anywhere.' On the other hand, he said, keen not to go over the top, there were some women on the present course 'who couldn't lead the way out of a paper bag'.

Leadership is a peculiar craft to teach. At Cranwell, the RAF officer trainees started by organising a team to build Lego towers and continued with imagined scenarios: 'You have two forty-foot lashings, one 200-foot lashing, a pine pole, a pulley and a spade. Your team's mission is to retrieve the crashed Land-Rover from the ditch and bring it back to base.' Each officer stood up in turn and lectured the class on her plan of action, giving the situation, the mission and the execution, in that order, and awarding each person a specific job. Then to check the men knew what they are doing, it was the 'pose, pause, pounce' technique – picking a surprise victim to answer each question. Next, the officer humiliated herself before the class, giving a self-analysis of where she might have gone wrong, or had not been clear enough, and then the class weighed in with more supposedly constructive criticism. After this was completed successfully in the classroom, the officers were allowed out in the field, armed with full-size pine poles and pulleys, to do the real thing.

The RAF provided a fascinating document for officer applicants, a sort of gung-ho guide to the services:

> The successful officer candidate is someone who: a) Gets *worthwhile results*, b) Even in the most *adverse circumstances*, c) In a way which *wins the loyalty and confidence* of his colleagues (be they subordinates, equals or superiors).

There was also a section on the implications of being an officer and the oath of allegiance. Each candidate would be asked difficult questions on what he or she thought about the use of armed force with the intention of taking life and national possession of nuclear weapons as a deterrent. That was followed by an eight-point list of qualities, beginning with an effective intelligence, an effective personality, strength of character, determination, confidence and assurance, good reaction to pressure, good group compatibility and planning, and physical and practical abilities. With physical abilities coming in eighth position, there is no question that women could fulfil these criteria as successfully as men. The women officers, at around fifteen per cent of the intake, have had a pass rate at Cranwell in the last few years of about three per cent less than the men. At the Royal Naval Academy at Dartmouth, the pass rate for both sexes during the first year of the integrated course was eighty-nine per cent; and at Sandhurst, the pass rate for women was ninety-two per cent, compared to the men's eighty-seven per cent.

A group of Sandhurst recruits only a few weeks into the course had hardly had time to show the expected qualities of character, determination and confidence which would result in a pass. They were out in the field on a map-reading exercise in Ashdown Forest – home of Pooh Corner. During the previous night's exercise, the confidence of a group of female officers had taken a knock. Three weeks into training, exhausted from sleepless nights in the field, they had got lost reading their map at night and their sad tones could be heard on the radio. The next day, however, they were up early again, with the boundless enthusiasm of unjaundiced recruits, carrying rifles and getting covered in mud, generally doing what soldiers do. For twenty-two- and twenty-three-year-olds, they were frighteningly articulate and utterly sure of the paths of their future careers: no prissy desk work for them. They were going into bomb disposal in the ordnance corps, air defence in the artillery and helicopter piloting in the Army Air Corps.

They were among the first to benefit from the disbandment of the WRAC, which until 1992 was a completely separate support corps with its own chain of command and promotion. Jobs had just opened up to them in the previously all-male ordnance, air and artillery corps. Instead of being a WRAC officer permanently employed with, say, a signals regiment, they would become fully part of that regiment, wear the same insignia and no longer be seen as slightly apart from the men. Before 1980, women officers were only temporarily attached to other corps, including the headquarters of combat regiments away from the front, mostly as assistant adjutants in administrative roles. Because the women would usually be attached to various different regiments during their careers, it was hard to have an impact, and they could only build up a professional repu-tation with the WRAC and not a particular regiment. 'You were the only girl in the mess and the centre of attention,' said Second Lieutenant Lisa Giles, a graduate trainee officer. 'That might be fun at first, but I've met people who say the work gets a lot less challenging and interesting later on.'

The isolation will continue at first for pioneering officers entering previously all-male corps, doing officers' jobs on the ground rather than the civilisation of headquarters. It would be surprising if they do not have to fight some initial resentment. The infantry and the armoured corps will still remain closed to women, except as assistant adjutants. Instead of being part of the WRAC, they will be sent there from the new Adjutant-General's Corps, which will include the former Pay Corps and the Military Police. The disbandment of the WRAC also means that enlisted women will be able to compete equally with men for jobs in a greater number of trades, instead of there being a certain number of posts, in some cases reserved for women only.

Officer Cadet Anjela Tilley was in the ranks of the Royal Signals for over five years before applying for her commission, so she was well versed in the art of being a woman in a man's world. (Recruits from the ranks, schools, or civilian work are officer cadets and those with university degrees are probationary Second Lieutenants.) 'When I first joined the Signals no one would talk to me. There were three of us and forty-five men, and it wasn't until I really got my hands dirty working on the vehicles and showed I could do it that they started to respect me. But as soon as I went for my commission, about seventy-five per cent of them stopped talking to me again.'

Integration in the Signals has in fact been one of the most successful so far of all the corps. Officer Cadet Tilley expected to join the ordnance corps when she graduated, although she was worried that her career might be affected later on because of restrictions on the front line. 'I can get fewer postings compared to the guys and I don't see any reason really, because what we do is defensive. I'm not going to be fighting.' Second Lieutenant Carole Rankin said she would be joining the Royal Artillery, but the regiment was only offering jobs for women up to the rank of major because of combat limitation. Another future artillery officer, Second Lieutenant Wendy Morton, was unworried by that. 'It's up to the first girls going through to prove we can do the job and once we've got our foot in the door ...'

The academy itself turned out to be a lot more civilised than the trainees expected. They were worried before arriving that they would be cleaning the toilets with their toothbrushes and blacking the skirting boards, but in fact there was nothing worse than boot polishing and regular kit inspections. Sandhurst is a state of mind, and you have to develop your own attitude towards it and work out how you view your life as an officer,' said Second Lieutenant Morton. A trained graphic designer, she was keeping a journal and taking photographs throughout the course. 'The whole system fascinates me, the idea that you spend hours getting your kit immaculate, and then an officer finds a tiny piece of fluff on your beret and you've got to spend half the night or early morning doing it all over again for another show parade. And there's the atmosphere. You're standing out there in line in the sun and you hear the boys clicking, doing drill, and the sound of a band playing at Old College.' Officer Cadet Tilley was amazed at how her priorities had changed in just three weeks. The trainees are gated for the first five weeks and deprivation is always conducive to indoctrination. 'We're supposed to stay in our corridor, but the other day they let us go into the back of the bar to buy a Coke. And we thought that was just fantastic. It's very odd.'

They see very little of the male officers except at meal times and they would prefer more contact. It would also be good for many of the men, particularly those from all-male boarding schools. Second Lieutenant Rankin said, 'They either treat you like a big sister and bring you all their problems, or patronise you like a little sister. They need to get used to integrating with women in a social situation, because at the moment some of them feel bad about having you as a friend.' Two female physical-training instructors who were also by now in on the conversation said that keeping the sexes separate for fitness should not change. The women's initial fitness when they arrived tended to be much worse than the men's and the lack of compulsory sport in schools nowadays had affected everyone. Out of a platoon of thirty, about four men would be really unfit, compared to around ten women. Besides, even the men could not run together as a group and had to be graded into different sections.

Most of the women at Sandhurst had gained previous experience through the Territorial Army, or had university or school scholarships from the army. Many had parents in the services and others had joined because of boyfriends in the Officers' Training Corps at university. When they left, they were expecting to become troop commanders, often in virtually all-male units. 'We will just have to pay a lot of attention to the male staff sergeant and learn all we can from him,' said Second Lieutenant Giles. Such policies sound fine in theory, but in practice it may be hard to persuade a forty-year-old sergeant to take seriously a twenty-two-year-old blonde. She is not unaware of that problem. 'Sometimes as girls we have an easier time too. You can get away with a lot, get round a fierce old sergeant-major in a way a man never could.'

Quite a few women officers make use of their femininity, flirting their way through. This is perhaps understandable – a company of men may respond much better to that than cold professionalism, but it creates expectations that those who follow will behave similarly. Many consider that while they are in the minority, they will use every weapon at their disposal to further their careers. But for female officers to demand equality while making good use of their attractions is unfair on men and on the women who will later hold that particular job.

With equality in mind, the officers-to-be had held a debate in Sandhurst on whether women should go into combat. Second Lieutenant Bobby Scott thought she could kill if necessary. 'It may not be the same sort of aggression that blokes have, but it's there when really needed.' Officer Cadet Susan Jamieson said that during the debate she had been asked by a man if she could shove a bayonet in someone's face. Reasonably, she answered that she would not know until she had to and neither would he. Those against women in combat tried to prove their point by ending the debate with a man lifting a fifty-five-pound artillery shell above his head and saying a woman could not do that. He was invited to select a woman from the audience to prove his point and picked a small, skinny girl – who happened to do a great deal of physical training and easily lifted the shell above her head. Even the place most people assume to be a last bastion of army tradition is being shaken.

Female trainees know that lifting the occasional shell to prove a point is not enough. They have inbuilt problems, which add to the barriers put up by the institutions around them. Second Lieutenant Scott had been thinking about taking an eight-year short-service commission, which would finish when she was thirty. That was partly to do with the fact that pregnant women had to leave. Now that they can stay in she may change her plans and take a sixteen-year regular commission. 'I think it's possible. My mum's a teacher and she was away a lot of the time and left us with a nanny. We all grew up to be very independent, and I've got a really good relationship with my mother, more like a friendship.'

Sandhurst's staff – often officers in their late twenties and early thirties – are presently facing major decisions about their lives and careers. Some see the pregnancy-rule change and the opening up of more varied jobs to women as encouraging. But others doubt the value of continuing the struggle. Captain Gemma Fesemeyer is one of those. Her short-service commission was coming to an end and she either had to commit herself to the army for another eight years or get a civilian job. Out in the mess tent in Ashdown Forest, over mugs of grey tea and mini-pizza, mixed veg and chips, she explained her frustration. She felt her full capabilities had not been used in a couple of previous postings and aged thirty she was no longer sure that the army could provide her with what she wanted. 'I am a little disillusioned, because although there are now more jobs open to us in the regiment, it's a man's world out there and it's never going to change. And British men will resist change more than most. If you accept that and are willing to work in that environment, that's fine, but I think it may be time to move on.'

At least future intakes of trainee officers at Sandhurst will be used to working in mixed groups from the start, in the classroom and out on exercises. Platoon commander Captain Fiona Grundy said, 'At the moment, the boys have the idea that they're first-class citizens and having girls there doing the job with them doing the job as well will give them another perspective. They're very chauvinist still and they don't like having to rely on a woman.'

That attitude is still preserved in aspic at high levels of large parts of the forces. Women were seen as useful up to a point, but when they go closer to power, job opportunities became scarce. Part of the problem was that the army gave young officers so much responsibility so early on, coupled with opportunities to travel. 'Then suddenly you get dumped in a grotty staff job at a desk and you have to wait about five years for command. I've been a captain so long

I've run out of captains' pay increments,' said Captain Grundy. Another irritation was the variation in the job of assistant adjutant. Depending on the commanding officer she was working for, the job could mean little more than keeping the regimental diary and photograph album, or it could be much more responsible. As Captain Fesemeyer pointed out, most people do not join the army to do a boring nine-to-five desk job and when she did one that consisted almost solely of answering the colonel's phone, she felt wasted as a university graduate.

Until the disbandment of the WRAC – the results of which have yet to be seen – army women lived in a sort of limbo, neither fully part of the regiments they were attached to, nor truly separate. Before 1990, when WRAC officers were at last allowed to be permanently employed with a regiment, their role was semi-civilian in many ways and often office-bound. The rules were only changed to allow them weapons training as late as 1984, yet at that time 221 women were working in the separately administered Ulster Defence Regiment in the nearest thing the British had to a war zone. It was only in 1987 that weapons training became an integral part of training for officers and enlisted women. That year four 'Greenfinches' – the nickname for women soldiers in the UDR – were murdered by the IRA. Although not allowed to carry guns, they were employed at road checkpoints to stop and search women.

In that year too, the first trickle of women officers into previously all male regiments began. The newspapers showed photographs of the first woman assistant adjutant in the Parachute Regiment, wearing the coveted red beret, and the first to join the Coldstream Guards out in Hong Kong. Another joined the Gurkhas and a fourth, the 3rd Battalion The Queen's Regiment, breaking a 400-year-old men-only tradition in the infantry.

It is a different women's army from the one that senior WRAC officers had joined in the sixties and seventies. Then, it was a corps of ladies who played netball in plimsolls, not women who played war in combat boots. One the former directors of the corps, Brigadier Shirley Nield, explained it like this: 'The majority of the army, both men and women, is not composed of essentially belligerent combat soldiers, but is engaged in ensuring that the First XV arrive on the field in the best condition to win the match. I suggest that placing a couple of women in the side on the field is not the best use of their talents.' Interestingly, some of the strongest opposition to increasing women's opportunities comes form former WRAC stalwarts, although the latest director, Brigadier Gael Ramsey was very forward-thinking.

When the highest-ranking woman at Sandhurst, Lieutenant-Colonel Jackie Smith, first joined up in 1973, she was only allowed to command platoons of women as a young officer. Ordering men around would have been unthinkable and probably impossible. Her next job was in divisional headquarters, away from her female contemporaries, working solely among men. 'I didn't go out in the field if the headquarters was deployed. Girls didn't go into the field, so I'd stay behind and catch up with the paperwork. If I was lucky, one of the officers' wives who was also at home alone would come and talk to me.'

Now she runs a huge department, responsible for the welfare and education of all Sandhurst's women officers, and has a staff flat in Old College, furnished by the college in traditional army style, with the usual, slightly uncomfortable armchairs covered in red or brown synthetic material, reminiscent of those on the sets of early sixties sitcoms. Over tea, Lieutenant-Colonel Smith discussed the changes. She already had seen three women opt for the artillery, in locating and air defence, but each had joined for a different reason. She thought one would aim for the traditional former-WRAC role and stick to the administrative side. 'Another has the potential to be a great technical officer, and the third one is one of the best leaders and officers to come out of here. If the gunners stifle her, it will be their loss.' She pointed out that although not the furthest forward regiments, the gunners were 'pretty warry people' and a female officer joining them would still be limited to defensive areas. 'Time will tell, when it comes to selection for higher promotion, whether experience in only one area of the artillery will be a handicap.'

Lieutenant-Colonel Smith thought the women were courageous to go in as pioneers, or even, perhaps, martyrs for those who would follow behind. On the other hand, the barrier-breaking challenge actually appealed to some of the officers and they got greater satisfaction proving themselves in adverse circumstances than a man could. 'The woman who comes here is already a pretty rare bird.

Her motivation is much greater than the average man's.' She also tends to have higher entrance grades at the Regular Commissions Board, although lack of candidates of both sexes, due partly to demographic changes, means Sandhurst is taking officers with the C, D and E grades it once turned away. It takes few women with E assessments, because there are enough available with higher qualifications for the few places, but for men, E is becoming increasingly common. This resulted in the setting up in the late seventies of Rowallen Company, a twelve-week army outward-bound-style course, which brings immature men up to standard.

Not that immaturity is lacking at Sandhurst itself. Lieutenant-Colonel Smith still finds men's attitudes towards women unbelievable. 'The boys are totally ignorant of what the girls can do. The levels of resistance and chauvinism are worse the younger they are.' For that reason, although the new course will be mixed, there will be separate male and female platoons of thirty students each. This is partly because of physical difference, but also because each woman has to play the role of commander and soldier to learn about leadership, and adding men to the cocktail of problems would be an unnecessary burden. As a minority of ten per cent, she thinks that women in mixed platoons will get out of doing some of the heavy work and the idea is that they should learn to do every job. The argument is sensible and the experience of West Point has shown how difficult integrated leadership training can be. Yet when women officers leave Sandhurst, they will be commanding mixed or all-male units. It might be good for them to get some practice.

For Lieutenant-Colonel Smith, who for eighteen years worked her way up the all-female WRAC chain of command, the future is suddenly wide open. She is going to join the new Adjutant-Generals' Corps: 'at my stage I can't change my spots'. She is about to attend the joint-service defence course, which broadens officers' awareness of the role of NATO and the Ministry of Defence. It is important to have that on her CV, because she did not attend Staff College, a course for fast-track officers usually in their early thirties, at the appropriate time. Once, it was largely for men.

She thinks Britain is little influenced by other NATO countries, particularly with regard to its policy on female employment. 'There is a lot of talk about compatibility and compatible kit, but let's just say we pay more than lip service to it.' Like many of those who have spent their lives within the WRAC, which exercised much time emphasising its soldiers' genteel qualities, Lieutenant-Colonel Smith hopes that expanding opportunities will not change the type of woman joining. The new redesigned uniform is less about white gloves and more about practicality, and features trousers as well as skirts. 'The emphasis in training has changed slightly, and some of the more ladylike aspects can't be stressed as much any more. There is no point in a woman trying to match a macho male, because that way we will only be considered a second-class man.' Besides, if Sandhurst's *raison d'être* is to create officers and gentlemen, presumably that applies to officers and ladies too, she reasons. 'When we have dinner night, the girls put flowers on the table and out there in the units, men will still expect them to do that, just as women will expect men not to turn up for dinner in jeans and a T-shirt.'

The old WRAC uniform, which died with the corps, was designed in 1949 by Sir Norman Hartnell and intended to look feminine. Indeed the final version was chosen by a committee of men, and what pleased their eyes all those years ago was short jackets buttoned tightly down the front with on-the-knee narrow skirts and cheeky caps. Apart from a rather hairy green jumper, its shape was sexy, and downright impractical for work outside an office, which the Queen, of all people, discovered on a visit to Sandhurst in 1986. As she inspected the troops on parade, she asked why the new women officers were herded off into a corner while their male colleagues marched proudly round the parade square. 'Ma'am, I'm afraid their skirts are too tight,' was the answer.

10

WHORE OR DYKE?

As an American soldier put it, 'Being a woman in the army is a Catch-44 situation – pay men the slightest bit of attention and you're a whore, ignore them at all and you're a dyke. So whaddya do?'

Treading the extremely narrow path laid out by men between the two sexual extremes is an extra drill fresh female recruits have to learn alongside the normal military ones. The tricky thing is that militarily correct behaviour for a woman will vary depending on her boss at the time and his (it is usually his) opinions on the subject. For men, too, attitudes to sexuality and sex are a good deal more complicated than they used to be. In the past if they wanted to be proper red-blooded soldiers, they went out and grabbed the nearest piece of skirt. Now, some of their colleagues *are* pieces of skirt – yet they must be responded to professionally. Ballsy behaviour, in the metaphorical and literal sense, is encouraged while at the same time female colleagues are something apart, not to be touched. The situation is muddling for men and more so for women. As years of military tradition are ripped from under them, it is not surprising that attitudes lag behind reality.

Militaries worldwide have rules against fraternisation. But what that means, precisely, varies. In America, it was originally brought in to prevent male officers having serious friendships with men in the lower ranks, since that was believed to create favouritism and adversely affect discipline. With the advent of women, that definition was expanded to include sexual relationships between men and women of the same rank in the same unit. The British have a simpler no-touching rule between the sexes, but again, crossing the officer-enlisted barrier is not encouraged. Whatever the rules, they are constantly broken and that creates a growing disciplinary problem in the military, as the percentage of women continues to grow. Such activity is, after all, far from abnormal among young people at their sexual peak forced into single living by the demands and changing locations of their jobs.

The average soldier just cannot get it right. While encouraged to be desperately heterosexual, destined to reproduce the splendid American, British or Canadian race, he or she is banned from completing that task on base, unless married. Then there is the opposing pull of bonding and friendship, the ties that make a platoon a platoon and not a disparate set of wage-slaves. Friendships between man and man, woman and woman, can easily grow into something more sexual, particularly when they are isolated by their jobs from meeting a wider range of people.

Worst of all, militaries everywhere are inclined to outrageous doublethink and prefer to pretend none of this goes on at all. When thirty-six women got pregnant on just one American ship during the Gulf War, the US Navy said no fraternisation whatsoever had occurred on board. As one commentator put it in the *Washington Post*, 'It was a statement so astoundingly preposterous that my faith in the stupidity of the military, shaken by the success of the Gulf War, was immediately revived.'

Of course, armies have their genuine whores and dykes, and not just the ones in male fantasies. Two women soldiers were alleged to have been sent home to Fort Bragg during the Gulf War for offering their services at $50 a shot in the sexually parched desert. When it comes to lesbians, it depends on who is asked. If the military reflects civilian society, then ten per cent is a possibility, although armies prefer to maintain that 'people with those sort of proclivities' do not join up. An American study, however, showed homosexual women were *more likely* than heterosexual women to have had military service.

Outsiders only see who is caught in the act, but 13,000 men and women have been discharged from the American military in the past ten years for being gay or lesbian. In the US Army, five per cent of total discharges were of enlisted gay men and seventeen per cent were of enlisted lesbians, yet women are only ten per cent of the total force. The dismissals were oddly disproportionate. Between 1987 and 1990 (the latest figure available) the British forces discharged 171 men and 126 women, and court-martialled thirty-nine men for committing homosexual acts. Women were twelve times more likely to be dismissed than men, but were never court-martialled, perhaps reflecting the fact that lesbianism has never been a crime in civilian society. The discharge figures reflect the extent of the obsession with women's sexuality and that massive investigations are often directed against a particular female barracks or unit which gains 'a reputation' in a way that a male unit does not.

So when the reaction of men to the relatively new concept of the female soldier goes wrong, there are two results: lesbians are hunted down and discharged, heterosexuals sexually harassed. Discharging people for their homosexuality is of course written into the military rules of countries like Britain and America, although this should not necessarily entail full-scale witchhunts which put dozens of women at a time under suspicion. Sexual harassment, which can mean anything from suggestive words to physical assault, although in no way condoned, is not quite discouraged enough in the tone set by military leadership. The relationship between men and women in the military is a love-hate relationship – harassment being the extreme of love and lesbian discharges the extreme of hate.

The whore-or-dyke stereotyping is in fact not a problem for women at all. It is a problem for men; and men who have learned from their fathers and grandfathers that returning home to the love and services of a good woman is their reward for war cannot cope with a good woman next to them in drill formation. Here are the words of James Salter, a 1945 graduate of the West Point Military Academy, on the subject of integration.

> There were women in the barracks. There were cadets with beautiful, boyish hair, like that of a shipmate on a cruise. It was an appeal that touched fantasies – on a clear autumn morning or in the winter dusk, the image of a tender cheek beneath a military cap, the trace of a smile, the womanly figure in rough clothes ...

Although his harassment is fortunately restricted to a literary sort, Salter can hardly contain his excitement. Neither can most of the American military, if the figures are to be believed. (There are no British military statistics on sexual harassment.) A Pentagon survey published in 1990 found that about two-thirds of women claimed they had been sexually harassed, either directly or in more subtle ways such as by catcalls, dirty looks or teasing. Compare this to surveys of civilians, which show on average thirty to forty per cent experience harassment. The Pentagon questioned over 20,000 men and women on active service for the survey, which also showed that seventeen per cent of men were sexually harassed, although it did not say by which sex. A third of women were physically harassed in some way; fifteen per cent had been pressurised for sexual favours and five per cent said they had experienced actual or attempted rape, or sexual assault. Over three-quarters of women said they were harassed by one man acting alone.

The survey – the biggest so far of its kind in either civilian or military life – showed how persuasive and subtle the denigration of women can be. Nearly half of women said they did not believe or know whether their senior leaders or immediate supervisors made an honest and reasonable effort to stop the harassment, despite regulations. Few thought it was worth the trouble reporting incidents, since often they were one-to-one, without witnesses, and committed by a male superior whose opinion could affect their promotion chances.

The fact that there are no British statistics on harassment perhaps means it is not considered a problem by the leadership. That may be the case, but it certainly exists, as a day spent talking to women at any military base or ship would prove. It may also be a growing problem, since until 1992, women in the army were largely dealt with within a separate administration and now they will be more integrated. The early stages of integration of women into previously masculine jobs in the air force showed that. One woman aircraft mechanic working in a hot hangar, who was wearing, as the men did, only overalls over her underwear, was grabbed by the men in her unit and her overalls were riveted to a ladder. They kept her hanging there for half an hour and suggested she left the overalls riveted where they were, and climb out in only her bra and pants. She refused and when the men knew a superior was about to arrive, they cut her down.

There may be hundreds of incidents of physical harassment, but they only become public if considered serious enough to merit a prosecution. In August 1988 RAF Warrant Officer Peter Parkes was severely reprimanded, and said he would retire after a court martial heard he had used his swagger stick to lift the skirts of airwomen on parade and made comments like 'Look – you've got no knickers on!' The fifty-six-year-old officer, who was supposedly in charge of disciplinary matters at RAF Newton, also asked enlisted women if they 'fancied a quick one' and made comments about their under-wear.

It is strange to find professional adults behaving like this and there must be something about the enclosed atmosphere of the military which encourages it. The treatment of women at West Point was catalogued in the chapter on officers, but such activities are not confined to the US Army. In autumn 1990 at the US Air Force Academy, it was discovered that several male cadets hid in a cupboard to watch one of their friends having sex with a female cadet without her knowledge of their presence. The practice was nicknamed 'rodeo', based on the object of the game, which was to remain 'mounted' for as long as possible after the voyeurs had leapt from concealment. In this particular case, the men remained hidden throughout and the woman did not discover what had happened until her classmates joked about it the next day.

Cynthia Wright, an officer in the air force, wrote in the political journal the *New Republic*: 'Another prank of the military leaders of tomorrow is the practice of referring to female midshipmen as WUBAs – an acronym supposedly derived from "Working Uniform, Blue Alpha", but now commonly, if clandestinely, recognised to stand for "Woman Used By All". This sort of low-level harassment is so frequent that it's considered normal and isn't even reported in most instances.'

Institutional policies towards women do little to encourage respect and equal treatment. At the Air Force Academy, women are still taught make-up application, the importance of not swearing or crying in public, and 'the necessity of periodic eyebrow waxing'. The women are warned not to spoil their reputations by sleeping around, while in the same breath they are told not to expect the same standards from their male classmates. The *New Republic* article also claimed a particular class was given diet tips to maintain 'all those curves they [the male cadets] like'. Worst of all, that briefing was given by senior women in positions of command, who considered it necessary to adapt to men's expectations in order to survive.

Still, the first step to change is realising exactly what is going on and the US Navy has begun to do that. In 1990, appalled by a fifty-five per cent increase in reported rapes and sexual assaults over three years to 240 cases per year, it commissioned an investigation. At its main training centre in Orlando, Florida, the navy's inspector-general said that over eighteen months there had been six confirmed rapes of recruits or female students by other members of the navy. But no prosecutions were carried out. During the same period, women recruits themselves reported twenty-four rapes or incidents of sexual assault. The *Washington Post* said only one out of thirteen cases, a sexual assault, went to court martial. The rest were 'unsubstantiated or resolved'. Investigators said two of the women raped had made false statements. The administration's failure to punish offenders in numerous sex-related cases had, said the inspector, contributed to an atmosphere that made women 'feel like they were second-class members of the navy.'

Three of the sexual assaults were committed by supervisors or instructors of the women who claimed they had been attacked. There was also a great deal of fraternisation between the new female recruits and the non-commissioned officers who were their instructors. Some of the alleged attackers were returned to their jobs after investigation, working in close proximity with their victims. Others were discharged from the navy, thus avoiding prosecution. The inspector also assumed that some women were so intimidated by their instructors that they did not risk pressing charges, so the figures may well have been higher. Subsequently, retraining was recommended for the male and female members of the Navy Investigative Service, particularly in the area of sexual assault. 'They are perceived as insensitive towards victims, frequently assuming at the outset that the victim is either lying or "asked for it" and as disinclined to pursue a charge if it involved "date or acquaintance" rape.'

The situation was little better for officers in the navy. In 1990, a second-year trainee midshipman Gwen Dreyer at the US Naval Academy in Annapolis resigned over the failure to investigate her complaint of harassment and to punish properly the men involved. She was dragged by male midshipmen to a urinal and handcuffed to it as other men stood around her, jeered and took photographs. Six of the men received letters of caution, and the two handcuffers lost good behaviour marks for one term and were restricted to campus for a month. Their victim felt forced to leave the academy. Dreyer said the attack was a culmination of many incidents of harassment and discrimination by other students. She told the *Washington Post*, 'I still believe in the academy, but it needs to be changed.' She had hoped to follow the paths of her father and grandfather, both academy graduates. 'I felt like I'd given enough to the academy and the academy didn't give enough back to me,' said Dreyer, who has now gone to take a non-military engineering degree. 'I never pictured myself anywhere else than in the navy. All my dreams were taken away from me and now I have to rebuild them.'

Cases are being taken increasingly seriously. In late 1991, an American admiral lost his command after failing to take seriously a complaint by an aide that she was sexually harassed during a convention of navy pilots in Las Vegas. The aide told Rear-Admiral John Snyder that she had to run a gauntlet of pilots who called out jibes, and tried to rip off her clothing and grab her crotch, but all he said was: 'Boys will be boys.' A spokesman said the admiral's lack of timely action to investigate the allegations caused the chief of naval operations to question his judgement in command.

Another report, running to 500 pages on the position of women in the navy, came out of the sexual assault and rape investigations. It said sexual harassment was a pervasive problem throughout the service, and particularly affected blacks and enlisted women. 'Inconsistent and ambiguous' job-assignment policies were limiting women's careers, and policies intended to curb discrimination were haphazardly applied and misunderstood by commanders and service personnel. 'Both law and policy still restrict the assignment of women, reinforcing the perception that women are not equal contributors and impacting women's career horizons negatively.'

Despite the jargon of good intentions, at about the same time as the report was finally produced, the US military had rented the Cunard liner *Princess* for the rest and recreation of its troops in the Gulf War. The soldiers, sailors, and airmen and women were in need of a place to drink and dance after the restrictions of Saudi Arabia. Indeed the ship was nicknamed 'The Love Boat', since the drinking and dancing had the expected results. But the US military made one mistake. It tried to hire three female strippers, just as it used to in

Vietnam, to entertain the troops. The American women soldiers were livid and, following complaints, the show was cancelled.

The Pentagon probably has the largest 'pending' tray in the world, where surveys such as the last two are stored, awaiting action, some time. But taking action on something as amorphous as personal opinion by soldiers who are attracted to the military precisely because of its ancient, largely manly, traditions is a near impossible task. Directly addressing the problem often creates more hostility towards the perceived creators of it – women. Consciousness raising often results in the raising of tempers.

The sensitivity of sexuality in the forces sometimes means reports never even make it to the 'pending' tray at all. The work is done, yet never published. A good example of this is the document PERS-TR-89-002, an unprepossessing name which belies rather interesting contents. It was a survey commissioned by the Pentagon in 1989 on homosexuality in the American military and never officially released. That is possibly because it came to an unacceptable conclusion – that homosexuals and lesbians *are* suitable for military service and it recommended the Defense Department should change its policy of dismissing all those discovered to be gay.

This must have come as a shock, since military law stated a number of reasons why gay men and lesbians should be banned: special investigations units had spent years, and a great deal of the defence budget, rooting out such people and bringing them to court martial. Allowing 'contamination' by homosexuals was deeply feared because of the adverse effect it might have on the image of true manliness – and womanliness – promoted by the clean-living forces.

The British ban was also questioned more recently, in 1991, when a House of Commons defence select committee, after long hearings, recommended that since homosexual activity was no longer an offence under civilian law, it should not be one under services law. The ban, said the committee, 'causes very real distress and the loss to the services of some men and women of undoubted competence and good character'. The Ministry of Defence said the ban was necessary for morale and discipline, but it would consider the committee's suggestions and report back in summer 1992.

The Americans allowed people of lesbian or homosexual *orientation* to join the forces up until 1982 and only barred the committing of homosexual acts. But following the moral backlash in civilian life during the Reagan era, the Department of Defense declared that any homosexuality was incompatible with military service, citing the following reasons:

> The presence of such members adversely affects the ability of the Armed Forces to maintain discipline, good order and morale; to foster mutual trust and confidence among the members; to ensure the integrity of the system of rank and command; to facilitate assignment and world-wide deployment of members who frequently must live and work under close conditions affording minimal privacy; to recruit and retain members of the military services; to maintain public acceptability of military services; and, in certain circumstances, to prevent breaches of security.

The PERS-TR-89-002 report disputes these points, pointing out that since only a minuscule number – less than one per cent of personnel – are ever caught, there must be large numbers of homosexuals serving undetected. Examining the service records of veterans who have subsequently come out shows that job performance of homosexuals in the military is as good as, if not above, average. As for privacy, homosexuals, like heterosexuals, prefer to conduct their relationships outside the public arena, so there is no reflection on their professionalism at work. In terms of public acceptability, the report says that a public admission of homosexuality or lesbianism carries much less stigma than it did previously in civilian life.

On security, a Pentagon report published in 1991 largely dismissed fears that homosexuals were vulnerable to blackmail and could not be trusted with military secrets. 'Sexual orientation is unrelated to moral character' or patriotism, it said. The Pentagon examined espionage cases from 1945 and out of 117 Americans who had tried to spy for foreign countries, only seven were identified as homosexual. Their motives were the same as heterosexuals – 'primarily money, secondarily resentment'. Even Defense Secretary Dick Cheney has dismissed the security argument as 'a bit of an old chestnut', but he said the policy would stay for the foreseeable future, for reasons of morale and discipline.

There have been several attempts to challenge the military's policy on gay men and lesbians in the civilian courts. The most recent ones included that of Army Sergeant Perry Watkins, who was prevented from re-enlisting on grounds of his sexuality, although he had disclosed it by ticking the appropriate box on his draft papers during the Vietnam War. In time of need, the military was willing to turn a blind eye. In 1990 the US Supreme Court refused to hear his case, saying it was not within its remit to examine the constitutionality of Pentagon policy. The court also refused to hear the appeal of Army Sergeant Miriam Ben-Shalom in the same year. She argued that banning her from re-enlisting after she declared she was a lesbian violated her rights to equal protection and free speech. Pentagon officials expected that the Supreme Court might take on the cases, and an internal memorandum from the Headquarters Office of the Department of the Army was prepared proposing homosexuals should be allowed to join and remain in the military so long as they exercised 'restraint, and discretion'. But there was no challenge and the memo was consigned to the 'pending' tray.

Those who continue to be dismissed are often a loss to the military. In late 1991, Army National Guard Colonel Margarethe Cammermeyer was discharged for being a lesbian, although the four army colonels at her dismissal hearing praised her 'superb leadership' and said she had been 'a great asset' to the military. She had been in the army for thirty years, won a Bronze Star in Vietnam, gained a doctoral degree in nursing, a Meritorious Service Medal and an entry in *Who's Who of American Women*.

Colonel Cammermeyer had acknowledged her sexuality in an interview required of officers seeking top-level security clearance. By her own account, when she enlisted at nineteen she had no idea she was gay. She married, had four sons and got divorced, before realising in the 1980s that she was only sexually attracted to women and considered it a 'very private, very personal' matter, which 'had no bearing on my work'. A *Washington Post* report said when she confessed to the investigator, she had not considered her case a cause. She said she was hoping now that she, as a senior military person, had come out, people would see that 'we are not out of the ordinary, that homosexuality is a part of life, and is part of our society'.

A book published in 1990, *My Country, My Right to Serve*, by Mary Ann Humphrey, chronicles dozens of lives of homosexuals and lesbians in the US military, from the Second World War to Vietnam and the present day. One woman, Sergeant Johnnie Phelps, worked as an assistant during the war to General Eisenhower. The general had been sent a report that there were lesbians in the Women's Army Corps battalion, and ordered Sergeant Phelps to take action. 'I want you to find them and give me a list. We've got to get rid of them.' She looked at him and said, 'Sir, if the general pleases, I'll be happy to check into this and make you a list. But you've got to know, when you get the list back, my name's going to be first.' His secretary, also a WAC member added, 'Sir, if the general pleases, Sergeant Phelps will have to be second on the list, because mine will be first ... I'm going to type it.' The general told them to drop it.

Again in time of war, attitudes were much more lax than in peacetime. During Vietnam, self-declared homosexuals were accepted, because it was assumed they were faking in order to dodge the draft. Often they stayed on afterwards, being more or less open about their sexuality, but keeping the specific details of various relationships quiet. Occasionally one would slip up and the investigation service would come down hard to make an example of him. Both men and women have been imprisoned for six months to a year. During the clamp-down in the eighties and nineties, homosexuals had to lead even more of a double life, talking in near-code on the telephone, and destroying letters and evidence of any relationships. They found the constant self-vigilance stressful. Sometimes lesbians and gay men who were friends would enter into sham marriages as a cover. For mess dinners and special events, it was embarrassing to be constantly noted as partnerless.

Many of the lesbians and gay men dismissed had exemplary service records, a fact also well known to the military. An extraordinary document was leaked from the commander of the US Navy's surface

Atlantic fleet which said lesbians who had been discovered were found to be 'hard-working, career-oriented and among the command's top performers', but they still must be vigorously rooted out. Women were eight times more likely to be dismissed than men, despite the fact that lesbians tended to give longer service, created no problems with time off for maternity and, lacking a family, showed greater dedication to the service.

The facts say one thing, the regulations another. There was a time when facts and regulations coincided. In classical Greece, homosexuality between soldiers was seen to be a useful bond, an asset to the performance of fighting men, increasing patriotism and courage. Cultures change and now the modern Greek forces, along with America, Britain, Italy and Turkey's, decry homosexuality. On the other hand, Canada, Israel, the Netherlands, Spain and Sweden have changed their policies to permit gay soldiers, without any obvious affect on military competence.

Gay men and women are as patriotic as any other soldiers. A number served in the Gulf War, for both Britain and America. Some went undercover, but at least two lesbians admitted their sexuality and were sent all the same. In America, Specialist Donna Jackson declared in January 1991 that she was volunteering to 'kick ass' in the Middle East and at the same time she faxed a declaration of her homosexuality to the commander at her base, Fort Ord, in California. 'I want to serve my country and go to war,' she told the *Washington Post*, 'but I also want them to know who I am and I want to be honest about it.' Her commander at the Reserves' 129th Evacuation Hospital thought Specialist Jackson should be allowed to go to the Middle East, although a military attorney said she would be likely to be discharged on her return.

A British nursing officer, who had just left the Queen Alexandra's Royal Army Nursing Corps (QARANC), was put in a similar position before her deployment to the Gulf. When she went to volunteer as a reserve, the colonel interviewing her said she knew of her lesbianism and was worried about sending her out to the desert among young girls. The nursing officer was extremely angry, saying her sexuality, whatever that might be, had nothing whatsoever to do with her professional life and walked off. Later than day, she returned to the office to sort the matter out, and said, 'I've never done anything unprofessional, or anything that I'm ashamed of.' She was signed up for war duty and served in Saudi Arabia.

In that case, necessity outweighed prejudice. In others, prejudice is taken to extraordinary lengths. Interviews with serving soldiers have to remain anonymous – going on the record would mean instant dismissal. But talking to a number of nurses in the British QARANC and soldiers in the former WRAC, it is clear that there is a network of gay women in the forces. It is a network which is quietly tolerated, so long as it does not interfere with working life. Every so often, the Special Investigations Branch gets wind of an 'outbreak' of lesbianism at a certain base and rolls in, supposedly to clear it up. But as one WRAC sergeant explained, referring to a mid-eighties' investigation of Woolwich Barracks, 'we told the investigators that they had better start with one of our senior officers and that shut them up'.

In 1991, an investigation began into HMS *Dryad* near Portsmouth, after Wren rating Sharon Pickering was discovered to have had an affair with a female officer. That sparked all sorts of allegations in the tabloids about a 'lesbian sex ring' and it was claimed that some younger women had been 'bullied' into bed. Rating Pickering was given an administrative discharge. The isolation of the base, away from pubs and cinemas, was partly blamed by a Ministry of Defence spokesman for the increase in lesbianism. It was a fairly closed community and the women lacked contact with men.

A senior nurse, who was present during a 1986 investigation at the Queen Elizabeth Military Hospital in London, said lesbians generally kept quiet about what went on and it was experimentation among heterosexual women which had aroused the SIB's suspicions. She said the main reason that lesbians were turned in by their colleagues was not disgust at their behaviour, but often professional jealousy, or the desire to remove an obstacle between themselves and promotion. In general, men were much more horrified by lesbianism than women, couching their fear in language like 'mutants' and 'diesel dykes', and complaining – erroneously – that a blind eye was turned to women, but not to homosexual men. Most heterosexual women interviewed elsewhere in this book said they did not mind lesbians, so long as they had relationships in privacy and not in the barracks.

The WRAC used to have quite a reputation for lesbianism, probably due to exaggerated tabloid newspaper reports. Typical of the sensational tone was a story in the *Sunday People* on 21 September 1986, which began: 'Butch Army girls are at the centre of a massive vice probe at a barracks where lesbianism is said to have been "rife for years".' It included the usual interviews with 'a squaddie' at London's Woolwich Barracks, who said things like 'There are 28 women drivers in the motor pool and at least 20 are gay ... It's disgraceful because most of the girls are away from home and easy prey.' The so-called interviewee did not say how he knew precisely the sexual preferences of the twenty women. Investigations like that one do spark off tremendous adverse publicity and the desire to show that something is being done often has a negative effect.

Lieutenant-Colonel Jackie Smith, in charge of women at Sandhurst, said: 'I don't know why we have this image. There was an advertising survey in the eighties which showed a lot of the public had this idea that we were butch or lesbians. Yet all the time, we were trying to emphasise the feminine aspect.' Sandhurst has had its share of dismissals for lesbianism, although they could not be described as an epidemic. In 1989, one student at the college, Second Lieutenant Hilary McCauly, was questioned about her sexuality and eventually resigned her commission to avoid further investigation. Afterwards, she told the *Guardian* her resignation was not due to peer pressure. 'My colleagues were very supportive; all the WRAC women on my course said they didn't give a damn about the allegations. When I apologised to a staff sergeant about all the trouble I was causing, she interrupted me to say, "It's only you that's getting hurt. I wish you the best of luck."'

On average, about forty women a year are dismissed or resign from the British military following accusations of lesbianism. Why are they hounded out? Brigadier Gael Ramsey says homosexuality undermines confidence in the military as a whole and she is worried that older women 'lead astray the very young'. She considers an important part of her job is to protect the eighteen- and nineteen-year-olds, and is concerned that more senior soldiers might use their positions to bully younger girls into lesbianism. 'We do have a few problems,' she says. 'Every nation does.' She realises the military is going to have to address the matter soon, particularly following the defence select committee report. There is obviously a political input coming from the top: in 1991 Prime Minister John Major had a meeting in Downing Street with actor Sir Ian McKellen, of the gay lobby group Stonewall, and the situation in the forces was discussed.

Brigadier Ramsey, however, thinks the regulations should remain. Her main worry is about barrack blocks, where enlisted women live in close proximity. 'It is an invasion of people's privacy. We live such an open public life in the forces, the time when we have a private life should be protected. No one is dictating what these people do outside barracks. The only dictum comes within barracks. But in a sense an officer or a soldier is never off duty. The reputation of the army is in the hands of its individual members in all they do.'

Once investigations start, however, they often go beyond barracks and two soldiers or nurses renting a private flat off base can easily come under scrutiny. Decisions about these matters are arbitrary. If someone senior on a base is obsessed with homosexuality, or homophobic, investigations and dismissals often occur. Otherwise, life goes on as normal. The extent of homosexuality within the forces is in no way reflected in the dismissal figures.

People throw figures in the air, saying 'nearly all' their platoon is gay, or calling the QARANC the 'Queer Angels'. It is certainly easier to meet lesbians in the forces than in civilian life, but the percentage is probably only a little higher. It seems obvious that the masculinity and physicality of the army will attract a certain type of woman, but her sexuality need not always follow that. The average army woman is heterosexual and this can easily be measured by the numbers who left before the lifting of the pregnancy ban in 1990 to have children, or who married fellow soldiers. Occasionally, though, she will have experimented with an all-female relationship in the forces and then sometimes decided it is not for her.

The former pregnancy rules are worth looking at, because obviously only those who were willing to forgo children for a military career would stay on into their late thirties and forties. It would be reasonable to assume a slightly higher percentage of women who stayed on were lesbians. As one thirty-one-year-old midwife who had recently joined the military said, 'I felt strange at home. All my friends were getting married and setting up house. But when I joined up, I felt comfortable about being single. No one considered it was weird, me not being married at my age.'

The public image of the forces is the great worry cited by many if the ban on homosexuality were lifted. But in countries like Canada, where that has already happened, there has been no directly related fall-off in recruits and no great public outcry. In some ways, if the women's services are presently perceived as harbouring lesbians, would not lifting the ban end the prurient interest and bad publicity gained by dismissals and investigations? Would the *Sun* and the *People* not be silenced? Would decriminalising lesbians not also lessen an expensive and time-wasting burden for the military? Would bullying, such as it is, not be brought out into the open if women could complain without fear of being accused of the military crime of lesbianism themselves? After all, changing the rules would not be a licence for sex in barracks – that is a disciplinary offence for heterosexuals too.

The military lost 126 qualified women because of this rule over three years. These women were all treated like criminals, for an offence that does not exist in civilian life (largely because Queen Victoria refused to believe such an act was possible). The story of the investigation, interrogation and dismissal of one QARANC nurse, Elaine Chambers, shows how disturbing and painful being branded a lesbian in the forces can be.

Now in her rented flat in Beckenham, Kent, and working in a nursing home next door, Chambers is much worse off financially than she was in the military. Emotionally, she is just beginning to feel she is better off, as she has now come 'out' and as she no longer needs to lead a double life, or be anything other than honest about her relationships with other women. On the walls she can display a vast selection of posters of the Eurythmics' Annie Lennox, without being seen to be at all suspicious, and she can write what she likes in her diary without fear of discovery. Now thirty-one, she is slim and good looking, with short hair and nothing like the army stereotype imagined by many detractors.

The then Lieutenant Chambers had been an army nurse for five years and was serving in a military hospital in Hanover when she was suddenly called to the matron's office, 'The date was Friday 21 August 1987. It's imprinted on my mind. Matron said: "I've got a very serious matter to deal with here. Allegations have been made that you indecently assaulted two of your fellow officers."' She was astounded. The charge was a serious one, far worse than one of just being a lesbian, and she feared it might result in court martial.

Although she had never assaulted anyone, Lieutenant Chambers' first thought was to protect herself and friends from further discovery. She went to her room and put her letters, diaries and photographs into two plastic bags, thinking she would give them to a friend for safekeeping, and left them on the bed while she finished her shift, not expecting the investigation to begin immediately. But a few hours later, a male regimental sergeant-major and a female lance corporal from the Special Investigations Branch of the Military Police appeared and took her to her room which they proceeded to search, inch by inch, wearing latex gloves, while all the evidence they might have considered incriminating sat in bags on the bed.

The search took almost three hours. They went through every pocket, leafed through every book, pulled out every record, opened a huge tin of years of photographs, packet by packet. 'They pointed to different women and asked who they were, and they were nearly all heterosexual friends.' Then the investigators went off for the weekend with their bags of evidence and she was left alone in her room. She felt ravaged. 'I just burst into tears. For two days I was left, without anyone to talk to, not knowing what was going to happen or exactly what I'd been accused of. I went between crying, and anger and fear. I kept trying to write down everything I could remember and wondered why girls I had thought were friends had done this to me.' On Monday, she was interrogated by the SIB for fifteen hours.

It took a while for Lieutenant Chambers to work out the mess which had resulted in the charges, which were later completely dropped. A few months before the investigators arrived, she had been having a night out with a group of friends, and after a regimental function they went to a nightclub in town and had some drinks. On their return, one of her friends, a heterosexual officer, who had evidently heard rumours about Lieutenant Chambers, asked to spend the night with her. They slept together. 'The next morning she got up and said something like, "Thanks, that was lovely, but I don't think it's for me."' She left the other officer's room. They continued to see one another socially in the same group. The second incident was also with a straight officer. They went to the bar and afterwards had 'what I can only describe as a necking session', and then went to bed in their separate rooms. Again, the woman remained in the same group of friends.

Lieutenant Chambers thought it unlikely that either of her friends would have turned her in. They had not. Another lesbian, who was a senior officer in the hospital, ambitious and keen to cover up her own activities, had informed the matron about the events, following a chance casual remark made by one of the heterosexual women who had been intimate with Lieutenant Chambers. To cover themselves, knowing lesbianism was a sackable offence, they had said they had been egged on and had not wanted to get involved. The officer whom she had slept with lied to the investigators, saying Lieutenant Chambers had been upset about something, and she had put her arm round her on the bed to comfort her and this had started the supposed indecent assault, after which she pretended she had returned to her own room.

The women's conflicting statements were what saved her, as did evidence from other officers that Lieutenant Chambers had clearly been invited to stay in the so-called victim's room all night.

The whole investigation became rather ludicrous and bureaucratic, but the most upsetting aspect was still to come. Lieutenant Chambers' legal counsel had told her the confiscated diaries proved she was a lesbian, so she might as well come clean and get out with as much dignity as possible. 'But the investigators wanted to know all the details of the sexual side. They pushed and pushed for more information. They asked me about distinguishing features on my friend's body – as though you notice those things in the height of passion – but they wanted me to prove my version was true.' She did and the assault charges fell. 'You could see the SIB man thinking, "Ooh, the numbers of women I can arrest are going up".'

Because Lieutenant Chambers' story was found to be true, the women who had tried to cover themselves by pretending they were sexually assaulted were now themselves accused of being gay. One had a breakdown and got a medical discharge, and the other got married to prove she was heterosexual and left. There was a second interrogation with Lieutenant Chambers, lasting nine hours, when the SIB tried to get other names. The interrogator held up letters in individually numbered plastic bags, which he referred to as 'exhibits'. Three other women were discovered through the 'exhibits' and they subsequently lost their jobs. One was her first lover, who had since got married. Another was a sergeant, with fifteen years of exemplary service, based in Hong Kong, and the third was the sergeant's friend. The investigators wanted even more names, but Lieutenant Chambers refused to discuss it. 'I told them not to drag me into some kind of witchhunt. Just because my career was over didn't mean I would give away everyone else. I was not going to lower myself to that level.'

What kept her going was reminding herself first that she had done nothing wrong under civilian law and second that she was the only one telling the truth. In the meantime – the inquiry dragged out for five months – she continued working, and was often made duty officer and occasionally night superintendent, in charge of the whole hospital. This was in stark contrast to the fact that she was about to be thrown out of the military for a breach of discipline. She worked hard, and continued to be sports officer and run charity fund-raising events. 'I did these things out of principle. I wanted them to know they were losing someone good.' She was protected somewhat by being an officer. One enlisted woman who was caught up in the tentacles of the investigation found her case took far longer to process and was treated much less politely by the investigators.

Sometimes, Lieutenant Chambers felt close to suicide and in the first week or two of the investigation she drank a lot. She felt almost physically invaded by the idea of strangers going through her private love letters and diaries, and pointlessly guilty about the others who were incriminated by the written evidence. There were sinister shades of McCarthyism; she felt she had no rights as the investigation penetrated every area of her life. Many of her heterosexual friends came under suspicion for the mere fact they were in photographs with her. But it was those who had made the military their life whom she was most upset about. 'The irony of it was they were the very people who were not going to get pregnant and waste their training, and they were quite likely to find a stable partner within the forces who would understand the complexities of service life. Getting rid of someone after fifteen years' service because they're gay is like throwing someone out because you suddenly discover they've been wearing blue contact lenses. It affects nobody and does no harm to their work.'

Obviously, lesbianism can go unnoticed for years without any noticeable effect on a woman's professional life, so it seems strange that the military displays such a high level of paranoia about it. Chambers thinks the laws have been there so long that there has been an inbreeding of fear, fuelled by secrecy and scandal. She claims there is massive hypocrisy. 'If you got rid of all the women who have had, at some time, a lesbian experience, the army would be decimated overnight. It could not function.' She has now helped to set up Rank Outsiders, an organisation for gay man and lesbians still in, or discharged by, the military, or those who have left of their own accord. Calls and letters to the organisation have shown that lesbians 'definitely make up more than ten per cent of the forces'. Chambers believes that, especially in the WRAC, women posted to an isolated place with hundreds of men have it very tough. 'It is not surprising that they have closer friendships with women, when in the eyes of men they are either lesbians, or what the squaddies call "the unit groundsheet".'

Just before Lieutenant Chambers was finally discharged in January, she was sent to see the then head of the QARANC, Brigadier Rita Hennessy, who told her she was a disgrace and had let down the corps. Lieutenant Chambers answered, 'I think the corps has let me down, Ma'am.' She was thinking that if she had committed the same act with a man, she would just have been fined, or given a ticking off.

Through the endless interviews, interrogations and lectures, Lieutenant Chambers felt she was up against a wall of pure loathing. 'The one time anyone high up ever showed me any feeling or kindness was the only time I nearly cried in front of someone official. I went to sign the last discharge papers at the training centre in Aldershot and I saw the commandant there. She said, 'I don't know a lot about your case and I'm not going to enquire, but I know a bit about what happened to you and I want to say how sorry I am to lose someone like you. I want to thank you for the time you've given to the corps."' Lieutenant Chambers, with a lump in her throat, left to walk down the long drive to the gates. 'It's where you've marched twice in your passing-out parades. You're so chuffed then with everybody seeing you in uniform and marching with the band. Walking back down that drive and thinking, "This is the last time", that was the only moment when I was genuinely sorry to be leaving the corps. I knew then what I'd lost.'

The military is losing people with exemplary work records like Lieutenant Chambers and the American Colonel Margarethe Cammermeyer far too often. Obviously, in Chambers' case, it was irresponsible to spend the night with someone in the barracks, but had that been a man, the consequences would probably have been a short lecture on behaviour at most. If such investigations have to take place under the present rules, why are they designed to drag on and on? Lieutenant Chambers – despite the fact she was seen as a moral danger to others – worked for four months while awaiting her discharge. The Special Investigations Branch also seems to treat homosexuality as an appalling crime, with its all-day interrogations, and reading of personal letters and diaries, when its time and money could be better spent elsewhere. If the army tightened up the application of its rules on sex in barracks – whether homosexual or heterosexual – all this would be unnecessary and soldiers could do what they liked off base. To civilians, the whole situation seems old-fashioned and the military are perhaps stuck in another era on the subject. Many senior officers privately admit that that is the case and that if politicians make another assault on the homosexuality ban, it is likely to succeed.

11

ICONS IN UNIFORM

What is it about women in uniform? What is it that men, women photographers, pornographers and readers of the *Daily Telegraph* find so fascinating? It is not, surely, their continuing advancement into military jobs traditionally held by men, or their splendid service records. The obsession with women in uniform goes much deeper: soldier girls are sexual icons.

The sight of a woman trimmed neatly into a tight skirt and a brass-buttoned jacket arouses all sorts of textbook passions. Attraction; a desire to be dominated by a woman so obviously wearing a badge of power; and the desire to peel away the anonymity of the uniform to reveal the (hoped-for) softness beneath. Is it surprising that large swathes of pornography are dedicated to the donning and removal of uniforms? That there are nightclubs which specialise in such activity? That kissogram girls often begin their striptease dressed as policewomen? That grown men from the City of London go to a restaurant called School Dinners where they allow themselves to be teased and spanked by uniformed head girls?

Naturally newspapers and magazines know of the public's proclivities, and provide a regular service. Often British newspapers will not really have a story at all, but if the soldier-girl's photograph is 'sexy' enough in the widest sense, it goes in with a one-line caption. Even the more serious upmarket papers indulge in this, the *Daily Telegraph* being the worst culprit. A writer on that newspaper said, 'It's no different from page three in the tabloids. A pretty girl in uniform is there for slurping, lascivious old colonels to look at. She is just an appendage. There's usually no news value to it.' Indeed, the pictures are often used on page three, or even page one. The serious American papers do it less, although they too went through a bad patch during the Gulf War.

The British tabloids, however, take no beating in this area. Often, clippings from the last few years read as if they were written in the sixties or seventies, so old-fashioned are their attitude and language. A woman soldier is identified by her rank, and whether she is 'pretty', 'sexy' or 'raven-haired', although this is always perfectly obvious from the accompanying picture. Even achievements like the opening of pilot training to women in 1989 met with the headline in the *Sun*, 'I Say, It's Biggles in a Bra!' The first female RAF recruiting officer was rewarded with 'I'm Veronica – Fly Me!' which would not have sounded quite the same with a man named Trevor. At least some are funny, but read together, year after year, the tone consistently puts women as sexual beings first and members of the forces second.

Around eighty per cent of the British public reads the tabloids, so they are the major source of information on the subject of women in the forces. Television coverage is rare, so it is not surprising that the stereotype created by newspapers is pervasive. The stories divide largely into two sorts – the heterosexual sex scandal and the lesbian one. A short study of the tabloids at the time women were first sent to sea provides an insight into a world of ancient prejudice. The arrival of women was greeted by the *Sun* with the headline 'Dolly Jack Tars' and followed with 'Wrens Sign Up for Love Boats'. It then proceeded to run a series of features on the subject of mixed ships, which all bore the logo 'HMS *Loveboat*' on a life ring. This included a number of 'Saucy Sailor' jokes along the lines of 'A group of Wrens on board a warship turned out for parade TOPLESS! When the captain arrived on deck, he stared at the lines of semi-clad dollies and screamed, "I said a KIT inspection".'

There was no explanation of the sort of work the Wrens would do on board and the articles largely concentrated on navy wives complaining that Wrens would lead their husbands astray.

That Wrens might go to war was not as interesting as whether they would go to bed. The problem was, of course, that once they got to sea they did just that, but only in tiny numbers. By contrast, the stories were huge, often meriting front-page treatment. These included 'Wren's Nude Romp with Lt', which began, 'A Randy Wren was caught naked with a dashing navy lieutenant on board a warship in the Gulf.' The emphasis is of course on the Wren, who was 'randy', clearly taking the initiative, while the male lieutenant is an old-fashioned 'dashing'; in fact both parties were found naked on a bunk.

When a Wren got pregnant, supposedly on shore leave, this was reported as 'Navy Wren Wendy Clay's actions during the Gulf War weren't what England expected – she became pregnant.' But her husband-to-be, who was also a sailor on HMS *Brilliant*, was sometimes not even mentioned in stories. There was no suggestion that England even blamed him – or that the country would have preferred if he had worn a condom. Double standards were everywhere.

Meanwhile, on the days when no sex-at-sea scandal could be unearthed, the tabloids went back to their previous theory, which was that all Wrens were lesbians. 'Gay Wrens Force Sailor Girls into Lesbian Orgies' was a typical headline. There was a 'sex ring probe' at HMS *Dryad*, where lesbianism was 'rife'. Better still was 'Tattoo Wren's Lesbian Romps with Shipmate' in the *News of the World*. Blonde Trish, thirty-seven, who had Popeye tattooed on her arm, informed the readers that eight out of ten 'sailor girls' were lesbians during her eight years as a Wren. Nowadays she estimated it was more like fifty per cent. The ever-changing sexuality of the randy Wren must have caused the readers some puzzlement.

The average British person's – and squaddie's – view of women in the military will be coloured by this set of Neanderthal prejudices laid out week by week in tabloids. Even in the broadsheet newspapers, although women's non-sexual achievements are reported, the underlying tone and the huge picture display often hint at old-fashioned attitudes ready to rear from below the surface.

A similar pattern is seen in the American press, which although it would never dare to be as overtly chauvinist as the British is by no means fair in its coverage of women soldiers. During the Gulf War, the University of Southern California's Women, Men and Media project analysed the representation of women in the major American newspapers, including the *New York Times*, the *Washington Post*, the *Los Angeles Times* and the *Chicago Tribune*. They found that eighty-five per cent of front-page news was devoted to men, which was acceptable, since women make up eleven per cent of the forces. But what articles there were stereotyped women. The study made the following points:

The great majority of stories focussed on men – their jobs, their weaponry, their opinions. There were few stories about women soldiers and those that did appear were centred on the women's parental status. Female soldiers were seldom quoted and photographs of women were mostly of them at home showing concern for absent family members. Editorials and news stories about the war's impact on families were critical of mothers for going to war, and expressed concern about the effect on children. There were no articles or editorials on the impact of a father leaving his children published during the study. A photograph of Army Captain JoAnn Conley with a badge picture of her daughter affixed to her helmet was widely circulated, but there were no photographs showing men with pictures or mementoes of their children. There were almost no photographs of women with weapons or performing their duties. A series of articles was devoted to what male soldiers carried to the front to remind them of home – primarily women's underwear. The few female soldiers interviewed said they carried pictures of their partners or families.

Much the same could be said for the British press and had it not been for a few television films, the public might have thought that there were no women fighting at all. There were a few mentions of those at sea, but almost nothing on the women near the front. Take the *Sun*'s major effort, a colour photograph of a female soldier sunbathing in a T-shirt and shorts, lying beneath a washing line of socks and towels. It was taken at a low angle, the photographer's lens obviously aimed at her crotch. The caption? 'Sox Appeal! Private Vicki Thrower, of Suffolk, soaks up the Saudi sun on wash day.' That was the entire story. There was no mention of the regiment she was attached to, the Royal Corps of Transport, or that she had been driving ammunition up to the front.

Such diminution of women soldiers in press reports is disturbing. Women are doing the same jobs as men and almost as likely to get killed. Yet they are portrayed as wives, mothers, sex-objects, or little extras taken along for the entertainment of the troops. There is no impression that they are hard-working soldiers. To argue that the way female soldiers are portrayed in tabloids is merely a reflection of the way women as a species are treated misses the point. There are topless, brainless page-three girls, but there are also strong images in these papers of women who are taken seriously – politicians like Mrs Thatcher, doctors in the NHS and so on. The difference for female soldiers is that there are no such strong images of them.

The images and myths of women perpetuated within the forces themselves are harder to find out about, since they appear sporadically in songs, on lavatory walls and bulletin boards, and refer largely to civilians. The walls of most of the shared bedrooms of eighteen-year-old Coldstream Guards at their London barracks are covered in *Playboy* centrefolds and blondes in leather. If this reflects their view of civilian women, it probably bodes ill for their social relations with military ones. The pilots of the US Air Force's 77th Tactical Fighter Squadron, based at Upper Heyford in Oxfordshire, published a book of their favourite songs. The *Gamblers' Song Book*, was 'a collection of 75 years of tradition', the private thoughts of pilots. The writer Joan Smith purchased a copy during open day at the base in 1987 and analysed some of the more horrendous songs in her book, *Misogynies*. The song book is full of images of death, whores – and worse. The following song is a 'straightforward tirade directed at women's bodies in which no attempt is made to disguise the contempt pilots feel for them, and particularly for their sexuality'; at the same time, the men also seem to find the image attractive:

> Ten pounds of tittie in a loose brassiere,
> A twat that twitches like a mouse's ear,
> Ejaculation in my glass of beer,
> These foolish things remind me of you.
>
> A pubic hair on my breakfast roll,
> A bloody Kotex in my toilet bowl,
> The smelly fragrance of your fat asshole,
> These foolish things remind me of you.
>
> A slobby blowjob in a taxicab,
> A cunt that's covered in syphilitic scabs,
> These foolish things remind me of you.

The official forces – rather than their individual members – are balanced about coverage. They often ask journalists to interview male and female soldiers together, so that women are seen as part of a group and not freaks. Understandably, however, the military PR machine tends to protect the minority of women from the wear-and-tear of hundreds of interviews. In the Gulf the British were perhaps too careful, to the point that the woman's role became invisible.

In military literature – recruiting leaflets, information packs – women are generally fairly portrayed. The RAF may have over-compensated, however, with its leaflets bursting with female aircraft mechanics covered in engine grease. Almost every second photo-graph in their glossy brochures is of a woman, which is not a true reflection of their small presence in real life. The WRAC's last recruiting leaflet before disbandment was still old-fashioned in tone and referred to recruits as 'girls', not women. The new recruit was told, 'You will wear a well-cut, feminine, lovat-green uniform suit, a crisp white shirt, dark green hat, court shoes, gloves, and you'll carry a black handbag' – almost everything, in fact, a modern woman would not be seen dead with.

American and Canadian recruiting literature is full of faces of pretty women doing men's jobs – it is interesting that the more 'mannish'-looking soldiers do not feature in the photographs, although there are plenty to be seen at military bases. There is careful emphasis on femininity. An American brochure from the eighties was still worried enough about avoiding a butch image that it showed a beautiful smiling woman wearing a camouflaged combat helmet, with the caption, 'Some of the best soldiers wear lipstick'. Yes, but not after three days out on exercise.

British recruitment advertising has changed in just the last few years from pushing an image of genteel ladies-in-uniform, helpmeets for the real soldiers, to women in combat gear *being* soldiers. Thirty years ago, in 1962, the WRAF began a new advertising campaign: 'Have you the mature mind that makes a good officer?' it asked, beside a picture of a woman smiling, wearing dark red lipstick, and with the glamour and arched eyebrows of a film star. The then deputy of the WRAF, Group Officer Felicity Hill, OBE, gave an interview and revealed the woman in uniform in the photograph was a model she had selected with the appropriate attributes. 'Well, there she is. What does she indicate to you? She indicates to me that she's a girl with a great deal of enthusiasm and a lot of charm, and looks as though she's going somewhere.' She added that the woman would have 'an awfully good career ... and excellent social facilities in the officer's mess. I don't think for this type of girl the fleshpots appeal.'

Cut to 1988 and magazines everywhere have a double-page advertisement featuring a tall, strong woman striding across the page in full combat gear, followed, at a respectful distance, by a platoon of male soldiers. Her boots are shining and her long red hair is tied in a bun underneath her beret. The caption goes, 'Behind every successful woman ...' But the advertising copy reassures readers that 'When you meet a bunch of Women's Royal Army Corps Officers, the first thing that strikes you is how feminine they are ... they like dancing, candlelit dinners with friends and good movies.' Women also bring (once again) 'the feminine qualities of tact and diplomacy to tricky situations' and are told 'If you lead from the front, they'll be behind you.' The advertisement got a response four times higher than normal.

By 1991, the army had become even more radical. A striking colour advertisement has the headline, 'As a woman in the Army, you'll be expected to cook, clean and do the dishes.' Beneath that, there are three photographs of a woman in combats. In the first she is alone in a snow-swept wilderness, boiling water on an open fire. In the second, she is stripping down her SA-80 rifle and cleaning it, and in the third, she is repositioning a huge camouflaged satellite dish. The advertisement is no longer for the WRAC, but for the army, and there is a marked difference in the text. It tells the potential officer that her very first job could be as assistant adjutant to a regiment of 650 men. 'Heaven or Hell?' it asks. 'You will probably be too busy to decide.' It mentions possible postings in Hong Kong, America, Cyprus or Brunei, and sub-aqua diving in Belize, cross-country skiing in Norway and trekking in the Himalayas.

This latest army advertisement is offering quite a different life from previous ones, even suggesting that a career can be combined with being a wife and mother, and it dares to say, 'The longer you are with us, the greater your responsibilities will be. You could end up as a General.' Such a suggestion would have been unthinkable and impossible a few years before. The last line goes, 'All things considered, it's no surprise we think a woman's place is in the Army.'

Of course, the civilian advertising copywriters are a good deal more radical than the average general, who probably winced on reading of the plans for a woman to take his job. But the advertisement does herald, at least in some parts of the forces, a new tone, which is very clearly pushing women to the limits and throwing away the ladylike shackles of the (surprisingly recent) past.

The image of military women is both ahead of and behind the image of civilian women. In one way, the female soldier is taking on the ultimate challenge and proving, in her combats, she can do the toughest jobs as well as a man, but at the same time, she is also seen as a sort of super-secretary in dress uniform. Perhaps not in the traditional news media, but in films, novels and even comics, a new image of woman as warrior, or at least as tough guy, is emerging. Being physically fit, independent and competent is part of the new, still sexy image. Heroines work out instead of waiting in for men to call and handle weapons as often as they used to handle lipstick.

Look at Sarah Connor, mother-of-one and heroine of the popular 1991 film *Terminator 2 – Judgement Day*, played by actress Linda Hamilton. As Arnold Schwarzenegger's sidekick, she does everything he typically does in these instant-retribution movies, with similarly messy results. Hamilton is a warrior who machine-guns her enemies, crushes a skull here, breaks a man's arm there, wires the occasional bomb and in the end terminates even Schwarzenegger. Her body is lean and strong, her muscles stand out even while her arms are at rest, she fights in black combat trousers and an army belt, and is decked with pounds of ammunition. She wears no make-up, but is good-looking in a different way, and clearly acceptable as a woman and not a freak to audiences worldwide.

If that image – however clichéd – replaces previous preconceptions of women as weak, then the generation of tiny *Terminator* fans may grow up slightly more aware that women come in more than one package. The *Rambo* factor is not, of course, universally admired and emulation is often condemned in young boys. It is unlikely, however, that it will affect young girls in the same way, who already have countless cultural barriers against violent behaviour.

Showing that these extremes are possible in women may at least encourage some new trains of thought.

The fighting female body shown in *Terminator 2* did not come naturally. *Entertainment Weekly* revealed that Hamilton worked with a personal trainer six days a week for three months, weightlifting, running, biking and swimming. An Israeli commando taught her judo and how to use a pump-action machine gun, change magazines and assume shooting position. This was serious stuff and had to be technically correct to satisfy an audience made up largely of young men. The director of *Terminator*, James Cameron, also directed the first *Alien* movie, when Sigourney Weaver played a similar role to Hamilton's, left alone to fight for her life in space.

The recent spate of strong fighting women has come in films all directed by men; they may be the subject of male fantasy, but they are also female fantasies. For men, they are challenging and possibly also sexually arousing. For women, they are empowering. The trend in films like *Terminator 2* has been identified in America as the 'cult of the hardbody'. Julie Baumgold wrote about its growth in *New York* magazine in 1991. They appear in films like *Thelma and Louise*, 'the first feminist road movie', which ends with the waitress and housewife driving, Butch Cassidy and Sundance Kid-style, over the edge of a canyon, following a shoot-out with the police; and *Nikita*, the story of a remorseless, though elegant hit-woman. In *Blue Steel*, Jamie Lee Curtis has a body more like a boy's, but that does not stop her, as a policewoman, from blowing men's heads off.

'By the end of *Thelma and Louise*, Geena Davies and Susan Sarandon, who start out with curls and curves, have bared their arms and gone to war,' said Baumgold.

> *La femme* Nikita turns in her stomper boots for heels but remains a killer. These women all have hardbodies like Madonna, pumped and toned. They are the inheritors of movie women like Katharine Hepburn and Rosalind Russell, who were always quick talking and strong, but these women are killers ... They are no longer molls and helpers, no longer love puppies who commit crimes of passion. They are combat-trained outlaws. They are

creatively vicious. Linda Hamilton jabs a pen in a psy-
chiatrist's knee; Nikita stabs a pencil in a cop's hand.

Creative or not, this is fake fun-violence and not to be taken seriously.
There is obviously no comparison with the real thing, but it raises
a question: if young men fed on a diet of *Rambo* films are keen to
join the army, what about the new generation of young women?
The combination of elegance and efficient violence is almost a more
frightening one; killing seems even cleaner and less couched in
reality. It's also worth noting that the fighting women only shoot
men who are clearly evil in some way. Would audiences find it easy
to stomach if they were killing other women? At the moment, their
violence is necessary for survival, but a point may come when it,
too, is gratuitous.

Films like *Terminator 2* reach tens of millions of viewers worldwide,
from America to Japan. Their cultural influence – however base –
should not be underestimated. It is a small step forward from Goldie
Hawn in *Private Benjamin* as a cute young widow at boot camp. There
are now also international television series dedicated to women who
can shoot *and* cook, like the female buddy-cop programme, *Cagney
and Lacey.*

There have always been novels about women detectives since
Agatha Christie's Miss Marple, but in the eighties and nineties, this
genre too experienced a growth in heroines who were physically
tough instead of being just mentally rigorous and were as comfortable
with a gun in their hands as the average male private investigator.
In America, Sue Grafton in her 'A-to-Z of murder' books, Barbara
Wilson, with her lesbian feminist protagonist, and Sara Paretsky,
with her Warshawski stories (filmed in 1991), all have hard-talking,
hard-hitting heroines. Women with weapons have become a standard
motif in this sort of mass-appeal literature.

The female detective V. I. Warshawski is smart, fit, lives alone,
drinks Johnnie Walker, has a few men, and displays her wit, street-
fighting skills and marksmanship. Paretsky said she created her
because of the female clichés in detective novels written by men.
'There are two major strands in detective fiction – the sexually active
woman who is by definition evil or the chaste woman who is unable
to solve any problems.' Although Warshawski's style has been a little

toned down for the film, Paretsky was pleased that generically this sort of film has suddenly become sought-after.

> Studios will see they can put a strong woman on the screen and make it work. Films like these are where we're going to start seeing different images of women coming out of Hollywood. That affects a lot more people than a book, and there only has to be a market success once for those sheep-like studios to start turning them out.

One of the more obscure, but increasingly popular, measures of cultural change are comics, particularly the so-called 'adult' type. In the early days there were clean-living female warriors like Super-woman and Spiderwoman. Now, there is the cult cartoon Tank Girl, so idolised that she has already been made flesh in the Wrangler jeans' 'Be More Than Just a Number' campaign, and is considering films and television deals, and has had a collection of her exploits published by Penguin as well as in numerous comic books.

In her regular cartoon books, Tank Girl is an independent hellraiser, but she trained with the Australian equivalent of the SAS and became fond of tank driving. She has retained her tank, and along with her friends Jet Girl and Sub Girl, goes around being generally drunk, violent and mean, as well as charming. She dresses in impossibly large biker boots, wears ripped cut-off jeans and shaves most of her head, which results in the occasional sticking plaster. She drinks beer, carries a spiked baseball club, or worse, and swears constantly. It sounds dreadful, but the comics are in fact witty and Tank Girl comes out as peculiarly sexy under her grotty exterior. She has a heterosexual relationship with a talking kangaroo.

Like the previous films, Tank Girl is written by two men, who treat their heroine with respect and affection – for safety, probably, as this is an orgy of reverse sexism. There is much R-R-RIP!, MASH!, STAB! and SPURT! as Tank Girl trashes various male villains with a wide range of weapons, including a Ninja knife and what appears to be a flame thrower, and trolls around in her tank. Often violence is not shown in detail and the frame will say, 'A few minutes later ...' – Tank Girl will be depicted with a cheesy leer, having just decapitated someone, saying '... cause of death? ... Lack of blood in the body by the looks of things ... after much con-sultation we decided it wouldn't be in our best interests to show you that scene!' Later, having made a two-way deal with Lucifer, she gets three wishes and uses one to make an appearance on the *Dame Edna Everage* show, where she offers to do her 'impression of a crocodile barfing'.

It may be very unpleasant reading for anyone beyond school age, with its basic sense of humour, rather like the successful *Viz* comic. But it has a woman doing all the appalling things men usually do in these strips, with a topcoat of irony. Wrangler's marketing depart-ment bought the rights to Tank Girl, because – amazingly – they thought she had great potential as a role model for young women. 'We looked at Tank Girl and liked what we saw. She's individual, independent, sexy and assertive,' they told the *Guardian*.

Tank Girl represents the most extreme end of the new images of women appearing on the periphery of the media and in some mainstream films. Although these are small signs of change, there is enough to begin to build a picture, and for young female recruits joining the military to have a very different set of aims and expec-tations from those of twenty or even ten years ago. There is nothing, now, inherently peculiar about a woman using a gun to defend herself and there is no expectation in any of these books, films or comics, that a man will appear to protect her. The woman warrior, be she detective, space traveller or cartoon, knows how to look after herself; and it is not 'unfeminine' to do so.

Women are greatly influenced by images of bodies and power in magazines and films. Their suggestibility is high – look at the growing problems of anorexia and bulimia in young women, who want to imitate the slimness of the women bombarding them in the print media. In pre-*perestroika* Poland and Russia, when there were only one or two housewifely knit-and-sew magazines, and no regular colour pictures of models, anorexia was virtually non-existent. After a few years of exposure to Western magazines and lifestyles, the anorexia rate has taken off. The two may be connected.

The image-building is all-pervasive and very powerful, especially if you get them early. There was a time when boys played with the Action Man soldier doll and girls played with Barbie. But then Barbie joined the army, the air force and in 1991 the navy. Barbie's military development, since her first post in 1989, will no doubt change the course of history as we know it. Her race towards equality in the forces – aided by the Mattel Toy Company – is breathtaking. It was charted in *Minerva's Bulletin Board*, a quarterly magazine on women in the military.

Army Barbie appeared in 1989 and had not, frankly, moved far on from the traditional air-hostess Barbie. She did not have a day uniform, but wore officers' mess dress with a long skirt, figure-hugging jacket and high heels. The box explained to little girls: 'pretty and proud Barbie attends official military dinners, embassy parties and many other formal affairs around the world with the men and women who serve their country'. The doll was not exactly gutsy.

But a few months later, with air-force Barbie, things were hotting up. Although American women had not been allowed into combat in fighter jets in 1989, an exception had been made for the pink plastic doll. On the box, she stood next to her fighter jet and wore a flight suit, A-2 jacket, blue flight cap, aviator scarf and boots. The caption informed: 'Captain Barbie epitomises everything that women can do today. She's a pilot in the Air Force, where only the best are chosen to fly.'

In 1991, navy Barbie appeared, with an eight-year career as a sailor behind her. She was a petty officer first class and a quartermaster, when only twenty-one women in the American Navy at that time were in that speciality. The box said Barbie 'knows everything about her ship from stem to stern'. Her decorations included the Navy Achievement Medal, the Good Conduct Medal (twice), the Meritorious Unit Citation, the Sea Service Deployment Ribbon and the Expert Pistol Ribbon.

As a cultural indicator, Barbie need not be taken entirely seriously, but she is part of a clear trend towards images of women as strong individuals able to fight their own battles, rather than girls waiting for men to do that for them. Public opinion is changing very quickly and indeed the British Army advertisements went from emphasising feminine traits three years ago to suggesting that women could become generals now. Opinion took a great leap ahead with the television pictures of real women fighting in the Gulf – the first sight for most people of the modern female soldier – and their impact should not be underestimated. Neither should the length of time such new images will take to percolate into the minds of those who still write about 'Biggles in a Bra'.

12

IN THE COMBAT ZONE

Put two opposing elements together and there is a chemical reaction, sometimes an explosion. That is what has been happening to the military over the last few years – and in the previous chapters. Soon, the unstable compound of male and female, tradition and change, should settle into comfortable acceptance. The misogyny, sexual harassment and lack of confidence in women are the results of fear of the unknown. But as time goes on, women become more of a known quantity, seen less as invaders or usurpers, and more as colleagues. Despite discrimination, most military women do not see the root of the conflict as male versus female, but as a generational issue. The older men in charge of the forces are entrenched in both senses. The trenches of the Somme, the Second World War and the foxholes of Vietnam still outweigh high-technology warfare in their minds, and their attitudes are immovable after years in a segregated environment. Women of the working rather than wifely sort remain a mystery to many of them. But when the next mixed generation moves up, the barriers will have fallen and a book like this will become obsolete. The stories of these women will become ordinary instead of extraordinary.

A minority of women want to join the army and of those, few choose to go into combat. Few men choose it either. But at least having that choice will mean all occupations are open to them, compared to the present situation which bars women from up to half of all jobs in some services – something which would be considered outrageous in civilian life. All the arguments against female soldiers serving as equals in combat – apart from the difference in strength – have been shown to be seriously flawed, rooted in prejudice rather than formed from observation. The protective attitude towards women may be couched in chivalrous words, but it is also about protecting the military from being forced to open up units, which run in cosy, undisturbed segregation. Besides, the Gulf War, a milestone in the advancement of female soldiers, disproved rhetoric about keeping them out of harm's way with their deaths and imprisonment. Predictions that the public would be unable to stomach such suffering were also unfounded. Afterwards the US Chief Defense Spokesman Pete Williams said, 'One of the lessons we've learned from Operation Desert Storm is the extent to which the nation accepted the significant role of women in that operation. Until then there had always been a concern that having women involved in combat would be traumatic for the country.'

The assumptions of those against female combatants were disproved, one after another. In the desert, women coped with the constant stress of Scud attacks – they did not fall apart psychologically and ask to go home. They showed courage, leading troops across minefields, flying ammunition into Iraq and following the battle in armoured ambulances. Menstruation caused no significant change in performance, nor did the fact that many of the soldiers were mothers, separated for long periods from young children. None of that was pleasant, but it was normal for wartime.

One positive aspect of that war was the change it wrought in military and political attitudes – the Americans and British altered their combat rules to allow women to fly fighter aircraft and discussed opening up more occupations. Defense Secretary Dick Cheney said, 'They did a bang-up job ... They were every bit as professional as their male colleagues.' He said he would not be at all surprised to see the role of women in combat 'expand in the years ahead'. The British Minister for the Armed Forces, Archie Hamilton MP, a former Guards' officer who is strongly in favour of female soldiers, said he thought they had 'performed splendidly – sometimes better than the men' and some commanders, in particular those in the Royal Corps of Transport, wanted to make greater use of them. Mr Hamilton expected further barriers to fall and saw no reason why women should not be driving tanks for Britain within the next ten years, and pointed to the fact that many new weapons being tested were being designed in terms of weight and handling with both sexes in mind.

Such enthusiasm probably would not be bursting forth if these countries were not experiencing a demographic shortage of young men, expected to last until the mid-1990s. To maintain quality, the military must employ women, as armies become more tail-heavy and increasingly reliant on complex technology. Even with NATO defence cuts, regular injections of young people are still needed. Most Western countries intend to increase their quota of females. As volunteer forces compete with civilian employers, their only chance of keeping intelligence levels up is to recruit from a pool of motivated and willing women. When enlisted women are asked why they join, they cite positive reasons: learning a skill, gaining education, as well as defending their country. Men, say recruiting officers, are more likely to give negative reasons like unemployment, or the lack of any other prospects.

Far more female soldiers compete for each place than do men. The figures make it clear: at Sandhurst, sixty-five per cent of female officers are graduates, compared to forty-five per cent of men. In America, statistics over four years showed 100 per cent of enlisted women in the army had high-school diplomas, compared to ninety-two per cent of men, and women consistently scored higher on entrance tests. In terms of maturity, anecdotal evidence from recruiting officers in America, Britain and Canada shows that women have a great deal more common-sense than their male contemporaries.

So far, so cost-effective. Women are better behaved too – military prison is expensive, as is the wasted training if offenders are discharged. In the British Army in 1990, 5.7 per cent of male soldiers committed offences which ended in trial and detention or fine, compared to 0.04 per cent of women. Even taking into account that women made up only four per cent of the force then, female crimes were only 0.6 per cent of the total. Female soldiers also have far fewer drug or alcohol problems. In initial training only eight per cent of women dropped out, compared to sixteen per cent of men, but long-term retention rates for women were much worse – fifteen per cent left the British Army in 1990, compared to eight per cent of men. Those figures are partially caused by women discharged on becoming pregnant. Now that mothers can remain, far more women are applying for sixteen-year regular commissions, rather than eight-year short-service commissions, so the personnel retention rate should start to even up. Many women – particularly officers – are also having children much later. Like civilians, they want to get established in their careers first.

Pregnancy will probably be one of the biggest issues for the military in the nineties. Although portrayed by traditionalists as a great burden, and a waste of time and money, the fact is that maternity leave is added on to British service. There is only additional time off if there are medical problems. In America, the six weeks allowed are considered as sick leave. Time off for pregnancy should be put into context with male absence. As Brigadier Gael Ramsey of the WRAC pointed out, 'Men who get sports injuries can be off the road and fully paid for it for up to eighteen months – they play rougher sports, so their injuries are far higher than women's.'

With more soldier-mothers, childcare will also become more of an issue but British and American soldiers must give a legal undertaking that they have a guardian ready to take the child immediately, should they be sent to war. As modern wars tend to be shorter than before – Panama, Grenada, the Falklands and Operation Desert Storm all lasting no more than a few months – separations will be manageable. Armies spend far more time training to go to war rather than actually doing the real thing, so childcare in peacetime will be important. Many think the forces should not be wasting time on crèches instead of weapons, but making childcare easier actually produces less stressed mothers and fathers, who are readily available to do long hours or night duty. The added complications of children, pregnancy and dual-career couples instead of officers' wives are the price paid for the feminisation of the military, but they are outweighed by the advantages of creating a normal atmosphere in the forces, which has been shown to make men more responsible, stable and better behaved, and, in the long run, happier.

Physically, it is clear from results in the Canadian infantry that women are not the best footsoldiers and should only be allowed to join that branch if they reach the same physical standards as men. In other combat arms, like the artillery, armour and engineers, they are physically capable of achieving those standards. But there should be no double standards, allowing some less qualified women to slip through; if they cannot make the grade physically, they should make use of their other talents. In future, rather than the existing system which permits blanket prohibitions based on sex, it makes more sense to allocate jobs according to the strength and fitness required for each, because as armies become more mixed in race – particularly the Americans – there is far greater variation in the size of men too.

With this in mind, the British Army completed an investigation into gender-free physical training in 1991. This means that a series of objective tests set minimal physical standards for each occupation, with ratings from, say, one to ten, with the lowest being a desk job that requires minimal strength and fitness, and the highest for the infantry. If the British go ahead with implementation, planned for April 1993, said Brigadier Ramsey, 'it begs the question, do we need deployment rules any more? Do we need to ban women from the infantry or armoured corps or can we take the best *person* who comes through the door?'

Gender-free testing will make combat restrictions obsolete, although already they are looking ragged in America and Britain, where each has one service – the US Air Force and the Royal Navy – which allows women on the front. After women pilots were allowed to fly fighters, a senior US Army official told the *Washington Post*, 'It's going to be hard to defend not doing a total repeal of the combat exclusion law. You've taken the heart and soul out of it.' The powerful American lobby group, the Defense Advisory Committee on Women in the Services (DACOWITS), tried to push for a four-year trial of women in combat arms following Panama and is stepping up pressure following the change of heart in the air force. As Democratic Representative and DACOWITS supporter Patricia Schroeder put it, 'It is not just a question of serving your country. It is also a question of being able to die for your country. If women have the courage to take that risk, who are we to stop that? Army policy allows women to be shot, but they can't be the first to shoot. The logic of that eludes me.'

The public agrees. Although there are no British surveys on the subject, a *New York Times/CBS* poll after Panama showed seventy-two per cent of people thought women should serve in combat if they wished. A post-Gulf Gallup poll in *Newsweek* found a surprisingly large majority – seventy-nine per cent – thought women should get combat assignments, and fifty-seven per cent felt they should meet the same standards of strength and endurance as men qualifying for the front, compared to thirty-nine per cent who did not. Even when it came to the draft, fifty per cent thought young women should be required to participate. Sixty to seventy per cent believed it would be an advantage to allow women into jobs in combat support, as a jet-fighter pilot and on a warship. But when it came to the infantry, fifty-one per cent were against, compared to forty-one per cent in favour.

So with politicians and the public agreed that women's role could expand, the remaining resistance, as has been seen, is within the military itself. Not surprisingly, army men think that they know best, because they have been doing the job for years. Even if the reality of statistics and performance tests show women are a perfectly good investment, there are still the questions of emotion and thousands of years of Western military tradition. Behind supposed statements of practicality – 'it would cost too much to adapt ships' or 'men and women can't share a tent' – lie moral and social qualms.

One is the argument that it is wrong in some way for the bearers of life to bring death, coupled with the possibility of mothers dying in battle. In a (now rare) long war, which wipes out a large section of the male population, having women at home breeding the next generation preserves the species. In Paraguay, following the War of the Triple Alliance in the 1860s, two-thirds of the male population was killed and the country became semi-polygamous for two generations. The modern species should be fairly safe, however, as most women are not interested in joining the military; the deaths of a small percentage of female soldiers should not greatly alter the balance. Besides, modern nuclear and chemical warfare can as easily affect those at home as on the front. It also has to be remembered that some women cannot have children, or do not wish to. To caricature everything female as a baby-machine also serves to negate men's increasing role as parents.

Mady Wechsler Segal in her paper 'The Argument for Female Combatants' offers an additional explanation for the resistance to change. Some men survive the rigours and savagery of combat by preserving a mental picture of the normal world back home to which they will return. 'One of the major components of the world back home is women, "our women", who are warm, nurturant, ultra-feminine, and objects for sexual fantasy ... one of the reasons for fighting is to protect our women and the image of the world back home.' It is a psychological defence which is severely dented if a woman is sharing your tank.

That is the effect of an imagined female stereotype, but the male stereotype brings its own rules – those of chivalry and protecting women. It is alleged that military units will not function properly because male soldiers will protect women at the expense of good judgement. But if women are as well-trained and as well-armed as men, and no longer perceived as a weaker species but capable of looking after themselves, that should not happen. The ingrained psychology of chivalry will ebb away. Being taught to attack and not just defend will increase women soldiers' chances of survival greatly, particularly with the unexpected techniques and blurring of the front in modern warfare. Oddly, although it is seen as disruptive if men are protective of women, when men are protective of men armies reward them. After the Gulf War, a US Air Force pilot was awarded a medal for valour for leading a nine-hour rescue mission for aircrew who had ditched on enemy soil.

It would make more sense if the military took advantage of perceived, and actual, differences between men and women. When soldiers complain about the problems of integration and the resentment on both sides, these are management and leadership problems, and not the fault of women. An army which accommodates women and uses them to best advantage rather than wasting time making excuses will find integration far less painful. Is it surprising that the military – structured by men, for men and encrusted in male bureaucracy – is sometimes uncomfortable for women? Yet women's skills, as managers, confessors and leaders, are often wasted. More than any civilian organisation, the military relies on building confidence and trust in leaders and colleagues, because survival may one day depend on such relationships. Although military leaders prefer not to admit it, the post-Cold War personnel shrinkage is an indication of a change in the style of conflict expected. There is a tendency for armies to spend more time dealing with civilians in crisis, as with the peacekeeping forces in Northern Ireland and Kurdish refugee aid in Iraq. Different skills are involved in dealing with these delicate situations, and they are skills which women possess as much as and sometimes more than men.

For Western armies, wars are rarely single-country affairs, but fought in alliances. That, coupled with plans for a European defence force which would be likely to include Britain, means that armies will cross-fertilise ideas and weapons. The committee on women in the NATO forces holds a conference each year and information is swapped on the progress of female soldiers. With women allowed into full combat in countries such as Canada, Belgium, Norway, the Netherlands, Denmark, and soon Spain and Portugal, the disease may be catching. Even the Australian Defence Force has opened combat-related duties to its women, who are expected to go from the present eleven per cent to fifteen per cent of the military, and the 1993 review of defence policy is to consider allowing women full combat duties.

So the change will come at a different pace in each country, but change is inevitable. If governments and societies set themselves up as defenders of equal rights, then that atmosphere will pervade the remotest corner, where the military lurks hoping its policies will continue to go unnoticed. Steady progress is probably better in some ways than a short, sharp shock when female troops are thrown in at the deep end; justice must always be balanced with military effectiveness. Women have crossed the sexual barriers preventing them from becoming fire fighters, armed police officers, miners and even prime ministers, so why not front-line soldiers? Apart from the priesthood, the military is the only institution still standing up to the onslaught. Its instincts to resist rest on thousands of years of tradition and deeply held beliefs. Secretly, it still believes weaker bodies are a sign of weak minds. But coming to the end of the millennium, as a new order begins and old values fade, the belief that anatomy is destiny may fade too.

NOTES

1 OPENING SHOTS

p. 1 'Over 34,000 women ...': statistics, unless otherwise noted, are from the Pentagon in America, the Canadian Defense Department and the Ministry of Defence in Britain.

p. 2 'Exposure to danger ...': General Robert Barrow, in the *New York Times*, 21 July 1991.

2 THE INFIDEL WHO BROUGHT HIS WIFE

p. 23 'We were deployed ...': Sergeant Sherry Callaghan in the *New York Times*, 25 September 1990.

p. 34 'What I am doing ...': Major Marie Rossi from CNN tape quoted in *Minerva's Bulletin Board*, summer 1991.

3 SAILING IN THE GOLDFISH BOWL

Parts of the section on HMS *Brilliant* were first published as 'Dressed to Kill' in *The Times*, 13 April 1991.

p. 39 'We trust our husbands ...': Jayne Green in the *Sun*, 17 February 1990.

p. 39 'Fair enough ...': Sub Lieutenant Jacqueline Ramsay in *The Times*, 14 June 1991.

p. 40 'I know people ...': Rating Wendy Clay in the *Daily Mirror*, 30 September 1991.

p. 44 'I know what ...': Sue Bradbury, *Daily Mail*, 7 February 1990.

p. 50 'Women's eternal role ...': Rear-Admiral Sir Morgan Morgan-Giles in the *Sunday Times*, 11 February 1990.

p. 53 'victims of the bubonic ...': Lieutenant Roberta Spillane, *Women in Ships: Can We Survive?*, US Naval Institute Proceedings, July 1987.

p. 53 'a perception among ...': Rear-Admiral Roberta Hazard in the *New York Times*, 26 May 1991.

4 ALWAYS AMAZONS

p. 60 'There is a Scythian ...': Hippocrates, quoted in Tim Newark, *Women Warlords*, London 1989, p. 12.

p. 61 'The origin of this ...': Richard Burton, *A Mission to Gelele, King of Dahome*, London 1864, p. 254.

NOTES

p. 61 'a woman is still ...': *ibid*, p. 259.
p. 61 'They are as savage ...': *ibid*, p. 255.
p. 62 '1. The Agbarya': *ibid*, p. 261.
p. 62 'The women are as brave ...': *ibid*, p. 264.
p. 63 'armed with the ...': Newark, *ibid*, p. 51.
p. 65 'The Maquis troop ...': James Gleeson, *They Feared No Evil*, London 1976, p. 73.
p. 66 'You are condemned ...': *ibid*, p. 145.
p. 67 'This is Frau ...': *ibid*, p. 148.
p. 67 'I could yet ...': *ibid*, p. 41.
p. 67 'I just want ...': *ibid*, p. 104.
p. 69 'One battle stands ...': *ibid*, p. 10.
p. 70 'We were immediately ...': *ibid*, p. 14.
p. 70 'I could not ...': *ibid*, p. 15.
p. 70 'Sometimes they amputated ...': *ibid*, p. 54.
p. 71 'It was difficult ...': *ibid*, p. 67.
p. 72 'I will not have ...': Bruce Myles, *Night Witches*, California 1981, p. 97.
p. 73 'Yes. Whoever it was ...': *ibid*, p. 220.
p. 73 'Battle life ...': *ibid*, p. 222.

5   THE BODY OF A WEAK AND FEEBLE WOMAN ...

p. 87 'Clearly we are ...': General Robert H. Barrow, quoted on cover of Brian Mitchell, *Weak Link: The Feminisation of the American Military*, Washington 1989.
p. 87 'We don't find ...': *New York Times*, 19 June 1991.

6   ... THE HEART AND STOMACH OF A KING

Parts of the section on Marine boot camp were first published as 'Platoon' in the *Sunday Correspondent Magazine*, 14 October 1990.
p. 96 'By being admitted ...': Dr Norman Dixon, *On the Psychology of Military Incompetence*, London 1976, p. 211.
p. 96 'size, muscle ...': *ibid*, p. 159.
p. 97 'A lifetime of ...': *ibid*, p. 162.
p. 97 'the social consequences ...': *ibid*, p. 197.
p. 97 'Since men are ...': *ibid*, p. 169.
p. 99 'It's not that ...': *Washington Post*, 29 January 1991.
p. 99 'Whatever the factors ...': *ibid*.

7   IN THE COCKPIT

p. 103 'I find great ...': *LA Times*, 1 July 1991.
p. 104 'It felt both ...': *Aircraft Illustrated*, April 1990, p. 202.
p. 104 'I had an hour ...': *ibid*, p. 202.
p. 104 'I had been considering ...': *ibid*, p. 203.

8   THE BATTLE OF MOTHERS

p. 116 'Depriving a tiny baby ...': *Daily Telegraph*, 1 February 1991.
p. 116 'the most blameworthy ...': *Sunday Telegraph*, 9 December 1990.
p. 116 'If we can't ...': *Washington Post*, 10 February 1991.
p. 122 'How could you ...': *New York Times*, 18 September 1990.
p. 124 'The men are finding ...': *ibid.*
p. 125 *Newsweek* poll on women at war: 5 August 1991.
p. 127 'He's only two ...': *Washington Post*, 9 February 1991.
p. 133 'If the army ignores ...': *Washington Post*, 25 September 1989.

9   AN OFFICER, NOT A GENTLEMAN

p. 135 'Men had to prove ...': Captain Carol Barkalow, *In the Men's House*, New York 1990, p. 36.
p. 135 'Even the simplest ...': *ibid*, p. 37.
p. 137 'Our support outfit ...': *Newsweek*, 5 August 1991.

10   WHORE OR DYKE?

p. 156 'it was a statement ...': *Washington Post*, 23 July 1991.
p. 157 'There were women ...': *Life*, May, 1980.
p. 159 'Another prank ...': *New Republic*, 21 October 1991.
p. 160 'feel like they were ...': *Washington Post*, 22 October 1990.
p. 160 'They are perceived ...': *ibid.*
p. 161 'I still believe ...': *Washington Post*, 24 May 1990.
p. 161 'Inconsistent and ambiguous ...': *Washington Post*, 4 April 1991.
p. 162 'causes very real ...': *Daily Telegraph*, 17 May 1991.
p. 163 'The presence of ...': official policy statement on homosexuality, US Department of Defense 1982.
p. 163 'Sexual orientation ...': *Washington Post*, 10 October 1991.
p. 164 'a bit of an old ...': *ibid.*
p. 164 'very private ...': *Washington Post*, 19 August 1991.
p. 165 'I want you ...': Mary Ann Humphrey, *My Country, My Right to Serve*, New York 1990, p. 40.
p. 166 'hard-working ...': *New York Times*, 9 September 1990.
p. 166 'kick ass ...': *Washington Post*, 11 January 1991.
p. 168 'My colleagues were ...': *Guardian*, 10 October 1991.

11   ICONS IN UNIFORM

p. 177 'I say, it's Biggles ...': *Sun*, 21 July 1989.
p. 177 'I'm Veronica ...': *Sun*, 1 March 1977.
p. 177 'Dolly Jack Tars ...': *Sun*, 7 February 1990.
p. 177 'Wren's nude romp ...': *Sun*, 14 June 1991.
p. 178 'Navy Wren Wendy ...': *Daily Mirror*, 30 September 1991.
p. 178 'Tattoo Wren's lesbian ...': *News of the World*, 19 May 1991.

p. 179 'The great majority ...': *Minerva's Bulletin Board*, summer 1991, p. 8.

p. 179 'Sox Appeal! ...': *Sun*, 4 February 1991.

p. 180 'straightforward tirade ...': Joan Smith, *Misogynies*, London 1989, p. 103.

p. 180 'Ten pounds of tittie ...': *ibid*, p. 104.

p. 182 'Well, there she ...': *Observer*, 21 October 1962.

p. 184 'By the end of ...': *New York*, August 1991.

p. 186 *Tank Girl*: Deadline Comics for Penguin Books, London 1990.

p. 187 'We looked at ...': *Guardian*, 18 June 1991.

12   IN THE COMBAT ZONE

p. 191 'One of the lessons ...': *Washington Post*, 16 June 1991.

p. 194 'It's going to ...': *ibid.*

p. 194 *Newsweek* poll: 5 August 1991.

p. 195 'One of the major ...': Mady Wechsler Segal, 'The Argument for Female Combatants' in Nancy Loring Goldman's *Female Soldiers*, New York 1982, p. 278.

Every effort has been made to credit copyright holders fully. However, if any credit needs amendment, this can be done in any future editions.

INDEX